THE MAIDEN WITH THE MEAD

A GODDESS OF INITIATION IN OLD NORSE MYTHOLOGY?

TLS

ISBN13: 978-1-959350-06-4
Set in: Georgia 11/12/15/17 pt, Symbola 9/10/11 pt

©The Three Little Sisters
USA/CANADA

Contents

Seek not the path of the ancients;
Seek that which the ancients sought.
--Matsuo Basho

„Sparkar atto ver konor,
ef oss at sparkom yrði;
horscar atto ver konor,
ef oss hollar væri;
þær or sandi
síma vndo
oc or dali divpom
grvnd vm grofo;
varþ ec þeim einn allom
æfri at raþom,
hvilda ec hia þeim systrom
siav
oc hafða ec geþ þeirra allt
oc gaman.

30.„Ec var avstr
oc viþ einhveria dǫmþac,
læc ec viþ ena línhvito
oc lavnþing háþac,
gladdac ena gvllbiorto,
gamni mær vnði."
---**Hárbarðsljóð**

18. Full of life sparks were
the women
-if they had only been
compliant to us
with their sparks!
Very wise were the women
-if they had only been
devoted to us!
They wound, from sand,
the ropes!
They dug the grounds
out of the deep valleys!
I was the one, out of all
who could rule them:
I rested with the seven
sisters
had all their wholeness
and their pleasure (…)

30. I was to the east
and judged between
everyone
I laid with the Linen
Bright Maiden
and had, with, her secret
council
I made the Golden Bright
happy
she granted me her
pleasure.
---The Song of Long Beard

LETTERS

Á/á = sounds like the "a" in "tall" or the "o" in "boss", but more prolonged
Ð/ð = soft "dh"-sound
Þ/þ = "th"-sound (this, there, that)
Æ/æ/ę = sounds like the "a" in "apple"
Ǫ/ǫ = ö - sounds like "ou" in "tough", "rough" or the "u" in "buffer", but more prolonged
Y/y = ü – sounds like the "ü" in "über"

EDDA POEMS PARTICULARLY RELEVANT TO THIS BOOK

» Vǫluspá [The Vǫlva's Divination]
» Hávamál [The High One's (Óðinn's) Speech]
» Vegtamskvíða eða Baldrs Draumar [The Song of the One Who Knows the Path or Balder's Dreams]
» Skírnismál [The Shining One's Speech]
» Hyndluljóð [The She-Wolf's Song]
» Grípisspá [The Grasping One's Divination]
» Helgakviða Hiǫrvarðssonar [The Poem of Helgi Hiǫrvarðsson]
» Helgakviða Hundingsbana hin fyrri [The First Poem of Helgi Hundingsbani]
» Helgakviða Hundingsbana hin önnur [The Second Poem of Helgi Hundingsbani]
» Fafnismál [The Embracer's Speech]
» Sígrdrífumál [Sígrdrífa's (Victory Drift's) Speech]
» Helreið Brynhildar [Brynhildr's Ride to Hel]
» Oddrúnargrátr [Edge Rune's Lament]
» Svípdagsmál: Gróagaldr & Fjǫlsvinnsmál [The Song of Swift Dawn: The Spell-Song of Growing & The Speech of Much Knowing]

Terms, Names, and Titles

» *Aegir: "Terrifying One" – the ocean, and the ocean giant, father of the personified waves and husband to Rán*
» *Aegisdætr: "Aegir's daughters": The personified waves*
» *Aesir/Æsir (masculine plural): The gods. Plural of Áss*
» *Álfr (masculine singular, plural: Álfar): Elf*
» *Allvissmál: "The Speech of All-Knowing" (Edda poem)*
» *Ásgarðr: The Settlement of the Gods/Divine World. Pronounced "oss-gar-dhur"*
» *Áss: (masculine singular. Pronounced like "auss"/"oss"): God*
» *Ásynja (feminine plural: Ásyniur): Goddess. Pronounced «oss-een-yah"*
» *Baldr: Balder – "The Bold", "Courageous One" – the god of goodness, fairness and open-mindedness, son of Frigg and Óðinn*
» *Blót: Sacrifice*
» *Blótgóði: Sacrificial priest*
» *Blótgyðja: Sacrificial priestess*
» *Edda: "Great Grandmother" – a term for Old Norse poetical lore regarding mythology.*
» *Einheri (masculine singular, plural: Einherjar): "Sole Rulers"/Lone Rulers" – those who are chosen by the valkyriur and who live on after death in Valhǫll or Fólkvangr*
» *Dvergr (m.sg): Dwarf*
» *Dís (feminine sg., plural: Dísir): Goddess or any other female supernatural power*
» *Dísablót: "Sacrifice to the Goddesses"*
» *Dísarsalr: "The Hall of the Goddess"*
» *Dísaþing: "The Parliament of the Goddesses"*
» *Fimbulþulr: "The Great Reciter" – an Óðinsheiti*
» *Flateyjarbók: "The Flat Island Book" – a collection of sagas and short stories 13th century*
» *Fólkvangr: "People Field" – Freyia's property and after-life heaven for her chosen dead*
» *Freyr: "Lord Sovereign – brother to Freyia*
» *Freyia: "Lady Sovereign" – a goddess of many names, blótgyðja and the first to teach seiðr to Óðinn*
» *Freyiuheiti: Nicknames/cover names for Freyia*
» *Frigg: "Beloved" goddess and wife to Óðinn, mother of Baldr*

» *Fjǫlkunnigr (adjective): Someone who has Fjǫlkyngi*
» *Fjǫlkyngi (feminine sg.): "Great Knowledge" – often translates as "sorcery". It refers to the knowledge of arts such as Skáldskap, Seiðr, Galdrar, shape-changing, summoning spirits and traveling outside of the physical body, often in the shape of an animal.*
» *Fjǫlsviðr: "Very Wise/Much Knowing" – the jǫtunn who guards the golden hall*
» *Fylgja (feminine singular. Plural: fylgjur): "Follower" – a feminine spiritual entity which may function a norn or valkyria for individuals or for entire families (ættarfylgjur – clan-followers), sometimes as omens of doom and death, other times as guardian spirits. May also be referred to as dís.*
» *Galdr (masculine sg, plural: galdrar): Spell-song, incantation, chant, also known as ljóð/ljóðar (neutral): songs, verses*
» *Gandr (masculine sg): Magic, Spell, Wand*
» *Gefn: Short form of Gefiun, and a Freyiuheiti*
» *Gefiun: "The Provider", a goddess who became ancestral mother to the Danish royal dynasty of the Skjöldungar*
» *Gerðr: "Enclosure" – a giantess, wife to Freyr, daughter to the jǫtunn Gýmir*
» *Gimli: "The Shimmering" – a hall in Ásgarðr*
» *Glitnir: "The Shining One" – a hall in Ásgarðr*
» *Grímnismál: "The Speech of the Masked" (Edda poem)*
» *Gullveigr: "Gold Drink" – a Vǫlva in the Vǫluspá*
» *Gunnlǫð: "Battle Drink/Invitation" - A giantess in the Hávamál and Skáldskaparmál*
» *Gylfaginning: "The Illusions of Gylfi" - Part one of Snorri's thesis about poetical metaphor in his Prose Edda*
» *Gýmir: "Hiding something"- a jǫtunn who is identified with Aegir*
» *Haustlǫng: "Prolonged Autumn" (Skaldic poem by Thióðolf from Kvina ca 900)*
» *Heiðr: "Heath" or "Bright" or "Clearing" – a clearing of light surrounded by dark forest, an open space of light emerging from within darkness. Name of Vǫlva in Vǫluspá*
» *Heiðrún: Bright Open Space Symbol (see Heiðr) – the "goat" who stands on the roof of Valhǫll feeding on the leaves of the world tree and produces the sacred mead of resurrection.*

» *Heimskringla: "The World Circuit" – a collection of sagas about the Norwegian kings by Snorri Sturluson*
» *Heiti: Nicknames, calling names or cover words/alternative words, used to create poetic variety*
» *Hel: "Death" ("Hidden") – the name of the goddess of the dead and the of her underworld*
» *Hlér: "Wind-Shield" (=immortal) a jǫtunn identified as Aegir*
» *Hlésey: "Wind-Shielded Island" (Island of Immortality and home to valkyriur): Aegir's abode*
» *Húgr (Masculine sg): The part of the self that desires, wants, loves, is passionate, thinks and intends. Able to move beyond the physical body, but very much a part of the innermost self, the soul.*
» *Iðunn: "Returning Streams" – a goddess who offers immortality through eternal resurrection*
» *Jǫrðr: "Earth" – the Earth goddess, wife to Óðinn, mother to Thor and to all living beings and human lineages*
» *Jǫtnar: Plural of Jǫtunn*
» *Jǫtunn (masculine singular) "Giant" – but the literal meaning is "Eater", "Devourer"*
» *Kenning: Metaphor, parable – two or several words put together to signify a particular character, place, entity or thing. Used to create variety in poetry, together with the use of Heiti.*
» *Loki: God of mischief and inventions*
» *Lokasenna: «Loki's Quarrel" (Edda poem)*
» *Menglǫð: «Blend Drink/Invitation» a fylgja and the ruler of the world of giants who sits beneath the Tree of Memory on the Mountain of Medicines surrounded by*
» *Njǫrðr: Vanir god of winds and waves and the ship harbor, father to Freyr and Freyia*
» *Norn (feminine sg, plural: Nornir): A goddess of fate*
» *Norse: the language of the primary source literature, as it was written down by medieval scholars, branch of the Germanic language family. Often used for the language and dialects of Scandinavia and Iceland during the Viking Age, although there are more specific terms for time periods and geographical regions.*
» *Óðinn: "The Spirit", "The Ecstasy", "The Inspiration", "The Mind", "The Poetry" – a great god, giver of breath and spirit to human beings.*
» *Óðinsheiti: Nicknames/cover names for the god Óðinn*

» *Óðr: "Spirit", "Ecstasy", "Inspiration", "Mind", "Poetry" – husband to Freyia*

» *Old Norse: This is an English translation which my supervisors suggested for the Norwegian term "norrøn", an adjective which is used for the language, culture and religion of the Norse-speaking people in pre-Christian Scandinavia and Iceland.*

» *Poetic Edda: A collective term for Old Norse poems of the Edda (mythological and legendary) style*

» *Prose Edda: A thesis on Old Norse poetical metaphors based on pagan mythology written by Snorri Sturluson in 1220-1225*

» *Rán: "Robbery" – the giantess of the ocean who receives the drowned in her halls*

» *Sámi: A Finnic-speaking ethnic minority in Norway, Sweden, Finland and Russia with a tradition of shamanism who have lived side by side with the majority populations in these countries for thousands of years.*

» *Seiðr (masculine) An Old Norse term for divination, witchcraft and what we may count as shamanistic practices.*

» *Siða (verb): To make seiðr*

» *Sígrdrífa: "Victory Drift"- a Valkyria*

» *Sígrdrífumál: "The Speech of Victory Drift" (Edda poem)*

» *Sígrlinn: "Soft/Mild Victory" – a Valkyria*

» *Skaði: «Harm», «Injury" – a giantess and wife to Njǫrðr and Óðinn and lover to Loki, also called Öndurdís – the Goddess of Skiing.*

» *Skáld: Bard, poet*

» *Skaldic poetry: Old Norse poetry composed by named and historical skáldir during the Viking Age in a bound form which means that they could not be altered over time, and are thus our oldest literary sources*

» *Skáldskaparmál: "The Speech of the Making of Poetry" – The second part of Snorri's thesis about poetical metaphors in Edda and Skaldic poetry, better known as the Prose Edda*

» *Skírnir: "The Shining One" – Freyr's servant*

» *Snorri Sturluson (1179-1241): An Icelandic scholar who wrote the Prose Edda and all the sagas of the Heimskringla during the 1220s. Our primary source to Norse Mythology.*

» *Són: "Atonement" = Blót*

» *Sváva: "The Floater"/"Sleeper"/"Sleep-maker" – a Valkyria*

» *Þórr (Thor): "Thunder" – the god of thunder and protector of Earth and Miðgarðr, son of Jǫrðr and Óðinn*

» *Þulr (masculine sg): Reciter, sage, priest, poet, wise man who knows and recites the lore*

» *Þurs (masculine sg., plural: Þursar): Thurse – a sort of giant or troll*

» *Þiódolfr af Hvinir: Thióðolf from Kvina, a skáld who lived during the 9th century and author of the Haustlǫng and the Ynglingatál.*

» *Urðarbrunnr: The Well of Origin*

» *Urðr: "Origin" – the oldest norn, the past and the origin, nourishes the universe and prevents its decay*

» *Útgarðr: "Outer Settlement/World" – the world of the jǫtnar*

» *Vafþrúðnir: "Powerful Head-Veil": a jǫtunn*

» *Vafþrúðnismál: "The Speech of the Powerful Head-Veil" (Edda poem)*

» *Valr (masculine singular): The slain, or those chosen by the valkyriur, Freyia or Óðinn for a special fate after death*

» *Valhǫll: The Hall of the Slain (Chosen Dead), Valhalla*

» *Váli: "The Slain", the name of a son of Óðinn and a son of Loki, the one who shall avenge Baldr*

» *Valkyria (feminine sg, plural: valkyriur): "Chooser of the Slain" – a warrior norn entity of Valhǫll*

» *Vanadís: "The Goddess of the Vanir" = Freyia*

» *Vegtamskvíða: "The Song of the One Who Knows the Path" (Edda poem, also known as Baldrs Draumar)*

» *Verðandi: "Happening" – the norn of the present moment*

» *Vǫluspá: "The Divination of the Vǫlva" (Edda poem)*

» *Vǫlva: Woman "Wed to the Wand [Vǫl]": An oracle, sibyl, witch or wise woman who has Fjǫlkyngi and practices Seiðr and Galdrar.*

» *Ynglinga saga: The first saga in the Heimskringla, based on the Ynglingatál*

» *Ynglingatál: A skaldic poem by Þiódolfr af Hvinir about the lives and deaths of the Ynglinga kings of Vestfold and Uppsala, counting near 30 generations*

PROLOGUE

The Maiden with the Mead began as a dissertation as my Master Thesis at the Master program in History of Religions at the department of Culture, University of Oslo, graduating in 2004, when it was published at the University of Oslo library. It was later published as at VDM Verlag in 2009. Now, in 2022, with a new publisher, I am happy to present you with a new, improved edition with some corrections, more details and in-depth analysis, as well as additions, not the least with more primary source quotes in the original Old Norse language next to my own, English translations. I have kept much of the original content but have made an attempt to adapt it somewhat to a broader audience, where the original thesis was of course directed at academics.

☛ *The illustrations are my own, based on various forms of Old Norse art, copied as detailed as possible.*

In The Maiden with the Mead, I was suggesting new insights into pre-Christian initiation rituals, as well as the notion of a goddess presiding over said rituals, a goddess or other female power whose role may have been similar to the role of a Great Goddess as savior which we often find in ancient Mystery religions of the Classical Age.

The new insights proposed were:

1. The studies of Old Norse myths have largely ignored one of its most central characters, a mead-serving supernatural woman in the underworld, whom I have titled the Maiden with the Mead – around whose figure most of the actions described in the Poetic Edda actually pivot.

2. The Maiden with the Mead is a central character because she symbolizes the stage of consecration and resurrection in Old Norse myths which seem based on actual initiation rituals.

3. Old Norse myths, especially those of the Edda category, are mostly concerned with initiation ritual and follows a typical initiation structure that is identical in all the poems, divine and heroic, no matter how different they appear to be on the surface.

4. The structure of initiation underlying all the myths follows a basic pattern of thematic stages which I have termed Vision Quest, Vision, Descent into the Underworld, Trials and Consecration. The surviving initiands become sages, kings, healers, priests and shaman-like figures. There is also a sense of seeking salvation or resurrection in death in a manner that is akin to the theologies of ancient Mystery religions.

5. The poems accurately describe ritual in so detailed a manner, even including techniques, teachers and teachings, that it is conceivable that they indeed are describing or echoing actual pagan ritual practice.

6. The initiation rituals are devoted to a female resurrecting power, whom I in 2004 identified as a Norse version of the Great Goddess of Classical Mystery religions, because she offers resurrection from the dark oblivion of Death.

7. The poems show that the initiation rituals are concerned with the resurrection of the soul after death and that they appear to describe initiation in general, not just into one particular office. The rituals, however, appear to be masculine, since all the initiands here are male. Females appear as teachers and guides, however, and the male initiands are the devotees of the Great Goddess. We do find two initiation stories involving women who become vǫlur or witches, and whose stages of initiation and sacred drink theme is similar to those of the males.

8. The teachings of the myths include knowledge about how the separate realms of cosmos are in fact one, how all beings are united in one great cosmological being, and that the dark and fearsome ogress of the underworld may be identical with (or the other face of) the bright and lovely goddess of initiation.

9. The dissertation stresses the importance of translating or at least attempting to translate names and place names in order to understand the true meaning of the myths, which were presented as allegories.

Since my graduation in 2004, I have kept researching on the side, and have come to the conclusion that the Old Norse initiation myths must be closely related to the parable-myths of Ancient Mystery Cults with their emphasis on resurrection or salvation through initiation and the love of the Supreme Being (mostly conceptualized as the Great Goddess – the great All-Soul behind all individual souls.) I do not see any Christian influence in these myths, since they are all thoroughly pagan in their character.

The idea of a Christian influence is derived from the concept of salvation being a particularly Christian trait. However, salvation as part of a initiation and sacred marriage ritual, as it appears in Old Norse myths, is closely associated with the Ancient Mystery Cults of Classical times.

This 2004 dissertation was published as a book by VDM Verlag in 2009 but is now re-published by The Three Little Sisters in 2022, and has been improved, corrected, added to and edited by the author, without losing the original content, unless there were some direct errors in the original. I have also added more of my own translations of the source material.

> *"I am all that is, all that has been, and all that will be.*
> *No Mortal has ever seen behind my veil."*
> *--Inscription above the Temple of Neith, Goddess of Existence, in Egypt.*
>
> *"Crawl to your mother, the Earth;*
> *-she will save you from the void."*
> *--Rig Veda 10.18*
>
> *"There Earth shall meet Thor, her son;*
> *she will show him the kinspeople's´ way to Óðinn's land*
> *--Hárbarðsljóð Stanza 56, Poetic Edda*

1.I have tasted the sweet drink of life, knowing that it inspires good thoughts and joyous expansiveness to the extreme, that all the gods and mortals seek it together, calling it honey.
2.When you penetrate inside, you will know no limits(...)
3.We have drunk the Soma; we have become immortal; we have gone to the light; we have found the gods. (...)
5.The glorious drops that I have drunk set me free in wide space. (...)
11. Weaknesses and diseases have gone; the forces of dark-ness have fled in terror. Soma has climbed up in us, expanding. We have come to the place where they stretch out our lifespans.
12. The drop that we have drunk has entered our hearts, an immortal inside mortals (...)
---Rig Veda, 8. 48

SÓLARLJÓÐ — THE SONG OF THE SUN

25. Dísir bið þú þér
dróttins mála
vera hollar í hugum;
viku eptir
mun þér vilja þíns
alt at óskum ganga.

25. Ask you the goddesses to
your aid
they who are of the speech
of the lord
to be benevolent to you in
their intent:
The week after
you shall have your will
all shall be as you wish

39. Sól ek sá
sanna dagstjörnu
drúpa dynheimum í;
en Heljar grind
heyrða ek á annan veg
þjóta þungliga.

39. I saw the Sun
true Star of Day
sink into Her roaring home
and by the Gate of Hel
I heard, from the other side
a heavy creaking.

40. Sól ek sá
setta dreyrstöfum,
mjök var ek þá ór heimi
hallr;
máttug hon leizk
á marga vegu
frá því er fyrri var.

40. I saw the Sun
beset with blood beams
I was fast declining from
the halls of the world
She seemed more powerful
in many ways
than She had been before.

41. Sól ek sá,
svá þótti mér,
sem ek sæja göfgan guð;
henni ek laut
hinzta sinni
aldaheimi í.

41. I saw the Sun
and it seemed to me
that I was seeing a glorious
deity;
to Her I bowed
for one last time
in this world of ages.

42. Sól ek sá,
svá hon geislaði,
at ek þóttumk vætki vita;
en Gylfar straumar
grenjuðu á annan veg,
blandnir mjök við blóð.

42. I saw the Sun
She beamed so splendidly
that I thought myself to
know nothing
and the streams of the river
of Hel
roared from the other side
blended much with blood

43. Sól ek sá
á sjónum skjálfandi,
hræzlufullr ok hnipinn;
þvíat hjarta mitt
var heldr mjök
runnit sundr í sega.

44. Sól ek sá
sjaldan hryggvari,
mjök var ek þá ór heimi
hallr;
tunga mín
var til trés metin,
ok kólnat alt fyr utan.

45. Sól ek sá
síðan aldregi
eptir þann dapra dag,
þvíat fjallavötn luktusk
fyr mér saman,
en ek hvarf kallaðr frá
kvölum.

46. Vánarstjarna flaug,
þá var ek fœddr,
brot frá brjósti mér;
hátt at hon fló,
hvergi settisk,
svá at hon mætti hvíld
hafa.

51. Á norna stóli
sat ek níu daga,
þaðan var ek á hest
hafinn;
gýgjar sól
er skein grimmliga
ór skýdrúpnis skýjum.

55. Sólar hjört
leit ek sunnan fara,
hann teymðu tveir
saman;
fœtr hans
stóðu foldu á,
en tóku horn til himins.

43. I saw the Sun
with quivering eyes
appalled and shrinking
because my heart
was to a great degree
torn apart in languor

44. I saw the Sun
and was seldom sadder
I was now far from the halls
of the world
my tongue
had turned into wood
and all around me was cold.

45. I saw the Sun
and then never again
after that gloomy day
for the waters of the
mountain
closed around me
and I was called from my
pains.

46. The Star of Hope flew
when I was born
cut out from my chest
She soared high
never settled
so that She might have found
peace.

51. In the Seat of the Norns
I sat for nine days
then I was placed on a horse
The Sun of the Giantess
shone in disguise
through the dripping clouds
of the sky

55. The Hart of the Sun
I saw arrive from the South
he was led by two together
his feet stood planted on
Earth
his horns spread into
Heaven

78. Arfi! faðir
einn þér ráðit hefi,
ok þeir Sólkötlu synir,
hjartar horn,
þat er ór haugi bar
hinn vitri Vígdvalinn.

78. Son! As your father
I have counseled you,
as have the sons of Sun
Cauldron Woman,
towards the Horn of the
Heart
that he brought from the
burial-mound
that wise Hibernation of
War

79. Hér 'ru rúnar,
er ristit hafa
Njarðar dœtr níu:
Ráðveig hin elzta
ok Kreppvör hin yngsta
ok þeirra systr sjau.

9. Here are runes
that have been carved
by the nine daughters of
Njǫrðr:
Counsel Power Drink the
oldest
Approaching Spring the
youngest
and their seven sisters.

These verses from the Edda poem Sólarljóð – The Song of the Sun - have been translated by the author. All Edda translations in this book by Maria Kvilhaug

1: Introduction

This thesis takes, as its starting point, a recurring theme in the Poetic Edda, namely the supernatural maiden offering a cup or a horn of precious mead to a hero. This theme is encountered in the various poems of the Poetic Edda, most specifically in the poems:

» Hávamál [The High One's (Óðinn's) Speech]
» Skírnismál [The Shining One's Speech]
» Hyndluljóð [The She-Wolf's Song]
» Sígrdrífumál [Sígrdrífa's (Victory Drift's) Speech]

The valkyria who offers the mead in the Sígrdrífumál is part of a story which stretches across several chronologically ordered Edda poems, beginning with the Grípisspá [The Grasping One's Speech], Reginsmál [The Ruler's Speech], followed by Fafnismál [The Embracer's Speech], all together leading to the climax of the Sígrdrífumál [Victory Drift's Speech].

Additionally, the valkyria Sígrdrífa is said to be a reincarnation (or a continuation, or other aspect/hypostases) of other valkyriur met with in the heroic poem of Helgi Hjǫrvarðsson and the two poems of Helgi Hundingsbani. These stories also do follow the same structure of stages, although the mead-serving is less obvious – all of which makes it necessary to study all these poems in order to form a complete picture of the "Maiden with the Mead".

I will also add to my study the double-poem "Svípdagsmál [Swift Dawn's Speech]", which consists of Gróagaldr [The Spell-Song of Growth] and the Fjǫlsvinnsmál [Great Wisdom's Speech], because the structure of the poem is comparable to the structure of the other poems studied in this dissertation.

Thus, many poems, each with their own history of research and interpretations, will be touched upon, and I may obviously not deal with all the details of each poem. The main aim, however, is to detect a common structure within each of the stories.

I wish to show that they are all, in essence, telling the same tale, even though they all have their particular poetic flavoring, their own particular contexts and purpose. My desire is to show that behind the different poetical scenarios, a common mythical pattern is to be observed: that of sacred initiation centered around the figure of a "Great Goddess", who may take many names and shapes. What is meant by a "Great Goddess"? This will be discussed as an academic term for when we find a goddess who can assume many different hypostases and who covers a very wide range of functions, is worshipped by every class and gender, both in the larger, public cult and in the home cults, often assuming a leading role in the pantheon of goddesses.

In this work, we will only slightly touch upon the kind of initiation that the poems are dealing with. Within the limits of this study there was not much room for discussing whether we are seeing the reflection of initiation to manhood, warriorhood, a secret society, a mystery cult, kingship or a religious office. Considering the number of participants and the diversity between them in the stories, I suspect that the "Maiden" as initiator is a part of a general pattern of initiation. The kind of trials and the kind of teachings that the supposed initiand must go through will be dealt with through the presentation of the poems, but since we are covering so many different stories there is not much space for an in-depth study.

Our focus will be on the structural pattern of themes, as well as on the figure of the "Maiden" and the mythology surrounding her.

I employ the word "Maiden" rather than "woman" or "goddess". Why?

» Firstly, the character in question is in the sources usually referred to as a mær/mey (f.pl[1]: meyiar), which means a maiden, in the sense of a young woman, usually but not necessarily unmarried.

» Secondly because her goddess-hood is ambivalent; she sometimes appears as a giantess, sometimes as a valkyria. It is possible that we are speaking of hypostases, a phenomenon which often appears in ancient religions with pantheistic sub-religions.

---

1 F.pl: = "feminine plural" noun in the gender-based grammars of Old Norse

WHAT IS PANTHEISM?

Within Hinduism, a polytheistic religious complex with roots reaching back into prehistory, we find a great array of countless different gods and goddesses, and yet, there are powerful religious, mystical, devotional and philosophic sub-traditions within Hinduism where pantheism prevails, often identifying any goddess as a hypostasis (aspect) of Mahadevi, which literally translates as "Great Goddess". She is often the object of worship in devotional Shakti and Shiva Bhakti traditions, but more famously (or infamously) in Tantra. Both Bhakti and Tantra tend towards Pantheism – the notion that All are One, and One is All. These notions are thousands of years old.

Mahadevi [Great Goddess] is also identical to the concept of Shakti, a serpentine creative energy known from Tantra and Kundalini Yoga, which represents the feminine and active half of the Supreme Being (the male and passive counterpart may be called Mahadeva – "the Great God").

Certain goddesses of great power and with a wide range of functions, such as Kali, Lakshmi, Durga, Sarasvati etc., are in different traditions seen as the "truest" face of Mahadevi, the Great Goddess, referred to by various names. Whereas all goddesses have different names, separate functions, personalities and ties, they are all, including the gods, ultimately mere aspects – hypostases - of the one true deity, the Supreme Being, which has a passive, masculine observer half, and an active, feminine creative part.

These esoteric traditions of Pantheism within the greater diversity of polytheistic folk religion are not only known from Hinduism. Pantheism also applies to an ancient form of salvation religions which preceded Christianity and other forms of Monotheism by thousands of years, what we today usually refer to as Classical Mystery Religions (or "Ancient Mystery Cults").

There may be tendencies towards Pantheism in very old places such as Egypt and the Middle East, but with the Classical Mystery Religions that were widespread in the Hellenistic and particularly the Roman Empires, we find a lot more source material. We know that particularly three goddesses of the Roman Empire, albeit with non-Roman origins, were regarded as saviors from death and as the true faces of the Supreme Being, the All-Soul, or the Great Goddess, by their devotional Mystery initiands: Greek Demeter, Middle Eastern Cybele, and Egyptian Isis.

We will return to this subject of Mystery Religions, suffice it to say here that these religions display many signs of Pantheistic philosophies. When it comes to Germanic, Pre-Christian religions, several scholars have addressed this theme of Pantheism in the form of a Great Goddess figure, from different perspectives, among others Folke Ström, Britt Mari Näsström and Else Mundal, who also argues a theory of hypostases, where the difference between the collective of deities and one singular deity may not always be so strict within the cult. It is my conviction that it is possible to form a more detailed picture of the "cult" (sub-religion within the greater religion) of the Maiden with the Mead and its philosophy through analysis of the patterns and structures of mythology hiding behind the medieval Icelandic poems.

ARCHAEOLOGICAL EVIDENCE OF THE MAIDEN WITH THE MEAD

The motif of a maiden serving mead is also found in many images from the Viking Age, carved on rock – especially memorial stones at burial places – or woven on hangings. The pictorial motif of the maiden with the horn is often interpreted as a valkyria welcoming the dead One-Harrier (or Sole Ruler) [einheri, m.sg[2]] as he arrives in Valhǫll [the Hall of the (Chosen) Dead, f.sg[3]].

Valhǫll is often understood as a kind of Heaven for those who die in battle, led by Óðinn, who in the tradition of Snorri is the ruler of all the gods. However, the Poetic Edda allows both giantesses and goddesses, as well as valkyriur, to serve the "precious mead", "the ancient mead", "the memory drink", "the adored mead" and the "poetry-stir" to worthy heroes. In none of these stories is it clear that we are reading about a dead one-harrier and a valkyria in Valhǫll, but the climax of the story involves an experienced or ritual death and a visit to the underworld, where the Maiden dwells. In the archaeological, pictorial sources, the link to an afterlife is strong since the images are found on burial monuments and within graves.

---

2   m.sg = "masculine singular"

3   f.sg = "feminine singular". Old Norse divides nouns into the masculine, feminine and neutral gender.

Michael Enright has shown how women's mead-offering in a hall constituted the central part of a very common and very significant ritual in all Germanic (and also in Celtic) societies, a ritual which had nothing to do with the afterlife but rather with kingship and hierarchical bonding within a warband - a theory that we shall return to in chapter 3.2. Through a survey of European archaeological finds, Enright has also proven the actual existence of what he calls "ladies with a mead-cup", that is, great ladies buried with liquor-serving device in hand and many associated objects.

The continuity and regularity of these finds shows that the mead-serving high-born woman was an important person in all Germanic societies for more than a millennium, and Enright questions whether she be a queen, a noblewoman, or, originally, a kind of priestess. Even if I take a different approach to this theme than Enright does, his work is valuable because it shows that there were indeed real women who held a social or religious status that was connected to a ritual of mead-serving, suggesting that the myths of the Maiden with the Mead may be based on actual ritual and religious traditions. We will come back to this question in chapter 9.5 with the hope of throwing some more light on the Maiden figure.

THE GODDESS IN HEL

Through a study of the symbols of the realm and kinsfolk surrounding the Maiden, we will see that whether she be goddess, valkyria or giantess, the essentials remain the same in all the poems. The symbolism is connected to the world of the dead and may be traced to the particular death-realm of Hel, where eagles, serpents and wolfdogs devour the corpses of the dead, where rivers and bridges carry loud sounds, where the fences and halls are high, and within which, mysteriously, a bright realm of immortality is to be found.

The fact that the symbolism of the Maiden's realm resembles Hel's is puzzling to everyone who are brought up to think that there are strict geographical borders between the Underworld of Hel and the Heaven of Óðinn, Valhǫll. One of the resulting conclusions of my study must be that there are no such geographical borders in the mythological sphere, and no actual borders between the races of giants, gods or valkyriur. What we are seeing must be aspects or levels of the same reality: The world where the valkyria offers life-giving mead to the One-Harrier may be an aspect of the same world where Hel keeps the bright mead covered by a shield.[4]

Yet it is a level of this same world where the hero has overcome the monstruous beings of absolute extinction in death. He has walked into the realm of death and has come out alive, following the pattern of Óðinn Helblindi [Hel-Blinder] and Hermóðr who jumps over the gates of death without touching them[5], returning to the world of the living with hidden knowledge. It is the idea of immortality in one form or another - I believe in close connection to an initiation rite - that can be detected within the myths of the Maiden.

DIFFERENT GUISES

The Maiden herself appears in different guises in each of the stories.

1. In those stories which may be placed back to the beginning of mythical time, where the gods are the heroes who undergo the trials, the Maiden is a giantess hidden underground.
2. Later, when human beings follow in the footsteps of Óðinn and Freyr, she appears as a dazzling goddess, or as a valkyria.

One could almost suspect that through her union with the gods of the ordered world, this primeval, giantess creature becomes an agent of this same world and thus a divine being herself. Not only may the goddesses be identified with the giantesses through their similar functions, but the valkyriur of the heroic poems illustrate the point of a common reality behind different names perfectly –for they are even directly said to be reincarnations of the same being over and over again. They have either been endrborinn [born again] or have slept since the last hero died, awaiting the return of his next incarnation.

---

4   Vegtamskvíða stanza 7
5   Gylfaginning 49

Through a study of a common structure in all the different poems that we are considering, we may draw the main conclusion: a common myth must lie behind the imagery of all these poems: the myth of a Maiden who dwells in the heart of Misty Hel, and who may be brought out to marry the worthy hero, a union which includes teachings and revelations of esoteric knowledge and seemingly even an alternative to extinction in death.

Within this myth we may see traces of a ritual, cult or ecstatic experience where the devoted hero undergoes trials of overcoming greed, pride, hatred and death in order to learn the arts of healing, eloquence, manliness and wisdom.

To prove my thesis, I will systematically try to detect significant structural elements that recur in all or most of these myths. We will see that the pattern detected could very much resemble a ritual of initiation. We will also throw some light upon what I shall call "Maiden-mythology" – a mythology of the goddess that I believe may be traced in the Poetic Edda, but which has been rather unexplored until now. To some degree I will make use of a philological method where I let the meanings of names and placenames determine my understanding of the texts.

As for translation of the original texts and names, I have basically used the dictionary from Old Norse to Norwegian called "Norrøn Ordbok", as well as Rudolf Simek's "Dictionary of Norse Mythology", and interpretations presented by various scholars in the secondary sources. In addition to Sophus Bugge's rendering of the original texts of the Poetic Edda, I have used the translations of these texts into English by Carolyne Larrington, and into the Norwegian by Ludvig Holm-Olsen and by Ivar Mortensson-Egnund. Since the respective translations differ from each other, I have in some places found it necessary to do some translation on my own according to my understanding.

2: Sources

2.1: The Poetic Edda

My main source will be the Poetic Edda, also known as the Elder Edda. In the year 1643, an Icelandic bishop called Brynjolf Sveinsson came across an old manuscript containing poems about gods and legendary heroes, poems largely unknown by the educated people of those days. Many of the stanzas that Snorri Sturluson had quoted and referred to in his prose work about pagan, mythology-based poetical metaphors, better known as the "Prose Edda", from 1220-1225 A.D. were recognized, and the bishop assumed that Snorri's Edda must have been based on this "elder, poetic Edda".

Brynjolf himself called the manuscript Sæmundar Edda, because he believed that the poems must have been written down by the famous monk Sæmundr the Wise, a belief which has not been confirmed by later scholars. The Latin name given to the old collection was Codex Regius, thus named because it was soon sent as a gift to king Fredrik III of Denmark.

Not counting the eight pages that had been torn out of the manuscript, the Codex Regius contains 29 poems, five of which are also found in another Icelandic manuscript from about 1300. In this manuscript is also found a poem that is not found in the Codex, namely the poem Baldrs draumar [Balder's Dreams], also known as the Vegtamskvíða [Way-Wont's Song or "The Song of the One Who Knows the Path"]. Both manuscripts have an older, common origin. Because of the letters and the language, it is believed that the Codex was written down in Iceland at the end of the 13th century, yet many of the poems are quoted in Snorri's Edda, which was written around 1220. It is believed that the older manuscript was written down a while before Snorri's works, sometime during the 12th century. The Edda poems are based on myth and legends that are older than the settling of Iceland; some legendary poems include historical characters from the 4th and 5th centuries A.D. For this reason, many 17th-19th century scholars believed that the poems were very old, but in 1871, Edvin Jessen concluded that the poems were created in the Viking Age and that only some parts are of older origin.

In the form in which they have been transmitted, they are mostly from the 11th and 12th century, some perhaps even as late as from the 13th century, and most of them were created in Iceland, although some are of Norwegian origin. There are, for example, three different versions of the poem Vǫluspá [The Prophecy of the Vǫlva] all with rather fundamental differences from each other. The poems are probably much older, but during oral transmission, scholars assume that changes and innovations have taken place, so that we cannot know how these poems were to begin with, we only now that this was how they were written down in the Middle Ages.

The idea that the poems are not "authentic" rendering of Pagan myth, however, has been criticized by many scholars who argue that poets were unlikely to invent mythical imagery that was not recognizable to the listeners already, and archaeology has shown that a great many myths rendered in the Poetic Edda have their far older pictorial versions: proving that these myths existed in pre-Christian times.[6]

The poems themselves may in part have been composed in their present form centuries earlier and transmitted orally. Many show signs of very old themes, often placing the stories in semi-historical context to the time of the Huns and the Roman Empire. Other themes show ancient links to other religious traditions – some even going as far back and away as ancient India and Iran. The god Þórr carries attributes that links him to Vedic Indra five thousand years ago, and to countless depictions of ancient thunderbolt-wielding gods from the ancient world reaching back to the Bronze Ages. As I myself am suggesting, there are interesting, conceptual similarities to Ancient Mystery religions going back to the Iron Ages and beyond.

Some linguists have suggested an origin of Edda poetry in the form we know them in 10th to 11th century Trøndelag, Norway, where the court of the earls of Hlaðir held many poets and were strongly devoted to the old religion, and in strong opposition to the new one. The language and content may suggest that many of the poems were based on very old myths but made in the form we know them as a conscious response to the new religion.[7]

---

6 Clunies-Ross, 1994, p. 16-19, Solli, 2002, p. 199, Mundal, 1974, p. 15-23

7 Steinsland, Gro & Meulengracht-Sørensen, Preben (1999): Voluspå, Pax Forlag

If you ask me, I will say that this sounds plausible, and that the poems seem to be bent towards showing that they, too, knew a meaningful path of "salvation" and deeper mysteries of initiation. After all, one of the most common arguments against the old religion that the early medieval Christians were using exactly during the time of conversion, was the notion that their pagan religion did not offer any hope of salvation in death, at least not one that was available for all the people who did not die in battle. In my opinion, the poets of the Edda appear to be consciously addressing the wealth of wisdom and paths towards enlightenment that also existed within their own religion – even if those paths may have been for the specially interested.

2.2: DIVINE POEMS

The Codex arranges the poems systematically in poems about the gods - Divine Poems and Heroic Poems. The manuscript contains ten Divine Poems, and from other manuscripts we know of three more poems, thirteen in all. Every poem stands on its own and has to be studied separately. The poems are referring to myths, tales about the fundamental actions of the gods in the beginning of time. According to Ludvig Holm-Olsen the original myths that the poems are based on have existed in poetic forms over the whole Norse-speaking area in pagan times.

Parts of the mythology clearly belong to a common Indo-European heritage, and there are some striking similarities to old Indian religion. Many of the myths may be closely connected to cult and ritual drama, where human beings would enact the roles of mythical beings. Holm-Olsen states that it has proven difficult to find the pagan cultic connection to the myths because the poems have been written down in Christian times and probably undergone some censorship and changes due to the new religion. The way the poems are presented, they are influenced by a time that saw the pagan myths as entertainment or material particularly interesting for skalds -bards, who would use mythical imagery for their poetic metaphors, the kenningar.[8]

---

8   This summary isbased on Holm-Olsen,1995 p. 256-260

This view has, however, been disputed by amongst others Mai Elisabeth Berg who sees the poems as purely literary constructions by Christian medieval poets.[9]

Yet Else Mundal argues that medieval poets used mythological material in a way that necessarily had to make sense to his contemporaries, who would be well-versed in the mythic cosmology.[10]

Margaret Clunies-Ross argues that Pagan ideas and mythology are proved to have survived as a living tradition several centuries after the establishment of Christianity in the North, a view that is also held by Gro Steinsland, who stresses the strength and reinforcement of the old religion during the period of conversion, when some of the poems were created.[11]

Scholars such as Einar Haugen and Gro Steinsland clearly state that genuine pre-Christian paganism may be detected in the poems.[12]

It appears today that most scholars agree that, with the use of discernment and criticism and always remembering that they were written down by medieval Christian scholars who may have meddled with the content here and there, we can clearly extract pagan elements that are recognizable from other and more provable sources or from comparative sources.

As I have shown in this thesis, we may even extract quite detailed descriptions of pagan initiation rituals that cannot possibly have been influenced by Christianity, both because the deeply pagan imagery is so thick and so shamanistic-like, and because even their hints towards a notion of salvation are near identical to the much older notion of salvation through initiation rituals that we find in Classical Mystery Religion.

---

9   Berg, 2001, p. 15, 20, 26
10   Mundal, 1994, p. 63-70
11   Clunies-Ross, 1994, p. 18-19, Steinsland, 1998, p. 81-84
12   See chapter 2.7 and. chapter 3.3

2.3: HEROIC POEMS

"In the traditional songs which form their only record of the past the Germans celebrate an earth-born god called Tuisto. His son Mannus is supposed to be the fountain head of their race and himself to have begotten three sons who gave their names to three groups of tribes."[13]---Tacitus, Germania 80 A.D.

The earliest proof of heroic poetry among Germanic peoples is given by the Roman historian, Tacitus, about the year 80 A.D., and by Jordanes in the 6th century. From the centuries that followed we have source material that shows how the Heroic Poetry of the Edda was a common Germanic heritage. The form is epical and dramatical, mostly presented in dialogues. The practical details are less important than the inner state of mind of the characters, their attitudes and their feelings.

I will add that the inner lives, desires, passions, sorrows and feelings of women are given remarkable space when seen in the context of a medieval world, even compared to the saga material, where the focus is more on the action, and more male-centered.

Changes and innovations in the oral transmissions have taken place before they were written down. The tales also existed in the form of legends, which may have formed the background of the poems, since the short, allusive style of the poems demands that the listeners possess knowledge of more detailed (prose) stories.

The poems of the two Helgi characters, which are rather young poems, clearly reflect the cultural milieu of the Viking Age –and are possibly of Danish origin, since they give numerous references to Danish place names. The compositions as we know them are probably not older than the 11th century, although the different parts are of different age.

Through prose interpolation, probably created by the directors of the manuscript, one of the Helgi characters is connected to Sígurðr the Serpent-slayer through close kinship. The stories of Siegfried-Sígurðr, however, came from the continent to Scandinavia during the 9th century, when they were already quite old, carrying legendary material from 5th century Europe.

Of all the poems, Grípisspá is probably the youngest, summing up the whole of Sígurðr's story in a "prophecy".[14]

---

13 Mattingly, 1970, p. 102
14 Holm-Olsen, 1995, p. 283-284, 288-299

2.4: SNORRI'S EDDA

Snorri Sturluson (1179-1241), a famous politician in his days, is today most famous for his great prose works, the Heimskringla, which contains the history of the Norwegian kings from their Pagan, divine origins and almost up to Snorri's own time, and of that work which has been called the "Younger Edda" or the "Snorri's Edda", which was composed some time between 1220 and 1225. It is both a thesis and a teaching book about the Old Norse art of poetry[15]. It is divided into a Prologus [Latin for Prologue] and three chapters; the Gylfaginning [Gylfi's Hallucinations] the Skáldskaparmál [Poetry Creation Speech] and the Háttatal [Verse List].

The Prologue and the Gylfaginning cover Norse mythology, whereas the next two chapters are concerned with teaching the ancient forms of poetry. The Skáldskaparmál is also rich in mythology, since myths form the basis for the poetic metaphors [kenningar] that Snorri is teaching[16]. The mythology that Snorri is relating is apparently founded on old poems but also on oral versions in prose.

Clunies-Ross argues that both forms of mythology existed in pre-Christian times. The allusive nature of Old Norse poems indicates that they only relate "the tips of narrative icebergs" and that the audience would already be acquainted with the "main part of the story below the surface"[17]. This story is supposedly what Snorri is relating, making it possible for us to understand much more of the poems and what they are alluding to, often explaining how this story may be applied in poetry.

Yet, Snorri probably had many versions of the same stories, and it is likely that his accounts do not represent the "final", "real" version, but the "most complete of many" versions.[18]

That Snorri's presentation of the mythic material was shaped by the Christian world-view of his era is visible, especially in the way he omits any explanations of known sacrificial myths such as Óðinn's hanging on the world-tree and the way the vǫlva Gullveigr defies death. Many scholars have suggested that Snorri omitted these important mythical events because they were just too alien for his Christian understanding.[19]

---

15 Clunies Ross, 1987, chapter I
16 Holm-Olsen, 1995, p. 211-220
17 Clunies-Ross, 1994, p. 25
18 Ibid, p. 30
19 Clunies-Ross, 1994, p. 32-33, Solli 2002, p. 159

2.5: OTHER SOURCES

There is a great wealth of written source material that scholars may use when studying Norse mythology. The different kinds of Icelandic sagas, the works of Saxo Grammaticus, contemporary literature from the continent, antique and Arab observations, as well as skaldic poetry may be used. For this thesis, I have focused mainly on the Eddas, and, out of concern with space will here refer to other material that has been directly applied when it seems necessary.

2.6: THE RELIABILITY OF THE SOURCES

We have already partially touched upon this subject in chapter 2.1 to 2.6. but we shall here quickly sum up our main standpoint.

It is important to bear in mind that, as Gro Steinsland pointed out, the Norse source-material in general are myths worked upon as literature. A myth may express the ideology – that is, the thoughts and ideas that are dominant in society or in certain layers of society, of a class or of a group, its self-understanding and its world-understanding.

One must, however, expect metamorphosis and transformations of various layers of ideas and be aware of individual, poetic creation. This means that the myth may have been removed from its original religious context. It is only through the revealing of and definition of mythological models in the sources, that one may have a hope of coming close to genuinely pagan beliefs. Through analysis of the texts, we may be able to detect the pre-Christian ideological contents of the literature, whereas a cultic frame of reference is far more difficult to reconstruct[20]. This is in accordance with my own approach as well.

As we shall see in chapter 3.2, most scholars, including Steinsland herself, have not refrained from interpreting the myths within a "cultic frame of reference" when the evidence seems to be sufficient. Through careful treatment, it appears possible to detect ideological models, structures and patterns within the poems. While some have seen the poems as actual "manuscripts" of recital or ritual drama, and thus of complete pagan origin, others have suggested remnants or patterns of practice and belief within the poetic creations.

---

20 Steinsland, 1991, p. 20

According to Eldar Heide, one could try and interpret myth through looking at the underlying structure in the myth behind the details. Heide reads mythology much like one would read a parable. This is in accordance with how I personally also read mythology, and lies the ground for my work on mythology.

In a parable, it is the structure that carries the meaning, not what fills out the structure. Variations in myths are thus no longer problematic. Heide builds his argument on the fact that this approach would be mindful of the rules for Norse poetic language. A most basic feature of Norse poetry is the endless variation in the expression of one thing or thought.[21]

My own perspective is a similar one to those of Heide and Steinsland; I aim at showing a recurring pattern in the poems that may reflect authentic pre-Christian myth and even cultic practice.

---

21   Heide, 1997, p. 92-93

3: Terminology and Previous Research

The Poetic Edda as a complete manuscript has a long history of research, and we will be scrutinizing several very different Edda poems, each of which also has its very own history of research. It will obviously be too much for this dissertation to cover the scholarly history of each poem and of the whole collection of poems. There will also be many details in the individual poems that we may not give sufficient attention.

Some keywords only will be our focus of investigation: The offering of mead to the hero –theme, the theme of ritual initiation reflected in the myths, and the study of the Maiden-figure in her aspect as giantess, goddess and valkyria. We will also touch upon some terms that will be used in this study.

Terms

"The term initiation in the most general sense denotes a body of rites and oral teachings whose purpose is to produce a radical modification of the religious and social status of the person to be initiated. In philosophical terms, initiation is equivalent to an ontological mutation of the existential condition. The novice emerges from his ordeal a totally different being."[22]

Initiation

Eliade and Adams divide initiation into three categories: "puberty rites", which may also be known as "tribal initiation" or "initiation into an age group", initiation into a secret society, and initiation connected to mystical vocation. The "puberty rites" introduce the novice into the world of spiritual and cultural values, making him or her a responsible member of society. The initiation requires some more or less dramatic trials: separation from the family, isolation from society and secret revelations. It often includes a ritual death, followed by a resurrection or rebirth into a new role, title or identity. Rites of entrance into a secret society correspond with those of puberty or tribal initiation: seclusion, tortures, "death" and "resurrection", the bestowal of a new name and the revelation of secret doctrines.

22 Eliade/Adams, 1987, VII, p. 225

Initiatory death signifies the end of a state of being and the entrance into a new spiritual state. This procedure is patterned on the model revealed by the gods or mythical ancestors. Elders or priests, masters of initiation, supervise the rites and convey the revelations. As for shamans and medicine men, the initiation consists in ecstatic experiences through dreams, visions and trances; the instruction may be imparted by a master of initiation but may also exclusively be imparted by spirits/supernatural entities. Sometimes the initiation is public and includes rituals, but in many cases the novice is initiated without rituals: it happens in his or her dreams or ecstatic experiences.[23]

Jens Peter Schjødt has argued that the universal pattern detected in initiation ritual in fact may be detected in many other kinds of rituals. It is only when the person undergoing the rituals actually becomes someone or something else than they were before the ritual, is given a new position, a new social or religious role, that we may actually be speaking of a genuine initiation ritual.[24]

SACRED MARRIAGE

Sacred marriage, also called by its Greek term; Hieros Gamos, is the name of a mythical or ritual union between a god and a goddess, or between a divine and a human being; most especially a king and a goddess.[25]

In early city-states of the Middle East, the Hieros Gamos ritual was very common for thousands of years. Hieros Gamos continued as an unbroken tradition and was the central rite in religious life during the whole time-span of the state of Sumer, which lasted from 4500 B.C to about 1750 B.C, and, moreover, continued into the following Babylonian and Hebrew times, influencing Minoan and Greek rites as well, particularly within mystery cults. The Sumerian ritual was associated with a descent by the goddess to her sister in the Underworld, where she would become a corpse and then be resurrected.

---

23 Ibid, p. 225-227
24 Schjødt, 1994, p. 114-115
25 Eliade/Adams, VI, p. 317, 319-320

As Anita Hammer has shown, the preparations for the descent were identical with preparations for the marriage.[26] The model for the ritual was given in myths, and the ritual itself was performed on stage by a king and a priestess representing the goddess. The ritual represented the union of the king with the city goddess, being the visible counterpart of a celestial union. Kingship demanded a sacred foundation that could be provided only through the omnipotence of the Great Goddess[27].

Sacred marriage in some form or another was also known in Scandinavia throughout the Bronze Age, shown in the rock carvings of that period. According to Camilla Helene Fari the contexts in which imagery of sexual intercourse from the Bronze Age are found strongly suggest a religious and cosmological framework. A great part of this imagery is clearly connected to a larger, official cult ruled by an elite.

The sacred marriage imagery seems to belong to a time when society was becoming increasingly hierarchical. Since the Scandinavian Bronze Age society had an Indo-European basic structure where the elite could maintain contact with other elites across Europe, Fari assumes that there must be a connection between the sacred marriage images of Scandinavia and the myths and rituals of sacred marriage in the Middle East. Fari speaks of a "basic myth" with great geographical extent that could have had some influence in Scandinavia. This basic myth was strongly connected to legitimation of the elite, to the peoples´ wish for fertility as well as philosophies around death and resurrection.[28]

Comparative studies show that the Norse goddess Freyia shares all her important mythological attributes with the Sumerian goddess Ishtar/Inanna, and many with other Middle Eastern goddesses who also played a role in sacred marriage.[29] In my opinion, this strengthens Fari's thesis of a strong connection between Middle Eastern and Scandinavian myth and cult.

---

26 Hammer, 1999, p. 1
27 Eliade/Adams, VI, p. 319-320
28 Fari, 2003, p. 20-25
29 Motz, 1993, p. 111

In his study on fertility cults in connection to sacred kingship, Folke Ström clearly connected the Middle Eastern traditions with the Norse. Ström found traces of a cult of the Great Goddess, intimately related to the "sacral king". In his study of Old Norse texts and the official Uppsala-cult in pagan Sweden, he claimed to find traces of ideas such as the king being identical with the god of fertility in his sexual relation to the Goddess and in his real or symbolic sacrificial death. Ström connects Óðinn's self-sacrifice in the World Tree with such a descent to the underworld through sacrifice.[30]

More recently, using the Skírnismál as a starting point, Gro Steinsland has shown that a myth of sacred marriage existed in the Norse society, and that it probably had its ritual counterparts. The Hieros Gamos myth was very important for the ideology of royal lines; the king or ruler represented a particular type of being different from others in that he was descended from a god and a giantess, representatives of cosmic polarity.

Steinsland dates this form of Hieros Gamos back to the 5th century A.D, when royal lines and central rule achieved greater importance than before; when the ancient custom of sacrificing outside in groves and bogs was replaced by a cult much more closely linked to the royal houses. The rituals of initiation into kingship or rulership was connected to a death and resurrection symbolism, a revelation of esoteric knowledge, and culminated in sacred marriage, reflecting the ancient myth of the divine ancestral father and the giant ancestral mother.[31]

"SHAMANISM"

Author's Note: Editing this manuscript in 2021, I am aware that the umbrella terms "shaman" and "shamanism" is problematic to some. Back in 2004, this was a common term, and used in the academic literature that I worked with. There is also no other general umbrella term for what "shamanism" has come to mean in an academic, phenomenological, comparative sense, so I will stick to this terminology in this book, while editing this in newer works of mine. Sámi "shamanism" is clearly related to Siberian, Uralic and Greenlandic "shamanism".

---

30 Ström, 1954, p. 6-8, Ström argues that Óðinn shares many traits with a fertility god on p.62-69

31 Steinsland, 1991; main theory of her thesis, Steinsland, 2000, p. 48 - 81

Britt Solli is the last in a long row of scholars who have argued the existence of shamanism within the Norse society. That shamanism was known among the Norse-speaking population is clear: shamanism was a central practice among their close neighbors, the Sámi.[32] Both sagas and laws testify to the close relationship between the Norse-speaking and the Finnic-speaking Sámi populations. Norsemen would approach Sámi shamans or sorcerers for help and even for teaching, even well into the Christian Middle Ages (even especially then, since only the Sámi still cultivated shamans by then).

In the strictest sense of the term, a shaman is a religious practitioner operating within Finnic, Turkic and Mongol tribes of Siberia and the Urals, but, as Åke Hultkrantz has shown, its most particular features are to be found also in North America and in Scandinavia among the Sámi. [33]Shamanism was also central in Greenland.[34]

According to Mircea Eliade, the shaman is primarily "the master of ecstasy" – an individual who succeeds in having mystical experiences in the form of a trance where the shaman's soul leaves the body and flies to heaven or the underworlds. They become an expert in orienting themselves in the unknown regions that they enter during ecstasy.

The descents to the underworld are usually undertaken to find and bring back a sick person's soul, or to escort the soul of the deceased to its new dwellings. The principal function of the shaman is healing. The shaman may operate side by side with other religious experts such as sacrificial priests and with cults of the home. [35]Eliade's definition made it possible to apply the umbrella term "shamanism" on several practices in other parts of the world, especially in Japan, Korea and among the Sora tribes in India. Thus, shamanism may occur not only in nomadic hunting-gathering societies, but also in agricultural and "civilized" settings. As to our own subject, where the hero is always married to the supernatural Maiden, it is interesting to note that the concept of a "spirit bride" or "spirit husband" is very common, often obligatory, in many shamanistic traditions.[36]

---

32 Solli, 2002, p. 169-197

33 Hultkrantz, 1978, p. 9-35

34 Demant Jacobsen, 1999, p. 1-17

35 Eliade, 2004, p. 4, Eliade/Adams, XIII, p. 202-207

36 Eliade and Adams, XIII, p. 202-207

Eliade saw clear traces of shamanism in Norse mythology, particularly in the figures of Óðinn and Hermóðr. But he, and many scholars after him, argued that there are no traces of real shamans, that is, human shamans, in the Norse sources[37]. In the descriptions of séances of seiðr, Eliade found no soul journeys to heaven or the underworld, and found that the séances were concentrated mainly on divination, which he regarded as a "lower" art. I would add that in the Classical world (Hellenistic and Roman Empires), and in the older worlds that this era descended from, oracular divination was considered very sacred and certainly belonged to the "higher" arts, even forming an integral, even central part of ancient, Classical religions.

Many have discussed whether seiðr and galdr may have been part of a genuine Norse shamanistic practice. Strömbäck, Ström, Hedeager and Solli are all scholars who argue that they are just that. Steinsland also points out that there are obvious contact points between shamanism and seiðr.[38]

The problem seems to be one of definition and interpretation.

Using Hultkrantz's definition of shamanism as not only mastery of ecstatic journeys, but also as an art of calling the spirits, it does indeed seem possible to interpret some séances of seiðr, galdr, as well as other arts such as útiseta (to sit outside in the night, often on a mound, or in a grove, to call the vættir - spirits) as a form of shamanism.[39]

Demant Jacobsen is also among those who argue that shamanism is as much about "mastery over spirits" as about soul journeys.[40]

Hultkrantz shows that, as opposed to Eliade's understanding, divination is both important and highly regarded within shamanistic traditions, thus again opening up for a fresh understanding of many Norse divinatory practices.[41]

---

37 Flood, 1999, p. 157-158, Eliade, 2004, p. 375, 380, 386-387

38 Hedeager 1997, p. 117 Ström 1967, p. 114, Strömbäck, Solli, 2002, p. 130, Steinsland,1997, p. 134

39 Solli, 2002, p. 135-140. Hultkrantz, 1978 p. 20. Mundal,1990, p. 311 also translates vættir as "spirits".

40 Demant Jacobsen, 1999, p. 5-7, 10, 15

41 Solli, 2002, p. 137, Hultkrantz, 1992, p. 18-19

Norse concepts of the soul included what Hultkrantz would call a "free-soul" – that is a soul which may leave the body and operate outside of it, often in the shape of an animal. Norse concepts of the húgr, hámr, fylgja and hamingja could all possibly fit into the "free-soul" concept that is so crucial to shamanism. The Norse soul-concepts seem compatible with the "free-soul" postulated by Åke Hultkrantz in his study of North American soul-concepts (and to the Sámi). Hultkrantz defines it as the soul active outside the body. Originally, the free-soul was combined with anormal states of consciousness, such as in dreams or visions, which is also seen in the Norse material, where a state of sleep or seclusion was connected to the wandering of the húgr.[42]

The Norse sources also show a belief in different kind of souls. The húgr, meaning "will", "thought", "intent", "desire", and "love", is the inner self of the human being. The húgr may separate itself from the body and move about on its own. When the soul moved outside of the body, it would take a hámr, a material shape, often an animal form. The ability to change hámr and travel on a hámr-journey (fara i hamförum) was the talent of the few and considered a capacity that you were born with. Such people were considered particularly versed in magic.

The sagas tell of bards, warriors and vǫlur who had this ability. The shape-changing was usually connected to a state of sleep or dreaming. The animal form of a human soul was also called fylgja (f.sg). The term is distinctly feminine. Some fylgjur came in woman form instead of animal form (even if the owner of the soul was male).

Else Mundal (1974) concluded that the woman fylgja was fundamentally different from the animal fylgja. While the animal fylgja represented a kind of "alter ego" to the person (and, according to Mundal, not a "free-soul") the woman fylgja (fylgjukóna) was considered a kind of guardian spirit, perhaps an ancestral mother, with her ultimate soul.

Ström (1985) had a different approach, sticking to the idea of the animal fylgja as "free-soul" and the woman fylgja as something related. Both agree that the fylgjur are connected to the dísir.

---

42   Hultkrantz, 1953, p. 241-291

Simek translates the fylgjukóna as a "fetch", although he adds that the literal meaning is "following spirit" or perhaps "skin", "cover". He defines it as the soul of people when it is separate from their bodies. The fylgjur may be identified with the personified fortune of a person, the hamingja. These are a kind of soul-like protective spirits. The word comes from hámr-gengja, which originally referred to people who could let their hámr walk. The idea of the woman fylgja and hamingja is to my view connected to the idea of the norns who follow each person through his or her life, as Snorri tells us in his Gylfaginning. They would appear to be intimately related to the collective of dísir.

As Mundal has pointed out, the fylgjur are often called dísir, especially in poems. She believes that the woman fylgjur originated among the collective of female spirits or goddesses called the dísir, while the animal fylgja has a different origin.

As for finding a (human) shaman in Norse society, the Vǫlva [f.pl: [43]vǫlur] is the latest and most obvious possible example. Her respected position and role in society and cult, as well as her art, seiðr, are most compatible with other descriptions of shamans. Another candidate is the male Seiðmaðr, who, at least in the written material, appears to have been more stigmatized than the female practitioner and often accused of unmanliness. Some have argued that seiðr was a women's business, and that men practicing it were regarded as unmanly simply because they operated in a feminine sphere of work.[44]

However, the amount of seiðmennir in the sources indicate that the practice was quite common also among men, and as Solli points out, even the highest god, Óðinn, practiced it without shame. It is possible that his arts included aspects that the Christian writers could not accept of a man. As for other and more ancient titles that may have covered the office of a Norse shaman, Solli suggests the þulr [45]and the eril, basing herself on discussions of the terms by scholars such as Ottar Grønvik and Bente Magnus[46]. Later in this study, we will meet both a þulr and a jarl – later version of eril - operating as what may be considered masters of initiation.

---

43 F.pl. = Feminine plural

44 For example Ström, 1954, p. 60, Flood, 1999, p. 146-150, Eliade, 2004, p. 385

45 Þulr (m.sg, plural: þulir), sage, wise man, poet, singer, storyteller, reciter, orator - from the verb þylja: to recite, to chant, tell. Related to Proto-Germanic *þuliz, and Old English þyle, with same meaning.

46 Solli, 2002, p. 157-162, 216

MYSTERY RELIGIONS

Näsström suggests that Óðinn's trials on the world tree are not necessarily reflections of shamanistic initiation; they might as well be compared to the initiation trials of antique Mystery Religions. In this 2004 study, I was still more leaning towards "shamanism", since it was so obviously present in the myths, but I also began to see a certain similarity between the hero's trials and relations to the Maiden – who in the context of her stories in the Edda does fit the bill of a classical "Great Goddess"- and those of ancient Mystery religions.

Originally, "mysteries" denoted a religious manifestation that is not open to everyone; they required a special initiation. The word has later become a technical term for secret cults and ceremonies. It is particularly related to the Greco-Roman age and Near Eastern religions. The Mysteries are special initiation ceremonies that are esoteric in character, involving the destiny of a deity and the communication of religious wisdom that enables the initiands to conquer death. Public processions and sacrifices, dances and music would frame the celebration, which was held in a closed room. The ceremony in itself was not open to the public. Since the Mysteries were secret, we know very little of the actual content of the rituals, which centered on initiation. We may only deduce that the central theme was the linking of the initiand with the destiny of the divinity (very often a goddess), resulting in the hope of a pleasant survival and resurrection after death – in fact salvation.

Many ethnologists have seen the Mysteries as remnants of ancient "rites of passage". The oldest Mystery cult is that of Demeter and Kore, known in Eleusis from the 7th century B.C until the destruction of its shrine by the Goths in 395 A.D. All classes, even slaves, were admitted to the cult. The initiands were considered blessed with life in the underworld, while others encountered evil. Other Greek mystery cults were that of Dionysus, open only to women, and that of Orpheus, who tried to retrieve his dead bride from the underworld.

Ström has seen a similarity between the woman-oriented Óðinn-cult and the Dionysus-cult. [47] In the Roman age, oriental cults such as those of Isis, Mithras and Cybele were adapted by Greco-Roman society and became very important as mystery cults. Cybele's cult involved the castration of male devotees. The cult of Isis was to become the most influential and important in late Antiquity. The initiand had to journey through the lower world and the upper world to be reborn by the grace of Isis, the Great Goddess, also referred to as "savior" centuries before the birth of Christ.[48]

MYSTICAL UNION

Mystical union is not necessarily a Mystery Religion thing, but more generally and in many different kinds of religions. It is a theme found even in sub-traditions within all the Monotheistic religions: The experience of a sublime, spiritual union between a human being or soul and its divine object, considered the supreme stage of mystical experience. It is found as a concept in most religions, and in the Greek and Roman mystery religions it was central.

A usual metaphor of mystical union is that of spiritual and heavenly marriage; a marriage of the soul with the deity. Mystical union may be understood as an experience of ecstasy. As with the shamans, who need to "die" in order to wander through the realms of death and spirits before being reborn, the "mystical death" and subsequent soul-journey is crucial in the stages leading to mystical union.[49]

---

47 Ström, 1954, p. 58-61
48 Eliade and Adams, X, p. 230-238
49 Eliade and Adams, X, p. 239-243

3.2: THE MAIDEN WITH THE MEAD

"Is it so hard to imagine that the land beyond the sun is more beautiful than the sun itself, and that Gunnlǫð may be sitting there on a golden throne, offering immortality to a mortal man? And this after he has experienced the horror of death and been born again, just as the earth is in Vǫluspá."
---Svava Jacobsdóttir

In his book Lady With a Mead Cup, Michael Enright discusses how the offering of mead by a royal or noble lady was part of an ancient Germanic (and Celtic) ritual the purpose of which was to establish kingly authority and hierarchy within the king's warband. The queen or lady would enter the hall in a prescribed manner, offering mead to the king with a formal greeting and giving of advice. Most significant would be her official naming of the lord and master of the hall during the mead-offering. She would then proceed to the other warriors in the hall, according to their status, offering the same mead. The ritual, according to Enright, would be a communal bonding rite between the warriors, but at the same time an expression of lordship, hierarchy and rank. Through her role in the ritual, the lady would also act as a delegate for the king, interrogating visitors or newcomers through her formal greeting, a greeting the visitor would be obliged to respond to, thus formally asserting his loyalty to the lord.[50]

Communal drinking had in itself some aspects of a cultic act. Liquor was the medium through which one achieved ecstasy and thus communion with the supernatural. The practice was widespread among the Indo-European peoples and seems to have been closely related to the earliest rites of royal inauguration. It was also closely connected to the sacred making of oaths. While this has been well-known among scholars, according to Enright the importance of the role of the lady in the ritual has been neglected.

---

50 Enright, 1996, p. 1-18

Through texts, Enright discusses how she was perceived very much in connection with the rite. He argues that she was the bearer of the consecrated liquor and the inciter of oaths. Her function was, according to Enright, quite like the diplomat who constructs bonds of allegiance between the outsider and a king and his court -she was the instrument that sanctified the lord's status by naming him as such, by "serving him before all others and by causing each of his retainers to drink after him".[51]

She sanctified the status of each warrior, made them all into a band of brothers which was also a perfectly hierarchical family. Her presence was essential, because the "binding rite" that she performed was her particular duty. Her cheering words and gifts "make a harsh life full of conflict and rivalry more bearable". At the same time, Enright argues she was a tool of her husband's dominance over his warriors, since it was his power that she symbolized and acted out as his representative. The queen, through the mead-offering ritual, was mainly a stabilizing influence, Enright concludes.

Enright uses the mead-ritual as a starting point for a discussion of the queen's political role within the warband of Germanic warrior societies. Since we are dealing only with religion and mythology, Enright's thesis moves beyond our purposes. It is however useful to note that the idea of an offering of mead by a "gold-adorned" lady had its powerful traditions within innumerable Germanic societies from the earliest times up to the Viking Age.

In chapter 9.5, we will further discuss Enright's works as he proceeds to showing, through an archaeological survey, that the lady with the mead cup was indeed an important and central character in Germanic societies, and that she might have originated as a prophetess or a priestess. As we shall see in this study, the mead-offering women of the Poetic Edda are supernatural characters, and the offering takes place somewhere apart from the world of humankind.

Enright showed that the event had its counterpart in a common and ancient ritual in the "real world", even though he focuses on the aspect of diplomacy, mediating between men and establishing hierarchy. The rite, as Enright asserts, was, besides being a repeated ritual during important gatherings, essential in royal inauguration. In fact, the queen and her "prophetess" ancestor appear to have played an important political role in royal consecration.[52]

---

51 Ibid, p. 22
52 Ibid, p. 24

As Steinsland has shown, the royal inauguration ritual in Norse society was also closely connected to a "sacred marriage rite", whether real or symbolic. Thus, mead-offering rituals would in such cases be accompanied by sacred marriage.

Svava Jacobsdóttir focuses on Gunnlǫð's serving of mead to Óðinn in the Hávamál, drawing a line between the magical drought of Gunnlǫð and those of Irish legends where a divine lady or goddess personifying the land offers a crystal cup of red mead to a young king or hero before they go to bed together.[53] Such a connection between Norse and Irish / Celtic traditions is also made by Michael Enright.

The lady is either named after the drink itself, such as "Intoxication", or after her function as ruler of the land: "Sovereignty". Only when the young hero accepts the drink and her holy embrace, is he fit to be king. This authority is granted through sacred marriage. In the Irish sources, the goddess is seated on a crystal chair, and the drink is emphasized for its (red) color and intoxicating effect. It is ladled out with a golden ladle and served from a golden cup. The hero has to swear an oath to the goddess.

In the Hávamál, Gunnlǫð is sitting on a golden chair, from where she ladles out the "precious mead" and serves it to Óðinn in a cup. The drink is called lítr in stanza 107, meaning "color", a fact Jacobsdóttir connects to the red color of the Irish mead. Óðinn has sworn a sacred ring-oath which Jacobsdóttir interprets as an oath of marriage (which Óðinn breaks). The intoxicating effect of the drink is emphasized in the poem's stanza 13-14.

According to Jacobsdóttir, the drink is not called poetry mead, only the "precious mead". However, in stanza 107, Óðrerir is mentioned, which could be translated as the "Poetry Stir", which Snorri gives as name for one of Gunnlǫð's three cauldrons. The name Óðrerir is directly made from the noun óðr which could mean poetry, but also ecstasy, drunkenness, inspiration and mind-power or intelligence. This noun is also the name of Freyia's lost husband, Óðr, and also happens to be the very word by which the name Óðinn was made of; literally meaning "The Óðr" [Óðr+hinn].

---

53 Jacobsdóttir, 2002, p. 30-53

After drinking it, Óðinn relates how he has obtained wisdom and become strengthened with the power of the Earth, bringing the mead up into the Shrine of the Earth [Jarðar Vé - stanza 107-108]. Jacobsdóttir suggests that the Earth is Gunnlǫð herself, personifying the land which the new king has married. The Shrine of Earth may have had its ritual counterpart in a cave or grave mound.[54]

Jacobsdóttir questions and discusses whether the Gunnlǫð story was a Norse imitation or adaption of an Irish original but concludes that it was part of the Norse tradition. Hieros Gamos was known in Norse society, and the theme of the sacred drink is also to be found in older Indo-European material.

In the Norse sources, the mead shows up in several places: The mead served by the valkyriur appears to have granted eternal life, and is, in Sígrdrífumál also associated with "holy embraces". The drink may also be found in the name of the maiden Menglǫð, whose embrace is also sought in the Fjǫlsvinnsmál. Instead of understanding her name as "men-glǫð", "Necklace/Jewel Pleased/Happy", as is the usual understanding, Jacobsdóttir claims that it could be derived from Old English mengan, to mix, and lǫð, which actually refers to a drink or to an invitation (to drink). The sacred drink would then be implicit in her name, she argues.

In fact, I would argue that the sacred drink or the invitation to drink it would then be implicit in both the name of Gunnlǫð and the name of Menglǫð. Their names would then, respectively, mean "Battle Drink/Invitation" and "Blend Drink/Invitation". As we shall see, both assume the role of the Maiden with the Mead within an initiation story.

Jacobsdóttir further connects the giantesses Gunnlǫð, Gerðr, the valkyriur and the maiden Menglǫð through the wall of flame that surrounds them and their enchanted state. Jacobsdóttir completes her essay by showing how the mead or ale from Norse and Celtic sources has its counterpart in Old Indian and Vedic religions where Soma plays an important role as a drink of knowledge and immortality. The herb which was used to make the drink and which

---

54 Ibid, p. 40. Symbolic death and re-birth was part of king´s consecration in many such societies, and was associated with the Great Goddess. It was connected to the idea of immortality, which may be found also in the Norse material.

gave it its intoxicating power was the soma.

In Sanskrit, another name for the Soma drink was madhu, a word which also meant "honey» and which is etymologically connected to Old Norse mjǫðr and its English translation, mead[55]. "Holy embraces" was a part of the soma ritual, and in one myth, Indra drinks Soma from the lips of Apala, daughter of the sun.

In another myth, an eagle called Garuda ("soma-thief") gives the sacred drink to the gods. Garuda is really Vac, goddess of the voice, in disguise. The guardian of the Soma was said to be a serpent. The parallel to Snorri's story of Óðinn's theft of the mead of poetry while in the shape of a serpent and then an eagle is striking.

3.3: RITUAL AND INITIATION REFLECTED IN THE NORSE MYTHS

In his essay on the Edda as ritual, Einar Haugen criticizes philology students who over-emphasize the literary quality of the Norse poems.[56] In their literary criticism, many have overlooked the religious values conveyed in the poetry. Students have criticized the poems for their repetitiousness, for their stereotyped forms, and the many lists of names have been considered dry and uninteresting. This, according to Haugen, is because these students have failed to penetrate behind the poems to the religious faith of those who composed and performed them. The value of formulaic repetition in creating a mood has been neglected. The "shamanic ecstasy that runs through these poems from one end to the other, the magic blessings that brought power..."[57] has not been appreciated.

Consequently, Haugen proposes that the high degree of performance-oriented quality in the poems must mean that we are close to having something like a text for cultic occasions in the poems of the Poetic Edda. The Skírnismál, for example, may very

---

55   Ibid, p. 48. This connection is also made by Näsström, 2001, p. 131, who speaks of a Norse Soma-tradition, and by Brockington, 1996, p. 16- Mead was used in libation sacrifice, something which is seen in the Sanskrit word medha; "sacrifice".

56   Haugen, 1983, p. 3-21

57   Ibid, p. 21

well be seen as a ritual drama promoting fertility.

The idea of the texts of the Edda as reflecting actual ritual is doubtful, as we saw in chapter 2.1, 2.2, and 2.7. Folke Ström believes that the original connection (which he assumes existed) between myth and cultic ritual has become weakened up to the point of complete dissolution where the myth takes its own life, making way for a more literary form. What may have begun as a cultic text is gradually turned into legend and saga. Yet in some instances, especially when the myth survives as a divine saga or legend, it may be possible to find the original pattern of cultic drama, a core of ritual, timeless reality. Ström uses Óðinn's self-sacrifice on the World Tree as an example of what he sees as a ritual where the king plays the role of the fertility god who dies and is resurrected, connected to a Hieros Gamos ritual with the Great Goddess. [58]

The stanzas about Óðinn's trials on the world tree, where he hangs, stabbed, without eating or drinking for nine days, before picking up the sacred knowledge of the runes, has caught the attention of many scholars from an early time.

Eliade saw the trial as strikingly reminiscent of Siberian shamans´ initiatory trials on the World Tree[59]. Solli argues the same thing, and proceeds to suggest that many so-called sacrifices by hanging may have been quite common as a ritual of initiation: the initiand would not be actually strangled, but hung up in a tree without food or drink for several days leading to the necessary trance state induced by pain and suffering which is so common in shamanistic practice. Following the argument of Ottar Grønvik, she suggests that the one hanging in the tree in Hávamál Stanza138-139 is not actually Óðinn but a þulr who identifies himself with the destiny of the god.[60]

Jere Fleck suggested that Óðinn's trials during his quest for wisdom may very well reflect a kind of ascetic mortification of the flesh for the sake of inducing visions of the unknown, a widely spread practice in many religions.[61]

Britt Mari Näsström sees the trials of Óðinn hanging on the world tree within the context of initiation into a religious office – an initiation which reminds her more of Hellenistic mystery-religions

58 Ström, 1954, p. 9
59 Eliade, 2004, p. 379-384
60 Solli, 2002, p. 154-162
61 Haugen, 1983, p. 20

than of shamanism.[62]

Whatever is our opinion about this subject, we may get from this discussion the idea of how pagan ritual and religion is being perceived by scholars in the history of religions as a historical reality hiding behind the medieval texts.

In her major work about Norse ritual and sacrifice, Näsström touches upon the theme of ritual reflected in myths several times.[63] In general, her view seems to be that myths which on the surface tell quite wild, romantic or funny tales may in reality reflect actual ritual.[64] She shows how Edda poems like the Hymiskvíða in its entirety deals with ritual eating and drinking, and how the Skaldic poem Haustlǫng is really describing an act of sacrifice. [65] In the Saga of Hrolf Kráki, she singles out elements of ritual initiation into manhood or a secret society.[66]

Näsström appears to be reflecting a general tendency among scholars of Norse mythology when she sees remnants of religious practice within the myths, although most are careful about suggesting that the poems as we know them are actual "manuscripts" for ritual drama.

As Holm-Olsen pointed out (see chapter 2.1) it is difficult to decide the age and authenticity of the poems. However, many are those who have seen at least reflections of the practices and concepts of ritual in the Edda (which we will examine below).

» Jan de Vries suggested that the myth of Balder's murder was describing an initiation rite for a young warrior. He points out that death (and resurrection) is part of the trials of initiation. [67]

» Kaaren Grimstad and Edith Marold[68] as well as Lotte Motz[69] point to the dwarf Regínn's role as a master of initiation for the young hero Sígurðr, while Grimstad adds the fact that in the Sígurðr-story there are several "elder" figures who also act in this fashion.

62 Näsström, 2001, p.167-172
63 Näsström, 2001
64 Ibid, p. 98
65 Ibid, p. 125-126
66 Ibid, p. 117-118
67 Näsström, 2001, p. 153 (De Vries, 1955, p. 44 , Arkiv för Nordisk filologi 70: Der Mythos von Balders Tod)
68 Grimstad, 1983, p. 187-205
69 Grimstad, 1983, p. 187-205

» Jens Peter Schødt also places the story of Sígurðr within the framework of a typical initiation ritual where the hero goes through trials that lead to numinous revelations and a new position in society afterwards.[70]

» In the Edda poem Vǫlundarkvíða, Grimstad sees a "double initiation": first, the one undergone by the elf smith Vǫlundr, suffering captivity, mutilation, and symbolic death before he is able to soar freely in the air, reborn with increased powers; secondly, he acts as the master of initiation to the kings´ sons. Slaying and dismemberment, Grimstad states, are integral parts in both shamanic and warrior cult initiations .[71]

» Gro Steinsland has argued that myths like the Skírnismál and the Hyndluljóð, both of which will be discussed in this work, reflect an ideology of "sacred" kingship based on the heritage of a sacred marriage between a god and a giantess. Since her theories have met with support and her ideas have been elaborated on the basis of more research, she has lately argued that both poems may very well reflect rituals of initiation into kingship through trials in the other world or world of the dead, culminating in sacred marriage.[72]

» In this context, Solli, who otherwise argues for shamanism, suggests that even kings or chiefs may have had to undergo "shamanistic" hanging rituals such as that of the king in Gautreks saga who (unsuccessfully) tried to let himself be symbolically hanged and stabbed. Solli supports her argument with the old Nordic concept of the widu-hundaR – "the chief in the tree".[73]

On comparing the myth of Gunnlǫð and Óðinn with Irish and Indian sources, Svava Jacobsdóttir decides that the myth must be treating the ritual initiation of a king through sacred marriage. Studying the details of the myth, she tries to form a picture of the ritual: It must have happened underground, and after trials of hardship, the young initiand is finally met by the representatives of the otherworld, a lady on a golden chair who grants him the holy drink and her holy embrace after he has sworn a most sacred ring-oath. The trials take place in the presence of his masters of initiation.

---

70 Schjødt, 1994, p. 113-123
71 Grimstad, 1983, p. 203
72 Steinsland,1991, Steinsland, 2000, p. 72-73
73 Solli, 2002, p. 162

Finally, Jacobsdóttir suggests that the myth encompasses more than just trials of kingship, since the realm of Gunnlǫð and the drink she conveys may appear to offer an alternative to death.[74] Einar Haugen criticized the strong focus upon kingship initiation among the scholars of the Edda. Although many poems may reflect the initiation of kings, to see them only in the light of kingship ritual is, according to Haugen, to restrict the myths too severely.

Haugen chooses to see the myths rather as part of the whole ceremonial pattern of Germanic religion in which the king-priest or sacred magician acts out the role of the gods he tells about. He points out that there is even a word for this kind of practitioner: the þulr, meaning "chanter" (from þylja –to "chant", to "recite") – a chanter, a reciter of numinous wisdom, a sage or a poet.[75]

To finish off this part, I shall add that I take a similar approach to this question as do Jacobsdóttir and Heide; the initiation rituals that I have detected within the structure of the Edda poems seem to point to all kinds of initiation rituals, not just royal inaugurations. This is why I have proposed the concept of a "goddess of initiation" – a goddess who not just grants kingship, but also esoteric wisdom, magical powers and even resurrection from oblivion in death, much like Isis, Demeter and Cybele did in Classical Mystery Religions.

3.4: THE GREAT GODDESS

Else Mundal has put forth the question of why the majority of Norse goddesses known from Snorri and the poets appear invisible in myth and cult. One common explanation has been that most of the goddess-names were poetic inventions. The poets supposedly needed goddess-names to use in their poetic metaphors for women. It is true that poets used the names of goddesses to describe women, but, as Mundal argues, "names of goddesses could not function as a basic word in kenningar if they did not give associations to goddesses people knew beforehand."[76]

---

74   Jacobsdóttir, 2002, p. 30-51

75   The þulr is found in the Poetic Edda as the reciter in the Hávamál Stanza 111, as a title for the Giant Vafþrúðnir ("an old þulr"), for the dwarf Reginn ("a hoary þulr"), and for Óðinn (the "master-þulr" in Hávamál Stanza 80, Stanza 142.) Haugen, 1983, p. 20

76   Mundal, 1990, p. 305

The poetic metaphors worked because they alluded to already known mythology. Mundal's explanation of the numerous named, but faded goddesses, is that female deities would mostly be worshipped as a collective. This "fact may partly explain why the individual goddess –with the exception of Freyia - disappears as an individual..."[77]

Another, complementing explanation is that the multitude of single, non-married goddesses, who far outnumber the male gods, did not fit into the patriarchal family structure that Snorri and his contemporaries tried to impose on the pagan gods.

Thirdly, Mundal argues that "concepts of one individual goddess and the female collective merge into one another. There is no sharp division between the dís (sg.) and the dísir (pl.)."[78] Mundal draws the line between the dís-dísir and the norns, the valkyriur, and the fylgjur, concluding that where the female deities are concerned, the conceptions of the individual and the collective merge together. To talk about "lower female deities" when talking about the collectives of norns, valkyriur, fylgjur and dísir is useless seen in this light: they are as important in the cult as the individual deity and are not separable from them.

Even the division between human and divine becomes blurred in the case of females: the valkyriur may be described almost as human beings, the vǫlur exist both as real women and as mythical beings, and even the word gyðja means both "priestess" and "goddess".

Mundal suggests that what we are seeing in the collective of female deities are hypostases of the greater, individual goddesses, such as Freyia and Frigg. And, she argues, "if we have hypostases, we will get more goddesses out of one, and the last one will be as "real" as the first one."[79]

Britt Mari Näsström defines a Great Goddess as the counterpart of a male high God; she takes a dominating position, she is independent, rules over fate, and is worshipped by both men and women. She often appears with many names and shapes, her character is ambivalent, a feature which often splits her into several beings. She is connected to the earth but may also be a goddess of heaven. Her cult is widespread and official.[80]

---

77 Ibid p. 300

78 Ibid, p. 312

79 Ibid, p. 304

80 Näsström, 1998, p. 79

The idea of "Mother Earth" as the Great Goddess may be limiting. As Jacobsdóttir intervenes, the goddess may be equally connected to heaven and sun, not the least in Norse mythology, where the connection of sunlight, brightness and the goddesses is very common.[81]

I wish to add that the sun in the Norse language is feminine, and in the myths, the sun is continually referred to as a woman or a goddess, sister of the (male) moon. This is a fact which appears to have been ignored by many scholars, who sometimes speak of a Norse Sun God, supposedly Freyr or Balder, although there is no reference to a male sun anywhere in the sources.[82] Even linguistically, all Germanic languages know the sun as a feminine noun.

As we shall see, the Maiden, who on some level may represent the land to whom the king must marry, is also associated with brightness and shine, and as a valkyria, her sphere is air and sea. As a giantess, however, she emerges from the depths of the earth as do Gunnlǫð, Gerðr, Hyndla, Hel, Fenia and Menia.

Folke Ström[83] and Näsström have both in their own ways expressed the idea of a Great Goddess behind the many shapes and names of female characters that appear in Norse mythology. Ström presents the dísir as the designation given to a collective of female deities without known individual names. As Mundal showed (above), these names may be the ones reflected in poetry.

The dísir were the objects of widespread cults of ancient origin, and they were closely connected to Freyia, the Vanadís. The idea of one Great Dís becomes clear from the name of the central hall of the Dísablót (the sacrifice to the dísir); the Dísarsalinn. Dísar here is a genitive singular, which means that we are dealing with the hall of the one (great) Dís rather than the hall of the many dísir who received sacrifice at this important celebration.

Ström suggested that it must be Freyia [Lady/ Sovereign] who hides behind the title, and is supported by Näsström, who points out that from the nameless collective of dísir, one great dís, one Great Goddess, emerges.[84]

---

81 Jacobsdóttir, 2002, p. 43
82 For example Dronke, 1997, p. 396-397, Turville-Petre, 1975, p.174
83 Ström, 1985, and 1954
84 Ström, 1997, p. 192-193, Näsström, 1998, p. 156

The dísir have their etymological origin from old Indian: Dhisanâ, a goddess who could appear in many shapes or hypostases, then called by the plural dhisanas. They were goddesses of wealth and happiness, described as the "wives of the gods", and, significantly, they took care of the sacred drink, Soma, the drink of immortality.[85]

In Norse mythology, the lines between the dísir, the valkyriur, the fylgjur, and the norns, are blurred; this blurred border between the various kinds may point to a common origin, or that the different designations just specify the kind of dís that we are dealing with. In the text material, we see this all the time: A norn could be called a fylgja or a dís, a fylgja could be called a valkyria, a norn, a hamingja and a dís, an ásynja could be called a dís, but so could a valkyria or a gýgr, as in a giantess – she too was a dís.

Absolutely all female supernatural entities could in fact be referred to as dísir.

Even human women could be referred to as dísir, especially in poetry. It was even a common ending in women's names, such as Hjördís, Thordís, Herdís, Freydís and so on.

Some dísir seem to have functioned as the guardian spirits of the clans and appear to have been particularly close to the head of the clan – especially the sort known as ættarfylgja – a "lineage follower".

The dísir called valkyriur have often been said to be the poetical expressions of the warrior ideal of the Viking ages, with their warlike appearance.

Sometimes, the dísir of the clan were called fylgjur, which means "followers".[86] It has been discussed whether the woman-fylgja could represent the soul of a person (see chapter 3.1). A person could have a woman fylgja or an animal fylgja, a form of soul that could travel independently of the body, as could the húgr ["will", "thought", "soul"] and the hamingja [fate, fortune]. [87] In their function as fate-deciding powers, the dísir were called nornir, who were thought to be present at a child's birth to give it a name and decide its fate.[88]

---

85 Näsström, 1998, p. 146, Ström, p. 192

86 Ström, 1997, p. 194-196

87 Ibid, p. 206

88 Ibid, p. 201

Ström and Näsström suggested that the goddess Freyia may be the head of all the different dísir, indeed, she may be the one Great Dís hiding behind the dís of the Dísarsalinn. Ström believes, for example, that the giantess Skaði – Qndurdís - is the winter-aspect of Freyia the goddess - Vanadís.[89] In her work on the Great Goddess of the North, Näsström identifies Freyia in the same manner, and sees Freyia, a name which is more of a title meaning "Lady" or "Sovereign", hiding behind most of the feminine deities in the mythology, whose names only denote the functions she plays in the myth, or refer to a local name for the Lady.

Many of the goddesses in the myth may be identified with Freyia through their character and their functions, and Freyia may also be recognized as the Great Valkyria, the Great Dís, and even the great old norn, Urðr [Origin].[90] The only female character whom Näsström does not identify Freyia with are the giantesses. They are seen as something completely different. Näsström even states that the giants are "bare ondskapsfulle" [only evil].[91] She also believes that the after-death realm of Freyia is completely separated from that of the giantess Hel. [92] However, without hesitating, both Ström and Näsström include the giantesses Gerðr and Skaði among the goddesses, showing how Freyia may hide behind even these figures.[93]

Gro Steinsland has shown that giantesses have had an important and positive role in the mythology. They played the part of ancestral mothers to the royal lines, contributing primeval creativity and power where the divine ancestral father contributed law and order. Besides, giants, particularly giantesses such as Skaði and the collective of giantesses known as the mqrnir, are now proven to have received sacrifice and had their own shrines and cults.

89 Näsström, 1998, p. 177, p.154-178
90 Näsström, 1998, p. 177, p.154-178
91 Näsström, 2001, p. 13
92 Näsström, 1998, p. 176-177
93 Näsström, 1998, p. 85, 112, 114, 122, 139-141, Ström, 1954, p. 6

This is not, according to Steinsland, because the giantesses were a kind of old, important goddesses who had become "lesser" with time. On the contrary, the giant stock is different from the gods, their opposites. Nonetheless, they were important and powerful cosmic characters, and it would be "...remarkable if Norse tradition should miss any ritual dealing with powers on whom the whole of existence finally depended. The giants are as necessary to the world as the gods are."[94] According to Steinsland, it is exactly from this polar opposition between god and giantess that the very power of the sacred marriage derives.[95]

Since I have detected "Maiden-mythology" (myths about the Maiden with the Mead) in poems concerning both obvious giantesses, goddesses, and valkyriur, I find Steinsland's theory of extreme opposition somewhat problematic.

As I have shown in this work, the Maiden does exist both in giant and divine form.

However, there is a remarkable difference between the role played by the giantess Maiden and the goddess Maiden;
» The giantess Maiden is related to the gods only
» The goddess and the valkyria Maiden deals with human heroes.
I think this is an important difference which I will touch upon in the chapters concerning the "Ogress-Maiden-opposition", without hoping to reach as yet to the absolute depth of this puzzling problem.

---

94 Steinsland, 1986, p. 212-220
95 Steinsland,1991, p. 268-269, p. 278-282, p. 127-129

4: GUNNLQÐ, GERÐR AND THE GIANTESSES

I n this chapter we shall explore the two main myths of the Poetic Edda where a giantess plays the role of serving the mead to the hero; that of Gunnlǫð as found in the Hávamál (and in Snorri's Skáldskaparmál) as well as the myth of Gerðr in the Skírnismál. In the two poems, a god, Óðinn and Freyr respectively, plays the hero's role of seeking the giantess with the mead, as opposed to the other poems of this study where the heroes are young men and the Maiden has, perhaps significantly, become a goddess or a valkyria.

Much research has been done on all these poems, and within the space of this work I have little leisure to explore all their implications: we will be concentrating on the common structural elements in the poems, to detect a common mythical concept and a ritual structure behind the different poetic expressions.

4.1: GIANTESSES IN THE REALMS OF DEATH

The jǫtnar (sg.m. jǫtunn) are always translated into English as "giants", while the female, the gýgjar (sg.f: gýgr) are called "giantesses". However, the actual significance of the word jǫtunn seems to be "eater", "devourer"[96]. The "giants" are the primeval beings, existing before the gods and the ordered world, and are, ultimately, their destroyers.

Giantesses operate as mistresses of the realms of death: Hel rules in Níflheimr – the "misty World" [97] where most dead souls must go – even the soul of the god Balder, for whom tables are decked and mead brewed – but hidden - in that dark realm.[98]

---

96 Simek, 1996, p. 232; translates Níflheimr to "Dark World" and Níflhel to "Dark Hel", although he admits that the words are derived from OE nifol –darl and Latin nebulae; "fog", "mist". In Norrøn Ordbok, the translation is "tåkeheim", that is, "misty world", my preferred interpretation, although the association with the realm and darkness is shown through the myths of Hermóðr and in Baldrs draumar/Vegtamskvíða.

97 Vegtamskvíða, Stanza 7

98 Steinsland, 1992, p. 321-322

Hel's hall is surrounded by tall gates that must not be touched by the living. Níflheimr is filled with poisonous rivers, with serpents and wolves, animals associated with other giantesses like Hyrrokkin, Skaði, Hyndla and the wolf-riding, serpent-handling, death-declaring fylgja that appears in the poem of Helgi Hiǫrvarðsson.

Hel's brothers are the World Serpent, who lays coiled around the ordered world [Miðgarðr] and the wolf Fenrir who is destined to devour Óðinn during Ragnarǫk. Níflheimr lies to the icy north of the world, where there is also a giant in eagle's disguise whose name is Hræsvelgr, "The Corpse-Swallower".[99] He is the origin of the winds of the world. The realm lies at one of the roots of the world tree where there is a well infested by serpents, from which many of the world's rivers originate. Hel is said to have power over nine worlds. According to Snorri, Hel's face is half pink as life, and half blue as death.

Another realm of death is below the sea, where the giantess Rán – "Robbery" [100] - dwells, catching those who drown in her net. She has nine daughters, who are often associated with the waves. Through poetic metaphors they are also connected to gold and poetry. Rán's realm is also associated with mead, cauldrons and decked tables, as we see in the beginning of the Skáldskaparmál.

Steinsland has shown how the experience of death often is depicted as something of an erotic feast or even a wedding to the mistresses of death. A drowned man could "climb into Rán's bed", another dying experience could be referred to as "pleasing Hel" in some way that seems erotically flavored.[101]

---

99 Simek, 1996, p.158

100 Simek, 1996, p. 260

101 Simek, 1996, p. 124-125

4.2: GUNNLǪÐ AND THE MEAD OF POETRY

Gotland, Sweden

Gunnlǫð means "Battle Drink/Invitation", a name which according to Simek would be rather more typical for a valkyria than for a giantess, suitable for the figure of the valkyria who hands out mead. The oldest written version of the story is to be found in the Hávamál poem Stanza 104-110, where Óðinn himself tells the story of his conquest.[102]

In the stanzas, which are quoted and translated below (translations by the author), Óðinn tells of how he entered the hall of the "old giant" – Suttungr - speaking so well for himself that he saved his life in that alien realm. His name may mean "Heavy with Drink".[103]

A lady sitting on a golden throne offers him "a precious drink of mead". The lady is Gunnlǫð, Suttungr's daughter, and her appearance is queen-like. We learn that Óðinn had sworn a sacred ring-oath before he had relations with her. The speaking in the hall of the maiden's father, the oath, the ritual offering of mead and the subsequent embrace between the god and the giantess all seem to indicate a wedding.[104]

Gunnlǫð proceeds to help Óðinn in his effort to get out of the hall of the giants, in fact, he admits that he would not have been able to escape without her help. Gnawing himself out through the mountain "with the mouth of Rati", risking his head between paths of giants, Óðinn manages to return up to "Earth's old shrine", bringing with him the drink that Gunnlǫð gave him, Óðrerir, or "Poetry Stir".

---

102 Simek, 1996, p.304
103 See chapter 3.2
104 See chapter 3.2

Óðinn concludes the story by naming himself Harm-Doer and oath-breaker, for he left Gunnlǫð behind, weeping, and he stole the mead by treason. He also tells how the frost-ogres ask themselves whether he had died by Suttungr's hands or had "come among the gods".

104.Enn aldna iotvn ec sotta,
nv em ec aptr vm kominn,
fát gat ec þegiandi þar;
mꜹrgom orþom
mꜹlta ec i mínn frama
i Svttvngs sꜹlom.

104. The ancient Jǫtunn I sought
now I have returned again
little did I get with silence there
with many words
I spoke in my favor
in the halls of Suttungr [Heavy with Drink].

105. Gvnnlꜹd mer vm gaf
gvllnom stóli á
drycc ins dyra miaþar;
ill iþgiold
let ec hana eptir hafa
sins ins heila hvgar,
sins ins svara sꜹva.

105. Gunnlǫð [Battle Drink/Invitation] gave me
on the golden chair
a drink of precious mead
A bad repayment
I let her have after
for her whole love
for her burdened soul.

106. Rata mvnn
letomc rvms vm fá
oc vm griot gnaga;
yfir oc vndir
stoðomc iotna vegir,
sva hꜹtta ec hꜹfði til.

106. With the mouth of the Drill[105]
I made a way for myself
and gnawed through the rocky rubble.
Above and below
were the paths of the jǫtnar [devourers (giants)]
Thus, I risked my head.

---

105 Rati – meaning drill, also the name of the drill used to enter the rocky abode of the giants. It is explained by Snorri in Skáldskaparmál 1 where a jǫtunn called Baugi [Ring] used Rati [the Drill] to drill a hole for Óðinn to go through in the shape of a serpent so that he could reach Gunnlǫð directly. In the older, Hávamál version, Rati is not a name, just the common word for a drill, and Óðinn does the drilling himself.

107. Vel keyptz litar
hefi ec vel notiþ,
fáss er froþom vant;
þviat Ódrerir
er nv vpp kominn
á alda vés iarþar.

107. The well-bought drink/color
I have enjoyed well
-the wise lacks for little.
For now, Poetry-Stir
has been brought up again
to the ancient Shrine of Earth.

108. Ifi er mer á,
at ec vęra en kominn
iotna gorðom or,
ef ec Gvnnladar ne nytac,
ennar goðo kono,
þeirrar er lagdomc
arm yfir.

108. I doubt this,
that I would have returned
from the settlements of the jǫtnar
if I had not enjoyed Gunnlǫð
that good wife
whom I laid my arms around.

109. Ens hindra dags
gengo hrimþvrsar
Hava ráþs at fregna
Hava Höllo í;
at Bǫlverci þeir spvrðo,
ef hann vęri með
bandom cominn
eþa hefdi hanom
Svttvngr of sóit.

109. For the next days
Frost-Thurses went
to ask the counsels of the High One
in the High Hall;
For Harm-Worker [Óðinn] they asked
if he had come among the bonds [the gods]
or whether he had died at Suttungr's.

110. Baugeið Oðinn
hygg ec at vnnit hafi;
hvat scal hans
trygðom trva?
Svttvng svikinn
hann let svmbli fra
oc grǫtta Gvnnlaðo.

110. A ring oath [marriage pledge]
I believe that Óðinn swore;
Who can now believe his words?
He betrayed Suttungr
when he stole his drink
and made Gunnlǫð weep.

111. Mál er at þylia	*111. It is time to speak*
þvlar stóli a	*from the chair of the*
Urðar brvnni at;	*þulr [reciting sage]*
sa ec oc þagþac,	*by the Well of Origin*
sa ec oc hugþac,	*I sat and I was silent*
hlydda ec a manna	*I sat and I thought*
mál;	*I listened to the speech of*
of rvnar heyrda ec	*people*
doma,	*Of runes I heard speak*
ne vm rádom þagðo	*They did not withhold*
Hava hallo at,	*their counsels*
Háva hollo i,	*By the High Hall*
heyrda ec segia sva:	*In the High Hall*
	I heard them speak like
	this:

Stanza 107 identifies the precious mead as Óðrerir, a cauldron of mead whose history Snorri explains in Skáldskaparmál. Snorri also asserts that it was this mead that Gunnlǫð gave to Óðinn. More to the point, Óðrerir was, according to Snorri, the biggest one of the three cauldrons in which the mead was kept.

Stanza 109 suggests that Óðinn "came among the gods" after he escaped from the world of the jǫtnar – the devourers, usually known to English translations as "giants".

Stanza 111 concludes that the god now may speak from the seat of the þulr – a sage, orator, reciter, wise man - a storyteller who knows and can ritually recite the sacred lore. The verses that follow show how he indeed does recite lore of wisdom to his students. As such, there is clearly a theme of initiation where the initiand risks his life in the underworld before he returns with gifts to the shrines of Earth, comes among the gods, and becomes a þulr.

We have two sources, the Skáldskaparmál and the Hávamál, that identify Gunnlǫð's precious mead with the "mead of poetry". It is a mead that is the essence of the primordial truce between the two tribes of gods, the Aesir and the Vanir. The mead contains divine wisdom and all the intelligence of the world. Anyone drinking it will become a sage and a great poet.[106]

In Snorri's version, a great point is made out of the fact that Óðinn manages to escape with the mead inside of himself, to be held forever after in the divine realm of Ásgarðr. The Hávamál version asserts that, because of his troubles and his relation to Gunnlǫð, Óðinn could now bring the mead "up" and "back" into the shrine of Earth.

---

106 Faulkes, 1987, p. 62-64.

Apparently, most scholars consider the trials of Óðinn on the world tree as something completely separate from his sacred marriage to Gunnlǫð.[107]

However, Óðrerir and the precious mead does indeed appear in a different set of Hávamál stanzas which, in my opinion, must connect the two events. Stanzas138-139 tell the tale of how Óðinn hangs in a wind-swept tree for nine whole nights, stabbed, thirsting and starving (or fasting, actually). He is given to Óðinn, he is giving "self to himself", and, peering down, he has a vision: screaming, he takes the runes "up", falling backwards. He also receives a drink of precious mead and nine powerful songs:

138. Vęit ec at ec hecc
vindga meiði a
nętr allar nío,
geiri vndaþr
oc gefinn Oðni,
sialfr sialfom mer,
a þeim meiþi,
er mangi veit,
hvers hann af rótom renn.

138. I know that I hung
in the wind-swept tree
all the nine nights
pierced with spears
And given to Óðinn
given self to my own self
on that tree
that few know
from where his roots have
run.

139. Við hleifi mic seldo
ne viþ hornigi,
nysta ec niþr,
nam ec vp rv́nar,
ǫpandi nam,
fęll ec aptr þaðan.

139. No bread did they
give to me
no drinking horn either
I peered down
I took up the runes
screaming I learned them
and fell back again

140. Fimbvllióð nío
nam ec af enom fregia syni
Baͬlþorn Bestlo faͬdvr;
oc ec dryc of gat
ens dyra miaðar
aͬsinn Oðreri.

140. Nine powerful songs
did I learn from the
famous son
of Bǫlþorn [Harm-Thorn],
Bestla's [108]father
and I had a drink
of precious mead
ladled from Óðrerir.

---

107 I have not been able to find anyone else who makes this connection.
108 Bestla is Óðinn's mother, here said to be the daughter of a certain Harm-Thorn, and thus a sister to Harm-Thorn's son, from whom Óðinn learns the spell-songs – his teacher here is thus his maternal uncle.

141. Þa nam ec frøvaz	*141. Then I learned to*
oc froþr vera	*become wise*
oc vaxa oc vel hafaz;	*and to be wise*
orð mer af orði	*and to grow and find*
orz leitaði,	*myself well;*
verc mer af verki	*Words me from words*
vercs leitaþi.	*found more words*
	Deeds me from deeds
	found more deeds.

As mentioned in chapter 3.1 and 3.3, Óðinn's trials on the World Tree is generally understood as a ritual of initiation. But as Schjødt pointed out (chapter 3.1), the initiation is only complete when the result is that the initiand achieves a new position, status or spiritual level.

Thus the stanzas 138-139 lose their meaning without the Stanza 141, which tells of how Óðinn became a sage after his trials. In between we have Stanza 140: explaining how Óðinn learns nine powerful charms from a giant, his maternal uncle, and, in the same breath, has a drink of precious mead, ladled out from Óðrerir.

Only then he learns to grow, be wise, and be eloquent.

To read the trials of Óðinn as reflecting a ritual of initiation, as most scholars do, it is necessary to consider all the stanzas from his trials to the result, that is, stanza 138 to stanza 141. Stanza 140 makes it clear that the precious mead, Óðrerir, and the learning of nine fimbulljóðar ["great songs", likely identical to galdrar – spell-songs] was part of the same ritual as the one where Óðinn hangs on a tree and grasps the runes. Óðrerir is certainly connected a description of Gunnlǫð's mead, as testified by Snorri and by Hávamál stanza 107. Stanza 141 asserts that only then did he learn to become ever wiser and more eloquent.

Snorri does not mention Óðinn's self-sacrifice in his Skáldskaparmál version of the Gunnlǫð story. However, he does not mention that important event anywhere.

As we saw in chapter 2.4, violent ritual sacrifice, even if symbolic, may simply have been too incomprehensible, too alien or even too pagan for Snorri to try and explain for his medieval, Christian audience.

Indeed, one does not need Snorri's Skáldskaparmál version to form a complete picture of one version of the story independently. The connection between stanza 140 and stanza 107 through the name of the mead that Óðinn drinks, Óðrerir, convinces me that there is a strong connection between Óðinn's self-sacrifice, not only with the discovery of the sacred runes, but also with the learning of charms from an old giant and the ritual drinking and marriage with a lady of the other world. I have no space to discuss what happens next in the Hávamál, when the god declares that it is finally time to speak from his new status as a sage, but I have left a translation of the verses that follow his initiation at the very end of this book.

4.3: AN UNDERLYING STRUCTURE OF THEMES

Assuming that the two sets of stanzas from the Hávamál that we have discussed are indeed connected through the mead-theme, we may form an image of at least one version of the story, and we may detect an underlying structure:

1. VISION QUEST

First, we have what I would call a "vision quest- theme": Óðinn, or the one trying to resemble him, undergoes trials of hardship, pain and fasting in order to achieve a vision.

2. VISION

Second, we have a "vision-theme": The I-person "peers down" and picks up sacred knowledge.

3. DESCENT

Third, we have a "descending- theme": Our hero descends into the world within the mountains, filled with the paths of otherworldly creatures, and ruled by giants, a deadly realm where one risks one's head. Only cleverness (the use of many words, eloquence), may save the life of the one who descends.

My reason for the use of the word "descend" is because I believe there is reason to assume that the realm in question is a kind of Underworld or, indeed, another image of the world of the dead. I will discuss this below.

4. TRIALS

Fourth, we have a "trial-theme": Óðinn has to face an old, dangerous giant, whether it be Suttungr, Gunnlǫð's father, or Bǫlþorn, his own maternal uncle, who will only receive him and teach him if he shows himself eloquent and smart enough.

5. MAIDEN/CONSECRATION

*After the learning of nine spell-songs, we are led over
to the fifth theme, the "Maiden-theme", which is where the
culmination of the hero's trials takes place: his meeting with
the queen-like Maiden on her golden throne, her offering of the
"precious drink", the "Poetry Stir", and her own soul, heart and
embrace.*

6. A NEW STATUS

*The result of the trials and the union with the Maiden-
figure is a knowledge of runes, of charms, and the escape
from that deadly realm which surrounds the Maiden. He also
becomes exceedingly wise and eloquent. The betrayal-theme in
the story of Óðinn and Gunnlǫð is very interesting but there is
no space to discuss it to any extent in this study.*

4.4: THE MAIDEN AND HER KIN: A REALM OF DEATH?

According to the Hávamál, Gunnlǫð is seated, queen-like, on a
golden throne within the hall of Suttungr and the jǫtnar, ladling
out a drink of the precious mead to the one who pretends to
be her groom before her father and all her people. In Snorri's
Skáldskaparmál, she dwells within a place called Hnitbjǫrg, the
"Beating/Clashing Rock/Mountain", where she guards the three
cauldrons of mead[109]. As opposed to the Hávamál version (which is
the older version), Óðinn here clandestinely sneaks in, pretending
to buy a drink from her and paying with sexual services before he
steals the whole batch of mead from all three cauldrons.

Both sources state that he stole the mead with trickery and
cunning, and that he came in through a drilled hole in the rock walls
– what may remind us of the pagan tradition of haugbrót, where
people ritually went into burial mounds in order to retrieve some
important and symbolic item, amply testified in both text material
and archaeological finds.

Hnitbjǫrg is usually understood to be a mountain, since bjǫrg
means "layers of rock", but is often also used to describe a rock
mound or a smaller mountain.[110]

---

109 Simek, 1996, p. 154, Jacobsdóttir
110 Norrøn Ordbok

Gunnlǫð stays within the rock-layers. This is in accordance with her role as a giantess, since giantesses are frequently related to rock, stone and mountain, described as their dwellings. The giantess Hyndla, for example, is said to live in a rock cave.[111] The guardian role is shared with other giantesses. Móðguðr – whose name may mean "Furious Battle" or "Furious Deity."[112] According to the Gylfaginning, she is the guardian of the river Gjǫll –"Loud Noise" and the bridge Gjallarbrú – the "Resounding Bridge"[113], covered in gold and which leads the way to Hel.[114] In the Edda poem Helreið Brynhildar [Brynhild's Ride to Hel] we see how the entry into Hel's realm is guarded by a gýgr – a giantess, an ogress, a "Bride of the Rocks" [bruðr or steini][115]

Is Gunnlǫð's dwelling also a death-realm?

To answer this, let us first look at some passages where the path to Hel is directly described, such as in the Edda poem Vegtamskvíða [The Song of the One who Knows the Way], where the god Óðinn rides down to Hel in order to seek answers to what the omen dreams of his son Balder might mean. He makes sure to ride to the east of the Hel-gate, where he sings galdrar to wake up a dead vǫlva:

1.Senn vorv Aesir allir a þingi ok asynivr alla a mali, ok vm þat ræðv rikir tifar, hvi væri Balldri ballir dravmar.	*1.Later, the gods all* *assembled at parliament* *and the goddesses* *all to have a voice* *and of this they spoke* *the powerful gods* *why Balder was troubled* *by bad dreams.*

---

111 Hyndluljóð, stanza 1

112 Simek, 1996, p. 220 translates the name Móðguðr s "Furious Battle". I question this translation, however. Móð means fury, or furious, but the second part of the name, guðr, has clearly been taken to really be gunnr – "battle" – however, guðr actually means "deity".

113 Snorri Sturluson: Gylfaginning

114 Snorri Sturluson: Gylfaginning

115 Helreið Brynhildar, stanza 3

2.Vpp ræis Oðinn,
alldinn gɐtr,
ok hann a Slæipni
sǫðvl vm lagði;
ræiþ hann niðr þaþan
Niflhæliar til,
mætti hann hvælpi
þæim ær or hæliv kom.

3.Sa var bloðvgr
vm briost framan
ok galldrs fǫðvr
gol vm længi.
Framm ræið Oðinn,
Folldvægr dvndi,
hann kom at háfv
Hæliar ranni.

4.Þa ræið Oðinn
fyrir ɐstan dyrr,
þar ær hann vissi
vǫlv læiði.
Nam hann vittvgri
valgalldr kveða,
vnz nɐðig ræis,
nas orð vm kvað:

5.„Hvat ær manna þat
mer okvnnra,
ær mer hæfir ɐkit
ærfit sinni?
var ec snivin sniofi
ok slægin rægni
ok drifin dɐggv,
dɐð var æk længi."

2.Up stood Óðinn
that ancient human
and on Sleipnir
he laid the saddle
He rode down there
unto Misty World
met there the hound
who came out of Hel

3.The hound was bloody
across its chest
and, at the father of spell-
songs
it barked a long time
Forth rode Óðinn
the Earth-path resounded
he came to the high hall
of Hel.

4.Then rode Óðinn
to the east of the door
There he knew
of a Vǫlva's grave
He learned with wisdom
To recite the spell-songs of
death
Until the corpse rose
And spoke the words of the
dead:

5.»Who is that man
unknown to me
who has woken me up
from my death?
I was covered with snow
and struck with rain
and moistened with dew
I was long dead."

6.Oðinn kvað:
„Vægtamr ec heiti,
sonr æm æk Valtams;
sægþv mer or hæliv,
æc man or hæimi:
hvæim erv bekkir
ba'gvm sánir,
flæt fagrlig
floþ gvlli?"

6.Óðinn said:
«My name is the One who
Knows the Path
and I am the son of Death-
Tame
Tell me, out of Hel,
from the world I know:
For whom are the benches
and the rings prepared?
the seats so beautiful
covered with gold?"

7.Vǫlva kvað:
„Her stændr Baldri
of brvgginn miǫðr,
skírar væigar,
liggr skiǫlldr yfir,
ænn asmAegir
i ofvæni;
na'ðvg sagðak,
nv mvn æk þægia.

7.The Vǫlva said:
"Here stands for Balder
the brewed mead
the shining drink
is covered by a shield;
The Aesir await in tense
expectation
I spoke without wanting
to
now I will go silent."

In Snorri's Gylfaginning, we also hear of a journey to Hel with
the purpose of getting Balder back from the dead. Not that the hero
makes sure to not touch the Hel-gate, just like the god did when he
went to Hel, and that both are riding the magnificent horse Sleipnir,
who has the magical ability to move through the borders between
the worlds.

49. Dauði Baldrs ins góða.
(…) En er goðin vitkuðust,
þá mælti Frigg ok spurði,
hverr sá væri með ásum,
er eignast vildi allar ástir
hennar ok hylli ok vili
hann ríða á helveg ok
freista, ef hann fái fundit
Baldr, ok bjóða Helju
útlausn, ef hon vill láta
fara Baldr heim í Ásgarð.

En sá er nefndr Hermóðr
inn Hvati, sonr Óðins, er
til þeirar farar varð. Þá
var tekinn Sleipnir, hestr
Óðins, ok leiddr fram, ok
steig Hermóðr á þann hest
ok hleypði braut. (…)

En þat er at segja frá
Hermóði, at hann reið
níu nætr dökkva dala
ok djúpa, svá at hann sá
ekki, fyrr en hann kom
til árinnar Gjallar ok reið
á Gjallarbrúna. Hon var
þökð lýsigulli.

49. The Death of Balder the Good
(…) And when the gods had calmed down, then Frigg spoke and asked who among the Aesir was willing to gain her whole love and good will by riding the Hel-path and try to find Balder and beg Hel for his release, and let Balder return home to the divine settlement.

And so he is called Hermóðr [Army Power] the Initiator, son of Óðinn, who agreed to take on this journey. Then they took out Sleipnir [Glider], Óðinn's horse, and led him forth, and Hermóðr got up on him and went forth (…)

And this is said about Hermóðr, that he rode for nine nights through dark and deep valleys, so that he could not see anything until he came to the river Resounding and rode on the Resounding Bridge. She was covered in bright shining gold.

Móðguðr er nefnd mær
sú, er gætir brúarinnar.
Hon spurði hann at nafni
eða at ætt ok sagði, at inn
fyrra dag riðu um brúna
fimm fylki dauðra manna
- "en eigi dynr brúin minnr
undir einum þér, ok eigi
hefir þú lit dauðra manna.
Hví ríðr þú hér á helveg?"

Hann svarar, at -"ek skal
ríða til Heljar at leita
Baldrs, eða hvárt hefir
þú nakkvat sét Baldr á
helvegi?"
En hon sagði, at Baldr
hafði þar riðit um
Gjallarbrú, "en niðr ok
norðr liggr helvegr."

Þá reið Hermóðr, þar til er
hann kom at Helgrindum.

Þá sté hann af hestinum ok
gyrði hann fast, steig upp
ok keyrði hann sporum, en
hestrinn hljóp svá hart ok
yfir grindina, at hann kom
hvergi nær.

Þá reið Hermóðr heim til
hallarinnar ok steig af
hesti, gekk inn í höllina,
sá þar sitja í öndugi, Baldr
bróður sinn, ok dvalðist
Hermóðr þar um nóttina.
En at morgni þá beiddist
Hermóðr af Helju, at Baldr
skyldi ríða heim með
honum, ok sagði, hversu
mikill grátr var með ásum.

*Furious Deity she is called,
the maiden who guards the
bridge. She asked him for
his name and lineage and
said that the other day, five
armies of dead men had
rode over the bridge, "but
the bridge does not resound
any less beneath you alone,
and you do not have the
color of dead men. Why are
you riding the Hel-path?"*

*He replied that «I am going
to ride to Hel to search for
Balder, or have you perhaps
seen Balder here on the Hel-
path?*
*And she said, that Balder
had ridden across the
Resounding Bridge, and
down and north lies the
Hel-path.*

*Then Hermóðr rode until he
reached the Hel-gate*

*Then he went off the horse
and fastened the saddle, got
up again and urged him on,
and the horse ran so hard
and jumped over the bridge,
so that he did not touch it.*

*Then rode Hermóðr on
to the hall and got off the
horse, and went into the
hall, there he sat in the high
seat, Balder his brother,
and Hermóðr stayed there
with him that night. And
in the morning, Hermóðr
begged of Hel that she let
Balder ride home with him,
and said that there was
much grief and weeping
among the gods*

En Hel sagði, at þat skyldi svá reyna, hvárt Baldr var svá ástsæll - "sem sagt er. Ok ef allir hlutir í heiminum, kykvir ok dauðir, gráta hann, þá skal hann fara til ása aftr, en haldast með Helju, ef nakkvarr mælir við eða vill eigi gráta."

Þá stóð Hermóðr upp, en Baldr leiddi hann út ór höllinni ok tók hringinn Draupni ok sendi Óðni til minja, en Nanna sendi Frigg rifti ok enn fleiri gjafar. Fullu fingrgull. Þá reið Hermóðr aftr leið sína ok kom í Ásgarð ok sagði öll tíðendi, þau er hann hafði séð ok heyrt.

And Hel said, that she wanted evidence for Balder being so highly loved as it was said; "and if all things in the world, alive and dead, weep for him, then he shall fare back to the gods, but be kept here in Hel, if anyone speaks against it or will not weep."

Then Hermóðr got up, and Balder accompanied him out of the hall and took the ring Draupnir and sent it to Óðinn as a memory, and Nanna sent to Frigg many gifts and a fingering of gold to Fulla [the Fulfilled One]. Then Hermóðr rode back on his way and came to the divine settlement and told them all the tidings of what he had seen and heard.

THE "EAGLE-PROOF"

Gunnlǫð is the daughter of giants. In Snorri's version of the story of Óðinn and Gunnlǫð, her father, Suttungr, appears as a giant in eagle's disguise, much like Hræsvelgr. We already mentioned this "Corpse-Swallower" in chapter 4.1 and find the image of death as a giant in eagle hide worth scrutinizing, especially since it will show up again in the heroic poems of chapter 6. The eagle is mentioned as the origin of all winds in Óðinn's ninth question in the poem Vafþrúðnismál [Powerful Head-Veil's Speech] stanza 36 and 37:

36.Oþinn qvaþ:
„Segðv þat iþ níunda,
allz þic svinnan qveþa,
oc þv, Vafþrvðnir, vitir:
hvadan vindr vm kǫmr,
sva at ferr vág yfir?
ę menn hann sialfan vm
siá."

36. Óðinn said:
«Tell me the ninth
since you are known to be
wise
and if you, Powerful Head-
Veil, knows:
From where comes the wind
that passes across the waves
and which men never see in
itself?"

37.Vafþrvðnir qvaþ:
„Hręsvelgr heitir,
er sitr a himins enda,
iotvnn i arnar ham;
af hans vengiom
qveþa vind koma
alla menn yfir."

37. Powerful Head-Veil said:
"Corpse Swallower he is
called
who sits at the end of heaven
a jǫtunn in eagle's hide;
From his wings
it is said that the wind comes
above all men."

Snorri in his Gylfaginning gives further information about "Corpse-Swallower":

18. Um uppruna vindsins.
Þá mælti Gangleri:
"Hvaðan kemr vindr?
Hann er sterkr, svá at
hann hrærir stór höf, ok
hann Aesir eld. En svá
sterkr sem hann er, þá má
eigi sjá hann, því er hann
undarliga skapaðr."
   Þá mælti Hárr: "Þat
kann ek vel segja þér. Á
norðanverðum himins
enda sitr jötunn sá, er
Hræsvelgr heitir. Hann
hefir arnarham, en er
hann beinir flug, þá standa
vindar undan vængjum
hans.

18. Of the origin of the
wind
Then spoke Wandering
Learner: "From where
comes the wind? He is
strong, so much so that
he can move the great
ocean, and he quenches
fire. And even as strong as
he is, nobody may see him,
for this, he is made in a
strange way."
Then said the High One:
"I can well tell you that. At
the northernmost end of
heaven there sits a jǫtunn
called Hræsvelgr [Corpse
Swallower]. He has eagle
hide. And when he flies,
then winds emerge from
beneath his wings."[116]

Snorri's addition is valuable because it locates Hræsvelgr's residence in the northern end of heaven. The north is the direction of Níflheimr and Hel, the world of the dead.[117] In the Gylfaginning, Snorri makes Níflheimr the opposite part of the south in the primeval universe, which, logically, must be to the north . In the Gylfaginning, Hermóðr, who is riding to Hel, has to go "north and down".

---

116 Snorri Sturluson: Gylfaginning 18
117 Snorri Sturluson: Gylfaginning 49

The Vǫluspá declares that the hall on Nástrǫndr [Corpse-beach] has doors looking to the north, and this is where the great serpent Niðhǫggr [Shame Biter] sucks the bodies of the dead.[118] The eagle Corpse-Swallower, then, must belong to Níflheimr, the Misty World of Hel, where, perhaps, as his name indicates, he tears at corpses in the same manner as the serpent Niðhǫggr and the other uncountable serpents (such as Svafnir) by the well, Hvergelmir, at the root of Yggdrasill's Ash - the World Tree.

Another great eagle connected to Yggdrasil and the heavens, is the unnamed eagle sitting in the branches of the ash. It is exceedingly wise, yet it keeps an ongoing quarrel with the serpent Niðhǫggr. [119]Between its eyes sits a hawk called Veðrfǫlnir – "Wind-Diminisher",[120] apparently the wind-creating eagle's anti-thesis sitting right in between its own eyes. Are we, in the eagle of the World Tree, perhaps seeing yet another image of our wind creating Hræsvelgr?

Another giant in eagle's disguise is Þiazi, father of Skaði, a giantess turned goddess through marriage with at least two the Aesir. [121]In the Skaldic poem Haustlǫng [Prolonged Autumn] by Þióðolfr of Kvinir, who lived before and around the year 900 A.D., Þiazi captures the goddess Iðunn. [122]Snorri relates the poem and gives a summary of the story in the Skáldskaparmál 2-3. According to the far older source, Haustlǫng, Iðunn is the goddess "who knows the age-cure of the Aesir", that is, she is the keeper of the apples that give the gods eternal youth. When Þiazi takes her away, the gods grow old and feeble, and realize that they will die unless Iðunn is brought back from the giant world. Eventually, wearing a falcon's disguise, Loki manages to bring her back. He is followed by Þiazi in the shape of an eagle. The flight in bird's disguise with a stolen (or rather retrieved) treasure from the giant in eagle's disguise is quite reminiscent of Óðinn's flight from Suttungr in eagle's shape.

The giant's association with death seems to me obvious: when offered a piece of the holy meal, it takes the whole steak. It flies off with Loki who is mysteriously stuck to it when first daring to touch

118 Vǫluspá, stanza 38, 39
119 Snorri Sturluson: Gylfaginning 15 & 16
120 From veðr, neutral singular: "wind, stormy weather", and verb fǫlna, "go pale, go dry, go less (fǫlna, f., "diminishing"), Norrøn Ordbok
121 Skaði was married to Njǫrðr but got divorced and later had many children by Óðinn according to the Skaldic poem Háleygjatál, as explained also in Snorri's Ynglinga saga. In the Edda poem Lokasenna, it is said that she was also a lover to Loki at some point.
122 Haustlǫng, Stanza 2-13 (Jónsson, 1912)

it. The flight, we realize, means the death of Loki, unless he brings Iðunn to the giant's world. Yet his escape is only temporary; the theft of Iðunn by the eagle also signifies old age and death – for all the gods. The image of the falcon flying from the eagle reminds me of the image of the eagle with a "wind-diminishing" hawk in between its eyes. If we take the eagle's daughter, Skaði into account, we will realize that her name literally means "harm, accident, death".[123]

Skaði's association to death is further enhanced by her pleasure in wolves, mountains, and hunting. The giantess's presence appears to threaten the divine world itself, whose inhabitants do all they can to appease her. The link to the eagle in the World Tree is there: Þiazi is first seen sitting in the top of an enormous tree. The link to Hel is there in the figure of Skaði. Finally, the link to the corpse-swallowing wind-creator is not lacking either: both Snorri and Þióðolfr make a point out of how the wind is whistling when the Þiazi beats his wings.

It should be added, in this respect, that the serpent-infested well in Níflheimr, Hvergelmir, may possibly be translated as "Eagle Cauldron or Eagle Mill". Gelmir (m.sg.) may refer to something that makes a loud sound, as in bellowing, related to other names belonging to the world of the dead or the bridge between the worlds; the river Giǫll [f.sg: Resounding] and the Gjallarbrú [Resounding Bridge], the one marking and the other crossing the border to Hel. We also find the word in the Gjallarhorn [Resounding Horn], which is used by the giant Mímir to drink wisdom from the Well of Memory (or the "Murmuring Well"), and by the god Heimdallr to blow out a warning sound when the bridge to the gods was attacked.

However, Gelmir is also a known heiti for "eagle" – the sound-maker. A number of primeval giants have names that may be related to the sound-making (and wind-making) eagle, such as the first being in the Cosmos, Ymir [Murmuring Voice/Sound], who is also called Aurgelmir [Aurr: Mud/Gravel + Gelmir: Eagle/Bellower]. The aurr – mud or sand or gravel, may be the same sort of aurr that the oldest norn, Urðr [Origin], uses to nourish the World Tree

---

123 Norrøn Ordbok

so that it is ever replenished with water and mud from the Well of Origin. However, it is also a word that may mean "splendid", "shining", and is even a heiti for gold. According to Näsström, the heiti aurr for gold is also drink-related, the golden mead could also be referred to as aurr.[124] Aurgelmir may then be translated in various ways such as Splendid Eagle, Shining Bellower, Gold Eagle, Gold Bellower, Gravel Sound/Bellower – perhaps even Mead-Eagle or Mead-Sound/Bellower.

Aurgelmir's descendant is Bergelmir [Ber: fruit/clear + Gelmir: Eagle/Sound], meaning something like Fruit-Bellower or Fruit-Eagle. The word ber could also be an adjective meaning clear, visible, transparent, and this giant represents the next stage in the creation of the world, perhaps the stage were things become clear and visible, or where they start to bear fruit.

He is followed by the third world giant stage; Þrúðgelmir [Þrúðr: Power + Gelmir: Eagle/Sound] – the sound or the eagle of power. All three have names that may be related to either "Eagle" or "Sound-making", or both. In the first Poem of Helgi Hundingsbani, the shrieking of eagles is related to the creation of the world:

1.Ár var alda þat er arar gvllo, hnigo heilog votn af himinfiollom;	1.*In the beginning of time* *when the eagles crowed* *and holy water ran* *from the mountains of* *heaven;*

A giant in eagle's disguise, then, may be a symbol of the devouring world of death. To be able to take off with the maiden that the eagle guards, it appears to be necessary to "kill" it, as Loki and the gods do in the Haustlǫng. It is tempting to suggest that death itself, in its all-devouring aspect, is "killed" when the maiden is rescued, meaning the return to life for the one who "kills" the eagle, conquering death. The eagle is also associated with knowledge.

THE INSIDE OF A MOUNTAIN OR ROCK

The inside of a rock, filled with the pathways of giants, where Óðinn literally risks his life, may very well denote a realm of death:

124 Aurr may signify gold (Näsström 2001, p.148)

the burial mound or tomb. As Lotte Motz has pointed out, stones and boulders of magical endowment was a common concept in the Norse tradition, believed to be the dwellings of spirits and of the dead.[125] Hilda Ellis Davidson describes the burial mound and the mound as such as sites where certain people would go for wisdom and inspiration, and in which would sometimes dwell elves or other spirit beings that could be sacrificed to.[126]

Jacobsdóttir translates Hnitbjǫrg as "Collision-Cliffs", regarding it as "the cliffs which crash together". According to her, they are a perfect image of the Symplegades of Greek mythology; the cliffs which crash together around the perilous entrance to the world of the dead, the obstacle that the hero had to pass if he wished to find treasure in the other world. In the Old Indian epic Mahabharata, the eagle Garuda (like all "soma thiefs") has to pass through a wheel of flame to reach the soma, the Water of Life. The wheel is pictured as golden, razor-sharp reeds that crash together in the blink of an eye.

Jacobsdóttir also convincingly shows how the serpent- and eagle-symbolisms of Óðinn's disguise in Snorri's version have their counterparts in Indian soma mythology.[127] Our aim here, however, is not to understand the myth in light of comparative mythology, but to find the meaning within the Norse imagery itself. It is highly interesting that Óðinn takes upon himself the very imagery associated with the powers of death: the serpent and the eagle are both prominent characters in the realm of Hel.

NOISE

There are several allusions to noise in the names just mentioned. Gunnlǫð dwells in the "Beating Rock" (or "Collision-Cliffs"). As we shall discuss below, there is a puzzling similarity between the meaning of her father's name and his association with a drink, and the doings of the giant Mímir, who drinks through a horn called the "Resounding Horn". Suttungr's father is called Gillingr which means "the Noisy One" or "Screamer[128] ". His wife was murdered with a millstone because the dwarf who killed her was weary of her

---

125 Motz, 1983, p. 6-7

126 Davidson, 1964, p. 154-157

127 Jakobsdottir, 2002, p. 48-51

128 Simek, 1996, p. 08

howling.[129] The noise is associated with the realm of death with its barking dogs, boundary river Loud Noise and its Resounding Bridge. All in all, the main imagery of the story may all be traced back to Hel's realm, and to some degree, to Mímir's Well of Wisdom.

4.5: The Initiations and Arts of Óðinn

Above we have seen that Óðinn learned the official arts of spell-songs or charms (galdrar), the mastery of runes, and the use of eloquence in the ancient realm of the giants and in connection with a wedding to a giantess. There are reasons to believe that the specific area of Giant-world that he is visiting is the realm of death, through some symbolic characters and characteristics which resemble those of Níflheimr. Gunnlǫð may indeed be the mistress of death in disguise, and her embraces usually mean only the "pleasures" of death itself.[130]

Óðinn's escape alive from that realm, carrying with him the hidden and well-guarded mead of poetry and divine wisdom, means that he is in fact conquering death. Conquering death, gathering wisdom in the underworld, and returning with the arts of runes and galdr are not the only wisdom-quests that Óðinn undertakes.

I believe that one should see all the arts of Óðinn and his manner of learning them in connection with each other.

The Drink of Memory

Suttungr's name deserves mention. It means "Heavy with Drink" – one would perhaps assume him to be heavy with the very precious mead of memory and wisdom of which he is the owner. One other giant is associated with drinking in the mythology, and that is Mímir, whose name possibly means "Rememberer".[131] He is full of learning because he drinks from the Mimisbrunnr – the Well of Memory, one of the three wells beneath the world tree –in the heart

---

129 Snorri Sturluson: Skáldskaparmál. The dwarf is the same who killed Kvasir and Gillingr, and who were later killed by Suttungr before he took the mead-cauldrons from them.
130 See chapter 4.1 on how death may be described as a wedding or sexual union with the mistress of death
131 Simek, 1996, p. 216

of the giant world. The well contains wisdom and knowledge:[132]

En undir þeiri rót, er til
hrímþursa horfir, þar er
Mímisbrunnr, er spekð ok
mannvit er í fólgit, ok heitir
sá Mímir, er á brunninn.
Hann er fullr af vísendum,
fyrir því at hann drekkr
ór brunninum af horninu
Gjallarhorni. Þar kom Alföðr
ok beiddist eins drykkjar af
brunninum, en hann fekk
eigi, fyrr en hann lagði auga
sitt at veði.

*And beneath the root
that turns to the world
of the frost thurses,
there we find the Well
of Memory, and this
is full of wisdom and
knowledge, and he is
called Mímir who owns
this well. He full of
wisdom, for he drinks
from the well through
the horn Gjallarhorn.
There came All-Father
and asked for a drink
from the well, but he did
not get anything before
he wagered his eye and
laid it into the well.*

I believe it is worthwhile to note, here, that the mead served by the "Maiden" in other stories is often called minnisdrycc, minnisveigr or minnis aul - the drink of memory. Mímir uses the Gjallarhorn – the Resounding Horn - to drink from. Óðinn paid one of his eyes in order to have a drink from that well – we must assume through the same horn.

In the Vǫluspá, Stanza 28, the payment of Óðinn's eye is somehow connected to the sad and violent fate of the world, whereas in the Hávamál, we may get the feeling that Óðinn's breaking of the ring-oath has terrible, though unmentioned, consequences. This link in itself is thin, but I find that there is a connection between Óðinn in Suttungr's realm and in that of Mímir, through the character of the two giants Suttungr and Mímir, who are both connected with a drink of wisdom, and both connected with what we shall call "Óðinn's initiation".

The two giants may very well be identical. The well of Mímir is generally understood to be situated by a different root than that of Hel, just as the well of Urðr is thought to be by a third root. I believe we should not be too geographic in our understandings of the mythic universe. All the wells have that in common that they are

132 Snorri Sturluson: Gylfaginning 15

situated at a root of the world tree, and we will see that the borders between the realms may not be as strict as they seem.

We ought to remember that the runes which Óðinn "picked up" while hanging from the world tree, were indeed first carved into that very tree by Urðr and her norns, as is clearly stated in Vǫluspá Stanza 19-20:

19.Ask veit ek standa, heitir Yggdrasill hár baðmr, ausinn hvíta auri; þaðan koma döggvar þærs í dala falla; stendr æ yfir grœnn Urðar brunni.	*19. I know an ash by the name Yggdrasill a tall tree, poured over with the bright mud/ gravel/gold/drink From there comes the dew that falls in the valleys standing ever green above the Well of Origin*
20.Þaðan koma meyjar margs vitandi þrjár, ór þeim sal er und þolli stendr; Urð hétu eina, aðra Verðandi, skáru á skíði, Skuld ina þriðju; þær lög lögðu, þær líf kuru alda börnum, örlög seggja.	*20. From there come the maidens of great knowledge Three from that hall which stands beneath the tree Origin the first is called, the second is Happening They carved (runes) into the wood Debt is the third They made the laws, they shaped the lives For the children of the ages they decide the fate.*

Thus, Óðinn has to move into the world of the norns to pick up the runes of fate, into the world of the giants to pick up the drink of memory, and, as we will see, into the world of death in order to drink the precious mead of the Maiden. In every case, Óðinn is initiated into sacred knowledge by a well at the root of the world tree, and in every case the root is connected to a water source or a well.[133]

---

133 Folke Ström, 1954, also identified the three wells with each other through a

SEIÐR

Dóttir Njarðar var Freyja, hon var blótgyðja, ok hon kendi fyrst með Ásum seið, sem Vönum var títt.

Njǫrð's daughter was Freya, she was a blótgyðja (sacrificial priestess), she was the first who taught the Aesir to practice seiðr, like the Vanir used to know".[134]

Óðinn kunni þá íþrótt, er mestr máttr fylgði, ok framdi sjálfr, er seiðr heitir. En af því mátti hann vita örlög manna ok úorðna hluti, svá ok at gera mönnum bana eða úhamingju eða vanheilindi, svá ok at taka frá mönnum vit eða afl ok gefa öðrum. En þessi fjǫlkyngi (...)

Odin knew that sport, with which the greatest power followed, and practiced it himself, what is called seidr. And from this he could know the fates of people and things not yet happened, and he could give death or misfortune or bad health to people, or take the wit from some and give it to others. And with this great knowledge (...)[135]

That art which "contained the most power", that of seiðr, was taught to Óðinn and the Aesir gods by the Vanir goddess, Freyia Vanadís. Snorri explains that seiðr originally was an art of the Vanir. Freyia came to the Aesir after the war between the tribes. The art of seiðr, then, is related to the truce meeting between the Aesir and the Vanir – where the precious mead was first produced. The mead of poetry was created during that very truce, or, according to another text, originated solely among the Vanir.[136] With Freyia came the art of seiðr, but in the very same event where Aesir and Vanir met came, also, the Mead of Poetry. The art of seiðr must have come to the Aesir around the same time as the art of poetry that Óðinn later brought back from the Hnitbjǫrg and Gunnlǫð.

different kind of argument.

134 Ynglinga saga 4

135 Ynglinga saga 7

136 Snorri`s Skáldskaparmál claims that Kvasir, whose blood became the mead of poetry, was created from the spit of the two tribes of gods during their truce meeting. But in the Ynglinga saga in Heimskringla, Snorri claims that Kvasir was the wisest man among the Vanir and that he came to Ásgarðr together with the Njordr-family. Apparently there were at least two versions of the story.

We do not know any more details of this myth, but it places Freyia in a position of teacher and Óðinn as her student. She bestows a very powerful – the most powerful – art of Fjǫlkyngi – Great Knowledge – to him, just like Gunnlǫð bestows on him the mead of poetry, just like Mímir bestows on him the Drink of Memory, and just as we may deduce that the norn Urðr bestowed on him the runes from her abode at the Well of Origin. As we shall see later, Freyia is also identifiable as the Maiden with the Mead and thus with the giantess Gunnlǫð.

The links we have discussed convince me that Óðinn's initiation on the world tree is really associated both with his learning of seiðr from Freyia, runes (from the norns?), galdrar from the "old giant", poetry and wisdom from the drink of Gunnlǫð, and with Mímir's drink of Memory. His death-experience may also involve a visit to the third well, Hvergelmir in Hel, the resounding mill of death, or the eagle's mill – or cauldron.

4.6: ÓÐINN AS DIVINE ARCHETYPE

It is necessary to note that the main actor in the story is a god – even a god of creation. We also know that the story takes place in the beginning of time, just after the great battle between the Aesir and the Vanir, before the valkyriur enter the cosmic scene. If we consider the mead strictly as a mead that makes you into a poet, then poetry is one of the many arts in which Óðinn is supreme – and the first to teach to humankind.[137]

Snorri's account in the Ynglinga Saga makes Óðinn stand out as the teacher and inventor of all the magical arts that priests and priestesses were required to know: eloquence, battle-frenzy, sorcery against enemies, change-shaping into the hides of animals, communication with the other worlds, traveling with the free-soul, [138]manipulation of natural elements like fire, wind and sea, the singing of spell-songs, the foretelling of the future and the opening up of the hidden realms within earth, rock or mound.

Óðinn, the oldest of gods, is the teacher, meaning something significant: namely that all the arts and the practitioners just mentioned had a beginning: a divine archetype. His female counterpart, Freyia, also stands out as a first teacher – teaching even the god.

---

137 See Appendix IV

138 See chapter 3.1 about shamanism and the free-soul.

As we discussed in chapter 4.5, Óðinn appears to have learned his arts by the wells beneath the world tree. Indeed, other sources indicate that learning religious lore by a water source was common far into medieval times. As bishop Bjarni Kolbeinsson stated sometime in the beginning of the 13th century: "I never learned the art of poetry by the water-source. I never performed galdr, and I never sat below a hanged man".[139] As Lotte Hedeager points out, the fact that the bishop, as a good Christian, is stating what he is not doing is most probably what the pagan would do.

In his statement, we may detect practices that indeed were common for the religious professional in pre-Christian times, and they do seem to form quite an echo of Óðinn's actions: learning the art of poetry by the well, singing charms, and "sitting below a hanged man", possibly a way of communicating with the spirits of the dead.

Solli has suggested that the latter practice also could indicate a sitting below a person who is only symbolically hanged, that is, an initiand who, like Óðinn, lets himself be "hanged" and "stabbed" but only in a manner that, however dangerously, enables him to achieve visions and ecstatic experiences.[140]

As the Hávamál and other sources make clear, Óðinn did not just invent the arts out of nothing – he obtained them, he acquired them, through practices that set an example for others to follow. When we read about the exploits of Óðinn it is my conviction that they ought to be seen as divine archetypes for later (human) magical behavior.

4.7: SUMMARY: WHAT ÓÐINN LEARNS

Through comparative analysis of the different "wisdom quests" of Óðinn, I have concluded that they may all be linked together. They include a trial of hardship leading to visions and descents into the lower worlds, where he is taught by supernatural beings. The teachings and the trials eventually lead to a ritual drinking séance and a sacred marriage, and, finally, to Óðinn becoming a great sage. That we are speaking of an initiation, as defined in chapter 3.1, is confirmed by the result: Óðinn's new state of being.

---

139 Hedeager, 1999, p. 9, my translation of the statement from Norwegian
140 Solli, 2002, p. 159-163

But what kind of state is he initiand into?

The Hávamál offers the most obvious answer; After his trials, the god becomes a Þulr – a reciting sage. He also acquires a heiti; Fimbulþulr – The Great Reciting Sage. We know from the meaning of the title itself that this had something to do with recitals of poetical, religious and legal lore, and we know that it was associated with a state of sublime wisdom and esoteric knowledge. The myths themselves may suggest more of what this office was about.

Snorri's account of Óðinn's many great "sports" is presented Ynglinga saga chapters 6 and 7:

6. Frá atgervi Óðins.
Þá er Ásaóðinn kom á norðrlönd, ok með honum Díar, er þat sagt með sannyndum, at þeir hófu ok kendu íþróttir, þær er menn hafa lengi síðan með farit.

Óðinn var göfgastr af öllum, ok af honum námu þeir allir íþróttirnar; því at hann kunni fyrst allar ok þó flestar. En þat er at segja, fyrir hverja sök hann var svá mjök tignaðr; þá báru þessir hlutir til: hann var svá fagr ok göfugligr álitum, þá er hann sat með vinum sínum, at öllum hló hugr við; en þá er hann var í her, þá sýndist hann grimmligr sínum úvinum.

6. Of Óðinn's Deeds
When Ása-Óðinn came to the northern land, and with him the Díar [priests, identified as the other gods who were either of or had united with the Aesir], they practiced and taught such sports that people have been practicing and teaching for a long time after.

Óðinn was the greatest of them all, and it was from him that they all learned these sports, for he knew them first, or at least most of them.[141]

Now it shall be said why it was that he was so highly honored, it was for these reasons; He was so beautiful and dignified to look at, when he sat among his friends, that everybody present had to feel joy in their souls, but when he was out in the army, he appeared grim and dangerous to his enemies.

---

141 The specific art of seiðr was revealed in ch. 4 to originate with Freyia and

En þat bar til þess, at hann kunni þær íþróttir, at hann skipti litum ok líkjum, á hverja lund er hann vildi; önnur var sú, at hann talaði svá snjalt ok slétt, at öllum er á heyrðu þótti þat eina satt; mælti hann alt hendingum, svá sem nú er þat kveðit, er skáldskapr heitir.

Hann ok hofgoðar hans heita ljóðasmiðir, því at sú íþrótt hófst af þeim í norðrlöndum.

Óðinn kunni svá gera, at í orrostum urðu úvinir hans blindir eða daufir eða óttafullir, en vápn þeirra bitu eigi heldr en vendir; en hans menn fóru brynjulausir ok váru galnir sem hundar eða vargar, bitu í skjöldu sína, váru sterkir sem birnir eða griðungar; þeir drápu mannfólkit, en hvártki eldr né járn orti á þá. Þat er kallaðr berserksgangr.

And this was because he knew those sports, that he could change color and appearance in every way, after his own desire. Another was that he could speak so well and so eloquently, that anyone who listened thought it must be the only truth.

He spoke all his speeches in poetical verses, just like we today recite what is called Skáldskap (Poetic Creation). He and his temple priests were called song-smiths, since they brought this sport into the northern lands.

Óðinn could do this, that in battle, his enemies became blind or deaf of struck with fear, and their weapons did not bite more than sticks, while his own men went without armor and were crazy like dogs or wolves, they bit into their shields, they were strong like bears or young oxen, they killed the man-people, and neither fire nor iron could harm them. This is called berserksgangr [going berserk].

---

the Vanir, who taught this art to the Aesir, and it was the most powerful of all the Fjǫlkyngi.

7. Frá íþróttum Óðins.
Óðinn skipti hömum; lá
þá búkrinn sem sofinn eða
dauðr, en hann var þá fugl
eða dýr, fiskr eða ormr,
ok fór á einni svipstund
á fjarlæg lönd, at sínum
erendum eða annarra
manna.

Þat kunni hann enn at
gera með orðum einum, at
slökkva eld ok kyrra sjá, ok
snúa vindum hverja leið er
hann vildi. Óðinn átti skip,
þat er Skiðblaðnir hét, er
hann fór á yfir höf stór, en
þat mátti vefja saman sem
dúk.

Óðinn hafði með sér
höfuð Mímis, ok sagði
þat honum mörg tíðindi
or öðrum heimum. En
stundum vakti hann upp
dauða menn or jörðu,
eða settist undir hanga;
fyrir því var hann kallaðr
drauga dróttinn eða hanga
dróttinn.

Hann átti hrafna tvá, er
hann hafði tamit við mál;
flugu þeir víða um lönd ok
sögðu honum mörg tíðindi.
Af þessum hlutum varð
hann stórliga fróðr.

7. Of Óðinn´s sports
Óðinn could change his
hide/shape [skipti hömum
], then his body lay as if
dead or sleeping, while
he himself was beast or
bird, fish or snake, and
traveled in an instant to
distant lands, on his own
or on others´ behalf. He
could also do other things;
with only words he could
quench a fire, silence the
ocean or turn the wind
where he wanted.

He had a ship called
Skíðblaðnir, in which he
traveled across great seas,
but it could also be folded
away like a tablecloth.

Óðinn kept with himself
the head of Memory/
Murmuring [Mímir,
guardian of the well that
contains all the memories
and knowledge of the
universe], it told him
tidings from other worlds.
Sometimes he woke the
dead up out of the ground
or sat beneath hanged
man; for this he has been
called Draugardróttinn
[Lord of the Undead] and
Hangadróttinn [Lord of
the Hanged].

He had two ravens,
whom he had taught how
to speak, and they flew
widely around the lands
and told him many tidings.
From all this he became
very knowledgeable.

Allar þessar íþróttir kendi hann með rúnum ok ljóðum, þeim er galdrar heita; fyrir því eru Æsir kallaðir galdrasmiðir.

All these arts he taught away in symbols/runes and songs [rúnum ok ljóðum], those that we call spell-songs [galdrar], from this the Aesir are called spell-song-smiths [Galdrasmiðir].

Óðinn kunni þá íþrótt, er mestr máttr fylgði, ok framdi sjálfr, er seiðr heitir.

En af því mátti hann vita örlög manna ok úorðna hluti, svá ok at gera mönnum bana eða úhamingju eða vanheilindi, svá ok at taka frá mönnum vit eða afl ok gefa öðrum.

En þessi fjölkyngi, er framit er, fylgir svá mikil ergi, at eigi þótti karlmönnum skamlaust við at fara, ok var gyðjunum kend sú íþrótt.

Óðinn knew that sport, with which the greatest power followed, and practiced it himself, it is the art called seiðr [Óðinn kunni þá íþrótt, er mestr máttr fylgði, ok framdi sjálfr, er seiðr heitir]. Because of this, he could know the destiny of people and things that had yet to happen, he could give death and bad health, he could take the wit and the power from people, and he could transfer it to others. With this great magical knowledge [fjǫlkyngi] so much ergi [shame, unmanliness] followed that menfolk could not practice it without shame, and only the gyðjur [priestesses] could know this sport.

Óðinn vissi um alt jarðfé,
hvar fólgit var, ok hann
kunni þau ljóð, er upp
laukst fyrir honum jörðin,
ok björg ok steinar, ok
haugarnir, ok batt hann
með orðum einum þá er
fyrir bjoggu, ok gékk inn
ok tók þar slíkt er hann
vildi.

*Óðinn also knew about all
earth-dug treasure and
where it was hidden, and
he knew songs that made
everything open up for
him, earth and mountain
and rock and mounds,
and he bound with words
those who lived in there,
and went inside and took
what he wanted.*

*From all these crafts
[kröptum] he became
famous, his enemies
feared him, but his
friends trusted in him
and believed in his craft
[Krapt] and in him also.
Most of his sports he
taught to the sacrificial
priests [blótgóðir], they
were next after him in
all wisdom [Fróðleikr]
and great knowledge
[fjǫlkyngi].*

Af þessum kröptum varð
hann mjök frægr; úvinir
hans óttuðust hann,
en vinir hans treystust
honum, ok trúðu á krapt
hans ok á sjálfan hann. En
hann kendi flestar íþróttir
sínar blótgoðunum; váru
þeir næst honum um allan
fróðleik ok fjölkyngi.

Margir aðrir námu þó
mikit af, ok hefir þaðan af
dreifzt fjölkyngin víða ok
haldizt lengi.

*But others still learned
a lot of it, and from
them has great magical
knowledge [fjǫlkyngi]
spread widely and
maintained for a long
time.*

All the things that the god learned during his trials of initiation, are all to be recognized in the various myths of his initiation trials and may be identified with arts that we know to be common within Norse society as well as some arts that scholars are more uncertain about. The known common arts that Óðinn obtains during his trials are those of poetry, runes, galdr, esoteric knowledge and seiðr

» Poetry in Norse society was a highly respected art and required a profound knowledge of mythical "facts" in order to apply poetic metaphors and allusions. The skáld – the bard - may have had his older counterpart in the þulr, (see chapter 3.3) whose title basically means "reciter" and refers to a sage of some kind, specializing in chanting and reciting – of poetry? He may be a kind of priest, or even a "shaman" (see chapter 3.1). The one telling the tale of the initiation by hanging on the world tree is speaking from the "chair of the þulr" and may either be Óðinn himself or, actually, a þulr, as discussed in chapter 3.1 and chapter 4.2.

» Runes are a kind of letters, but their etymological significance is "hidden knowledge" or "whisper"[142], and they were related to fate and destiny, as they were first carved by the norns, mistresses of fate. They were often used for healing and spells and the casting of lots for divination.

» Galdr is derived from the verb gala, which means the sound that the rooster makes, denoting a high-pitched voice.[143] It was a way of making spells and had its counterpart in other magical songs such as the Varðlokur and the Seiðlæti and the Fimbulljóðar.

---

142 Norrøn Ordbok
143 Näsström, 2001, p. 57

» Seiðr has an uncertain etymology, but it may mean "to sing", something which connects it to the art of galdr. Indeed, magical songs were used to call the vættir – spirits - to aid in séances of seiðr. Seiðr appears to have centered on divination, magic and sorcery. As we saw in chapter 3.1, many are those who have connected the arts of seiðr and galdr with a supposed Norse form of shamanism. Other arts of Óðinn do indeed resemble shamanism insofar as he is said to travel with his soul to other "countries" in order to bring back information for himself or for others. His descent into the world of Gunnlǫð may be another such tale, but it may refer to something even more crucial than the gathering of information; it may include the art of conquering death. This is a quite common theme in the history of religions and known, among other things, in mystery cults of the goddess.

So far, we have not really discussed the drink that the Gunnlǫð offers. Steinsland calls this kind of drink "materialized knowledge".[144] As we saw in chapter 3.2, the ritual offering of mead may have been part of a general welcome into the hall of a ruler, a consecration into a sacred office, perhaps part of a kingship inauguration, or indeed, of marriage, in this case sacred marriage since at least one of the partners is divine. None of these possibilities need exclude the others.

The drink is identified as the drink of poetry created by the truce between the gods (or as coming from the Vanir). It contains hidden wisdom, all the intelligence of the world, and it will make the drinker a great poet and sage. Seen in the light of all the trials that Óðinn has to go through to get the precious draughts, the drinking and the subsequent "marriage" appears to be the culmination and the confirmation.

The Maiden, a giantess, is situated within a realm that bears resemblance to the realm of Hel, death itself. It is surrounded by obstacles which she helps the hero to conquer.

The hero, in this case a god, undergoes a trial involving fasting and physical hardships, in which he learns powerful arts: There is a connection between these arts and the art of seiðr through the arrival of Freyia and the Vanir to Ásgarðr – an event which induces both the creation of the sacred mead, Óðinn's subsequent trials on the world tree, and Freyia's teaching him the art of seiðr. There is also a link to Óðinn's sacrifice of his eye by the well of Memory.

---

144 Steinsland, 1997, p. 126

Ström, like myself, sees a parallel in Óðinn's eye-sacrifice and his hanging, and he also identifies the three wells as really being one and the same.[145] Many of the arts of Óðinn are conveyed by female characters: The mead of knowledge and poetry is given by Gunnlǫð, the art of seiðr is given by Freyia, and the runes that Óðinn brings up to Earth's sanctuary were, according to Vǫluspá Stanza 20, originally carved by the norns Urðr and Verðandi.

Thus, we see how teacher figures for the god are found in giantesses, goddesses, and norns, creatures of different realms, linked to each other through their functions. It is also interesting to note how all of them are associated with sacred liquids, as we shall see in the following chapters.

Only one of Óðinn's mentors is male; the unnamed giant who is his mother's brother. However, he acts in the manner of a helper, while the Maiden is the goal and the initiation itself. As we shall see in the Gróagaldr, the galdr that that the hero is taught is a means to reach the actual goal. Likewise, Óðinn is taught the nine galdrar from the unnamed giant before he has a drink from Poetry Stir.

In Snorri's version the giant Baugi [Ring] helps Óðinn on his way to the drink of poetry. In fact, these giant figures could very well resemble human mentors in a ritual setting. Gunnlǫð, the Maiden, appears in a different light, being placed right where the goal is, its guardian, its conveyer. Her offering of the mead is the consecration, her embrace the culmination and the step to freedom from death.

Óðinn's trials may be seen in the light of an initiation ritual, as shown among many others by Näsström, who regards them as the initiation trials of a religious professional, much akin to the trials of initiation in mystic religions.[146]

Óðinn as a god is setting an example for others to follow; as Snorri remarked, he taught the arts to the priests and priestesses, who practiced and taught them on to the people. Thus we have a thesis on which to build the rest of our study: that the trials and the teachings, and, indeed, the sacred marriage of Óðinn in Gunnlǫð's realm, are undertaken by human beings in his aftermath.

---

145 Ström, 1954, p. 88-91
146 Näsström, 2001, p.165-173

4.8: THE WOOING OF GERÐR

Gerðr means "Enclosure" (as in a fence of sorts) and is the name of another daughter of giants in the Skírnismál [The Shining/Pure One's Speech]. Her father is Gýmir – a name which indicates that he hides something. Who may these two be?

In the Skáldskaparmál 33, Snorri claims that Gýmir is identical to another giant called Hlér [Wind-Shielded], and that both are identical to Aegir [Terrifying]:

(...) Hér er sagt, at allt er eitt Aegir ok Hlér ok Gymir.

(...) Here it is said, that they are all one; Aegir and Hlér and Gýmir.

In the beginning of the chapter 33, Snorri lists some common names for Aegir as the personification of the ocean itself:

33.Sjávarkenningar. Hvernig skal sæ kenna? Svá, at kalla hann Ymis blóð, heimsækir goðanna, verr Ránar, faðir Ægisdætra, þeira er svá heita Himinglæva, Dúfa, Blóðughadda, Hefring, Uðr, Hrönn, Bylgja, Bára, Kólga, land Ránar ok Ægisdætra ok (...)	33.Metaphors for the Ocean How shall the ocean be known? So, as to call him the Blood of Ymir [the Murmuring Sound], Visitor to the Gods, Husband of Rán [Robbery], father of the Aegir's [Ocean] Daughters, they are called Himinglæva, Dúfa, Blóðughadda, Hefring, Uðr, Hrönn, Bylgja, Bára, Kólga [nine names for nine different kinds of waves, streams or currents], Rán's Land, and the Land of Aegir's Daughters and (...)

Aegir is first introduced in the first chapter of the Skáldskaparmál, where the giant comes to visit the gods, and they receive him well. During the banquet, the god Bragi offers a lengthy speech about the art of poetry and metaphors, which forms more than half of the content of the Skáldskaparmál:

1. Aegir sækir heim æsi.
Einn maðr er nefndr Aegir eða Hlér. Hann bjó í eyju þeiri, er nú er kölluð Hlésey.
Hann var mjök fjölkunnigr. Hann gerði ferð sína til Ásgarðs, en æsir vissu fyrir ferð hans, ok var honum fagnat vel ok þó margir hlutir gervir með sjónhverfingum.
Ok um kveldit, er drekka skyldi, þá lét Óðinn bera inn í höllina sverð ok váru svá björt, at þar af lýsti, ok var ekki haft ljós annat, meðan við drykkju var setit.

1.Aegir Seeks the World of the Gods
A man is called Aegir [Terrifying/Ocean] or Hlér [Windshield/Death Shield]. He lives on that island, which is now called Hlésey [Wind-Shielded Island (Island of Immortality?)]. He was very fjǫlkunnigr [of great, magical knowledge].
He made his journey to Ásgarðr, and the Aesir knew beforehand of his coming, and he was well received, even though many things were made with illusions.
And in the evening, when they were to drink, then Óðinn let carry into the hall swords, and they were so bright, that light emitted from them and no other light did they have while the drink was served.

Later on, when Aegir leaves the hall, he invites the gods to his own home, but demands that they bring a cauldron large enough to hold all his mead. The god Þórr [Thor] gets the task of getting the cauldron, a story that is told in the Edda poem Hymiskvíða, where the god also happens to get the World Serpent on his fishing hook, making the whole world tremble before the serpent sinks back into the ocean waves. Before Þórr may return from his quest for the mead-cauldron, which now covers his entire body, he needs the aid of a mysterious "Mother", who also calls him "son" – and we all know that the Thunder god's mother is Earth.

While the gods are waiting for Þórr [Thor] to arrive, they settle down in the hall of Aegir, what is described further in the Skáldskaparmál:

41. Æsir þágu veizlu at Ægis.

Fyrir hví er gull kallat eldr Ægis? Þessi saga er til þess, er fyrr er getit, at Aegir sótti heimboð til Ásgarðs, en er hann var búinn til heimferðar, þá bauð hann til sín Óðni ok öllum ásum (…) svá ok ásynjur(…).

Þórr var eigi þar. Hann var farinn í austrveg at drepa troll. En er goðin höfðu setzt í sæti, þá lét Aegir bera inn á hallargólf lýsigull, þat er birti ok lýsti höllina sem eldr, ok þat var þar haft fyrir ljós at hans veizlu, sem í Valhöllu váru sverðin fyrir eld. (…)

Rán er nefnd kona hans, en níu dætr þeira, svá sem fyrr er ritat. At þeiri veizlu vannst allt sjálft, bæði vist ok öl ok öll reiða, er til veizlunnar þurfti. Þá urðu æsir þessir varir, at Rán átti net þat, er hon veiddi í menn alla, þá er á sæ kómu.

41. The Gods Dare to Visit Aegir

Why is gold called the Fire of the Ocean? It is said, as before was told, that Aegir came to visit the World of the Gods, and when he was ready to go home, then he invited Óðinn and all the gods (...) and also the goddesses (...)

Thor was not there. He had traveled the eastern paths to slay trolls. And when the gods had sat down in their seats, then Aegir let carry into the hall floor light gold, it was bright and lit up the hall like fire, and this was all they had for light at the banquet, just as in Valhǫll they had swords for fire (...)

Rán is she named, his wife, and their nine daughters, as has before been counted. At this banquet, everything served itself, both food and drink and everything needed for the banquet. Then the gods became aware that Rán owned a net, with which she hunted men who had drowned at sea

Nú er þessi saga til þess,
hvaðan af þat er, at gull er
kallat eldr eða ljós eða birti
Ægis, Ránar eða Ægis dætra.

Ok af þeim kenningum er
nú svá sett, at gull er kallat
eldr sævar ok allra hans
heita, svá sem Aegir eða
Rán eigu heiti við sæinn, ok
þaðan af er nú gull kallat
eldr vatna eða á ok allra
árheita.

*Now from this story we may
see why it is so that gold is called
fire or light or shine of Aegir, Rán
or the Aegir-Daughters.*

*And these metaphors are so put,
that gold is called the fire of the
sea and all his heiti, so as Aegir
and Rán may be used as heiti for
the ocean, and from this now is
gold called the fire of water or of
the rivers, or of any kind of heiti
for rivers.*

The Skáldskaparmál does mention an event at this banquet, where Loki kills a slave out of jealousy and is chased out of the hall, but breaks back in, upon which he reveals that he is the one who really killed Balder. In the Edda poem Lokasenna [Loki's Quarrel], this story is elaborated further as something that happens until Thor returns with the cauldron and the ability to smite Loki out of the hall of the immortals. The prose introduction to the Lokasenna also claims that Gýmir is another name for Aegir:

Egir, er aðro nafni het Gýmir (…)

Aegir, who goes by another name, Gýmir, (…)

In the Edda poem Oddrúnargrátr [Edge Rune's Lament], the valkyriur are said to be dwelling at Hlésey. The valkyriur of the Edda poems are always the daughters of giants.

Gerðr, thus, may be a giantess, a personification of an ocean wave or a current, but also a valkyria, or something else that is sublime, esoteric. Since winds are common metaphors for death, dying or mortality in Norse poetry, whatever is wind-shielded must needs be metaphors for immortality, "shielded against death".

The poem Skírnismál begins with a prose description of the god Freyr sitting down in the Hlíðskiǫlf [Opening Watchtower [147]] usually the seat of Óðinn, from where he sees into all the worlds:

Freyr sonr Niarþar hafði
einn dag setzc i Hliþscialf oc
sa vm heima alla; hann sa
i iotvnheima oc sa þar mey
fagra, þa er hon gecc fra
scala faðvr sins til scemmo;
þar af fecc hann hvgsottir
miclar.
    Scírnir het scósveinn
Freys; Niorþr baþ hann
qveþia Frey mals. Þa mælti
Scaði (…)

Freyr, Njǫrð's son, sat
one day in the Opening
Watchtower and saw into
all the worlds; he looked into
the world of the jǫtnar and
saw a maiden so beautiful,
as she went from her father's
house to her own dwelling;
of this he got great soul-grief.
Skírnir was Freyr's shoe-boy
(servant). Njǫrðr asked him
to make Freyr talk. Then said
Skaði (…)

So, Freyr, looking into the world of the giants, spots a maiden in the courts of the giant Gýmir, who is likely identical to Aegir the ocean god, and falls violently in love. But this passion makes him weep from grief, for he is certain that the match is impossible. His parents ask his servant, Skírnir, to talk to him, and Freyr explains that nobody wants him to unite with the one he has fallen in love with.

As we shall see, there could seem as if the maiden is related to the Sun goddess, for she is so bright that her arms illuminate air and sea, and there is a direct mention of how the Sun goddess refuses to shine on Freyr's passion:

4. Freyr qvaþ:
„Hvi vm segiac þer,
seggr enn vngi!
mikinn móðtrega?
þviat Alfraþvll
lysir um alla daga
oc þeygi at minom mvnom."

4. Freyr said;
«What shall I tell you,
such a young boy
of my great mood-grief?
For Elf-Splendor [the Sun
Goddess]
she shines all days
but not on my desires."

6. Freyr qvaþ:
„I Gymis garþom
ec sa ganga
mer tiþa mey;
armar lysto,
en af þaþan
alt lopt oc largr.

6. Freyr said
«In the settlements of Gýmir
I saw her walk
a maiden most dear to me;
Her arms shone bright
and from that light
she illuminated air and sea."

---

147 Simek, 1996, p. 152. The meaning is disputed, but could come from hlid, "opening", and skialf, "watchtower".

7. Mẹr er mer tiðari manni hveim vngom i árdaga; asa oc alfa þat vill engi maþr at viþ samt sém."	*7. That maiden is more dear to me that from the days of origin no man has ever loved more But of the gods and the elves nobody want that we together be.*

Freyr 's servant, Skírnir [Shining/Pure/Transparent One [148]] offers to woo the maiden for him, if the god will only grant him "the horse that will carry him through the dark, sure, flickering flame", and the "sword which fights by itself against the giants".[149] Freyr grants him these treasures, and his servant sets off towards the realm of the giants on that magical horse. Regarding the name of the hero: Note that in the Gylfaginning 15 & 16, we learn that:

15 (…) Þriðja rót asksins stendr á himni, ok undir þeiri rót er brunnr sá, er mjök er heilagr, er heitir Urðarbrunnr.	*15 (…) The third root of the ash stands in heaven, and beneath this root there is a well that is very sacred, it is called the Well of Origin (…)*
16 (…)En þat vatn er svá heilagt, at allir hlutir, þeir er þar koma í brunninn, verða svá hvítir sem hinna sú, er skjall heitir, er innan liggr við eggskurn	*16 (…) And that water is so sacred, that everything that may come into that well, becomes so bright/ transparent as that membrane is called which lies on the inner side of an eggshell.*

Skírnir, who is clear, pure, bright, shining, transparent – as if he has gone through the Well of Origin and been resurrected and transformed there, now rides through a familiar darkness and dewy mountains, a landscape recognizable from the stories we earlier quoted (see chapter 4.4) about journeys into Hel.

---

148 Simek, 1996, p. 290, from skirr, "clean", "clear", "shining", "transparent". Note that in Snorri's Gylfaginning, it is said that anyone who enters the Well of Origin will come out shining and transparent.
149 Skírnismál Stanza 8

Let us look at what the Skírnismál has to say about this journey:

10. Scirnir męlti viþ hestinn:
„Myrct er v́ti,
mal qveþ ec ocr fara
vrig fioll yfir,
þvrsa þioþ yfir;
baþir viþ comvmc,
eþa ocr bada tecr
sa inn amatki iotvnn."
   Scirnir reíþ i iotvnheima
til Gymiss garða. Þar varo
hvndar ólmir oc bvndnir fyr
sciþgards hlidi, þess er vm
sal Gerðar var. Hann reiþ at
þar er fehirþir sat a haugi oc
qvaddi hann:

10. *Skírnir said to the horse:*
"Dark it is outside
now we must fare forth
across the rainy wet
mountains
across the flocks of thurses
   We will both reach the
goal
   Or we will both be taken
   By that almighty jǫtunn."

Skírnir rode down into the World of the Giants to the settlement of Gýmir. There were aggressive dogs bound before the gate of the enclosure that was around Gerðr's hall. He rode there were a herdsman sat on a burial mound and greeted him:

11.„Segðv þat, hirþir!
er þv a haugi sitr
oc vardar alla vega:
hve ec at andspilli komvmc
ens vnga mans
fyr greyiom Gymis?"

11.»*Tell me this, herdsman*
you who sit on the barrow
and are guarding all the paths:
How can I come to meet
the young maiden
and pass the wolves of Gýmir?

12.Hirþir qvaþ:
„Hvart ertv feigr
eþa ertv framgenginn
. . . .?
andspillis vanr
þv scalt ę vera
godrar meyiar Gymiss."

12.*The herdsman said:*
"Are you dying
or already dead?
....
Never shall you
for eternity meet
the good maiden of Gýmir.

13.Scirnir qvaþ:
„Kostir 'ro betri
heldr enn at klaŕcqva se
hveim er fv́ss er fara;
eino dǫgri
mer var aldr vm scapaþr
oc alt lif vm lagið."

13. *Skírnir said:*
«*One may choose better,*
if one wants to get forwards
than to wail and complain without
hope
I will not avoid
that one day
which is the end of life."

14. Gerðr qvaþ:
„Hvat er þat hlym hlymia,
er ec heyri nv til
ossom ra*nnom i?
iorþ bifaz,
enn allir fyr
scialfa garðar Gymis."

14. Gerðr said:
«What is that roar of roars
that I can now hear
here within our halls?
Earth is trembling
and all houses shake
here in the farms of Gýmir."

Stanza 10 clearly states that his is a very dangerous, nocturnal journey through the world of the þursar were the "too almighty giant" may very well take both the horse and its rider.

In **stanza 11**, Skírnir encounters savage dogs outside of the fence surrounding the hall of the Maiden. He asks a herdsman who is sitting on a mound how to come past the "greys [wolves] of Gýmir". These are also described as hounds guarding the gate to the hall, barking and bloody, perhaps, as the hounds of Hel that both Hermóðr and Óðinn met on the way (see chapter 4.4).

In **stanza 12**, the herdsman, surprised by the request, does not answer but questions whether Skírnir is dead or about to die, just like Móðguðr remarked that Hermóðr did not have the color of dead men, wondering why he was then traveling the Hel-path (see chapter 4.4). Some text is missing, but we learn that the herdsman, guarding all the roads while sitting on a haugr – a barrow, a burial mound, apparently decides that Skírnir is neither dead nor dying, and states that there can be no conversation between him and the daughter of Gýmir.

It could seem as if one has to be dead or dying in order to "converse" with the giantess.

In **stanza 13**, Skírnir states that he is not afraid to die.

In **stanza 14 - 17**, Gerðr, however, is alerted by now, as she hears the earth trembling, just like Móðguðr remarked on the trembling that came from Hermóðr compared to the vibrations of hundreds of dead men.

When she learns about Skírnir's presence, she asks him to come into her halls and drink inn męra mioþ - the "adored mead" - even though she fears that he is her brother's slayer. She realizes that he is neither god, nor elf, nor of the wise Vanir, and wonders what on earth he is then doing in her hall, not even being dead nor dying:

16.Gerðr qvaþ: „Inn biþþv hann ganga i occarn sal oc drecca inn męra mioþ! þo ec hitt óvmc, at her vti se minn broðvrbani.	*Gerðr said:* *«Bid him to enter* *into our hall* *and drink the adored* *mead!* *Although I worry* *that the one here outside* *may be my brother's bane.*
17. Hvat er þat alfa ne asa sona ne víssa vana? hvi þv einn vm komt ęikinn fýr yfir ór salkynni at sia?"	*17.You are not of elves* *nor of the sons of the gods* *nor of the wise Vanir?* *How did you cross* *the furious fire* *and arrived here at my* *hall to see me?"*

Evidently, the fence around the Maiden's hall is made out of furious fire, but Skírnir crosses the fire-fence, and the Maiden wonders what he could be, who is not elf, or a god of the Aesir or of the Vanir.

18.Scirnir qvaþ: „Emkat ec alfa ne ása sona ne víssa vana; þo ec einn vm komc eikinn fýr yfir ydor salkynni at siá.	*18. Skírnir said:* *«I am not elf* *nor the son of a god* *nor of the wise Vanir;* *Though I came* *from over the furious fire* *to arrive at your hall and* *see you.*

Skírnir responds that he is neither elf, Áss, or of the Vanir, what leaves us with the notion that he, a servant to a god, may actually be a human being, who is in a place where only dead or dying humans may usually go; the world of the dead.

What follows is a **long process of quarrel** and many a display of eloquence and magical powers, where Skírnir first states his purpose; immediately asking her to become Freyr's bride, offering her eleven apples of gold and the ring that drips nine new ones like itself every ninth night.

⬳ *Gerðr flatly refuses. She has more than enough gold in her father's hall.*

⬳ *Skírnir threatens her with the sword, but she again refuses, arguing that Gýmir, her father, could well fight back.*

⬳ *Eventually, Skírnir makes use of galdrar to curse her in the most deliberate ways.*

Suddenly, **by stanza 37**, the maiden changes her mind, welcomes him and offers him hrímcálki fvllom forns miaþar - the "crystal cup full of ancient mead".

⬳ *She declares that she will meet Freyr within nine nights, in the breeze-less grove of Barri.[150]*

⬳ *Freyr, when he learns about her conditions, does not rejoice, but complains about the durance of nine whole nights.*

Let us go through these stanzas:

37.Gerðr qvaþ:
„Heill verþv nv heldr, sveinn!
oc tac viþ hrímcálki
fvllom forns miaþar;
þo hafþa ec þat etlad,
at myndac aldregi
vnna vaningia vel."

37. Gerðr said:
«Be rather whole, lad
and take the frosty cup
full of ancient mead
Although I had never guessed
that I ever would
love the Vanir-kind well."

38.Scirnir qvaþ:
„Ǫrindi mín
vil ec ǫll vita,
aðr ec riþa heim heþan:
nęr þv a þingi
mvnt enom þrosca
nenna Niarþar syni."

38.Skírnir said:
"My errand
I want to fulfil completely,
before I can ride home from here:
When will you call to assembly
and offer your love
to the son of Njǫrðr?"

39. Gerðr qvaþ:
„Barri heitir,
er viþ bęði vitom,
lvndr lognfara;
enn ept nętr nío
þar mvn Niarþar syni
Gerþr vnna gamans."

39. Gerðr said:
«Barri [Conifer] it is called
as we both know
the breezeless grove;
And after nine nights
there may the Njǫrðr's son
bestow on him tender pleasure."

---

150 From barr, "barley" or "conifer". Simek, 1996, p. 32

When Skírnir returns home with this message, Freyr breaks down in further tears, for, as he cries;

42.Freyr qvaþ:	42.Freyr said:
„Lang er nott,	"Long is one night,
langar 'ro tver,	Longer are two
hve vm þreyiac þriár?	How shall I endure the third?
opt mer manaþr	Often a month seemed
minni þotti,	Less to me
enn sia half hynótt."	Than this night of yearning."

This reaction has often been taken to refer to Freyr's passion as a god of love and sex, who cannot wait even nine nights for the union with his beloved. But here we can clearly see some elements that are closely connected to the ones we saw in the story of Óðinn's initiation. It took nine nights to get there, just as it took Hermóðr nine nights to get into Hel. There is a precious, adored, ancient and powerful mead involved. Dangerous gates guarded by Hel-Hounds, furious fires to cross and not touch, and the goal of the whole thing is a union with the Maiden with the Mead in a "breezeless grove" – a grove where the winds of death may not reach. Let us go through the structure and thematic stages of the story.

4.9: The Structure of Themes in Gerðr's story

As in the story of Gunnlǫð and Óðinn, we may here detect the same structure of themes.

Vision Quest: The poem begins with a (prose) vision quest theme: Freyr sits down in Óðinn's seat, from where he may look out upon "all the worlds". This kind of universal vision from a special, divine kind of position could hardly resemble anything else than a visionary experience.

☛Vision: *The vision theme follows as Freyr lays eyes on a Maiden in a far-off world whose arms illuminate the oceans and the hills as she walks. She is clearly in another world, different from that of Freyr's, and may only be seen by him through such supernatural sight.*

☛Descent: *Then follows a descending theme where not Freyr, but his "servant", who is neither elf or god, moves into an underworld of death and giants.*

☛**Trials**: *Like Óðinn, he has to know how to talk in his encounter with the giant herdsman and the giantess. The trial theme follows as Skírnir moves past the flickering fires and the barking dogs to enter the hall of Gerðr.*

☛**The Maiden with the mead (Consecration)**: *He is greeted by her, and thus we proceed to the Maiden theme where she offers him a drink and, after a duel of words where Skírnir, like Óðinn, has to show his eloquence, agrees to marriage while offering a drink.*

As Skírnir returns to Freyr with the message, it becomes clear, at least to my mind, that the descending-, trial- and Maiden- themes will be repeated: Skírnir has made the initiatory journey on behalf of Freyr, after the latter's visionary experience, but now, Freyr has to make the journey himself.

The Maiden does not pack her belongings to join Skírnir on his way back to the divine realm. Instead, she decides the conditions of their union: that Freyr will have to endure nine nights before their meeting in a breezeless grove. Freyr is right to complain about the durance of those nine nights and worry how he shall survive even one or three of them, for they are probably as tough as the nine nights of Óðinn's hanging and will only culminate in a sacred grove where the winds - of the eagle Corpse Swallower - do not reach.

4.10: The Maiden and Her Realm

"...The raging guard-dogs of Gýmir (...) the shepherd on the grave-mound, and, together with the grave-mound, contribute to the scenery of the entrance to the world of the dead with its' perpetual tribe of Cerberus."
---Ursula Dronke[151]

Since we have established Gunnlǫð as dwelling in a realm of death, we must ask ourselves whether Gerðr also does so. Indeed, she does. The dark, wet road, the trembling earth, the wall (of fire) that must not be touched, and the barking dogs are all typical symbols of the world of Hel. The barking dogs motivate a conversation with a shepherd who sits on a grave mound. The shepherd assumes that Skírnir must be dead or dying, as one would usually be when traveling the Hel-Road.

---

151 Dronke, 1997, p. 390

When he realizes that Skírnir is a living soul, he assumes that there may be no meeting with Gerðr. If she is the lady of death itself, this is a logical assumption. We are so lucky as to have very detailed descriptions of the Norse world of the dead. In Snorri's story of Hermóðr, we are told how Hermóðr rides to Hel to bring Baldr back from the world of the dead, what I quoted in full in chapter 4.4. Here we learn that it took nine nights, that the valleys were dark and deep, that there was golden gold, a maiden guarding the bridge who interrogates the visitor, remarking that he does not belong here on account of being neither dead nor dying.

The bridge resounded and the earth trembled when he came, just like it did for Skírnir, another still living human who could enter this world while still alive. It is also important to cross above the fence, gate or flickering fire without touching it. As we saw in Vegtamskvíða, there were also Hel-hounds, now belonging to Gýmir and Gerðr. Skírnir's journey would easily fit into the pattern shown in these two sources. He rides a magical steed that has the particular quality of being able to jump through flames –the flames which constitute the fence around Gerðr's hall.

So do Óðinn and Hermóðr –they both ride the eight-legged Sleipnir, and a point is made out of how they avoid touching the gate of Hel. The road is dark and long. The earth trembles when Skírnir arrives, so does the Resounding Bridge when Hermóðr rides over it, and Óðinn's road resounds. Skírnir encounters savage dogs, just like Óðinn. He has to cross a fiery fence; Hermóðr and Óðinn have to cross a fence or a gate. The female warden at the Resounding Bridge remarks that Hermóðr does not have the color of dead men, the male warden or mound-dweller outside of the hall of Gerd asks Skírnir whether he is dead or marked to die.

Gerðr's father is Gýmir, which according to Simek could mean "Sea".[152] Simek suggests that he is a sea-giant, since he is identified with the sea-giant Aegir both in the Lokasenna and in the Skáldskaparmál 23. Aegir is the husband of Rán, mistress of the drowned (and dead), and is certainly associated with cauldrons and mead and daughters too, as shown in the beginning of the Skáldskaparmál and in the poem Hymiskvíða (see chapter 4.8).

---

152 Simek, 1996, p. 126, 127

In chapter 6.10, we shall see that sea-giants are connected to the Maiden in her aspect as valkyria The etymological meaning of Gýmir is unclear, but Simek suggests that it could, for example, come from the word geyma, which means to hide, keep safe. In that case, we are reminded of Suttungr who hides the mead (and the Maiden) within the rock-layers. For the time being, I would wish to emphasize that Aegir's realm also is a realm of the dead, where the giantess Rán receives drowned people in her halls. It is also associated with a notion of immortality – the Wind-Shielded Island, where the giants meet the gods. It is here, in the grove of immortality, that Freyr may join his beloved of the illuminating arms.

Much else is not to be said about Gerðr, except that she offers ancient or adored mead, has beautiful, shining arms which shine up all the lands and the sea, and that she is in possession of lots of gold and an independent mind – and, clearly cunning and wit. She even tricked Skírnir into believing that he had conquered her, not knowing before he returns home that she really demanded that Freyr go through these trials himself before she would have him. She is surrounded by a fence of fire.

All in all, it seems safe to place Gerðr right in the heart of misty Hel.

4.11: THE TRIALS OF THE HEROES

Freyr is a god and an ancestor of kings, and it is his servant and childhood companion, the Shining One (or the "Clear One" or the "Pure One"), who gets the task of actually traveling to the other world.

The servant asks, one could imagine as if in prayer to the god, to have a magical horse and a magical sword, which he is granted. The theme of a chief's servant actually undertaking the "wooing" part of the quest for the Maiden will be recognized in chapter 7.2, where this kind of servant resembles a religious professional.

Since Skírnir is not dead nor dying, the Maiden expects him to be an elf, Áss or wise Vanir, moving about in the Other Worlds. The riddle presented when Skírnir presents himself as neither elf nor god, could be explained by the possibility of him being a still living human.

The magical horse and the sword are something Skírnir shares with the hero Sígurðr (chapter 6) with the hero Hermóðr and with the god Óðinn. It is worthwhile to note how the journey to the world of the dead in the Norse material often is pictured on horse-back – horses being a common sacrifice in burial mounds.

An older and equally important "steed" to the underworld is the (funeral) ship, which we shall see is the more common vehicle in the Heroic Poems. For women, the journey was often pictured as driving a chart – an image we recognize in *Helreið Brynhildar*.[153] The magical sword is crucial also in the stories of the two Helgi characters, which we shall be studying in chapter 6.

Skírnir, like Óðinn, has to enter the deadly realm of the powerful giants in order to encounter the Maiden. It is in the encounter that his trial differs dramatically from that of Óðinn, who obviously receives teachings.

Skírnir does not appear interested in any teachings at all: he offers gifts to entice the Maiden out of her realm, and when she refuses he threatens and curses her. He appears successful in his task when Gerðr suddenly greets him as "lad" [sveinn[154]] and offers him the mead. We do not learn whether Skírnir drinks the mead, and he continues uninterested in teachings, eagerly asking when she will meet Freyr.

Freyr's devastated reaction to her answer is odd. Perhaps it considered a sign of the immense sexual desire of the fertility god, who cannot bear to wait for nine nights. I believe, however, that those nine nights really are long: As long as the nine dark nights that Hermóðr had to endure on his way to Hel, and as hard as the work of nine men that Odin in Snorri's version had to finish in the fields of Baugi, as dangerous as the nine nights that the god hang stabbed, starving and thirsting, on the world tree.

---

153 Ellis Davidson, 1964, p. 154,
154 Skírnismál stanza 37

Indeed, Freyr's nights must be as uncertain as the three nights that we will see that Óttarr is granted to learn his sacred genealogy, and as powerful as the nine spell-songs that transport Svípdagr to the halls of the goddess.[155] The number nine is no coincidence, it symbolizes something which we can only vaguely deduce from the other settings in which the number appears. Those particular nine nights shall be concluded in a breeze-less grove [lund lognfarna[156]] – a place where the winds of the death-eagle's wings do not reach.

The theme of conquering death may be subtly revealed in this allusion.

4.12: THE GIFTS AND THE THREATS

"She does not capitulate because he has frightened her, but because she sees some truth in what he says. (...) he has painted the alternative very well."
---Ursular Dronke[157]

A few words on the gifts and the threats that the Maiden receives are perhaps necessary. Steinsland has shown how the gifts: apples and ring, and the wand that Skírnir uses to curse with, all resemble royal symbols that may connect the myth to kingship (and thus sacred marriage).[158]

Näsström, moreover, sees the three methods used to conquer Gerðr as representing the three Indo-European "functions" (as described by Dumezil) in society. Gold and riches represent the "third" function: that of the peasants, the sword he uses to threaten her represent the warrior function, while the magical wand and the curses represent the first, priestly function.[159]

The curses are perhaps the most puzzling aspect of the myth: they take up a great part of the poem and are extremely aggressive. But as Ursula Dronke has suggested, Skírnir with his curses is only really summing up what Gerðr may in fact expect if she stays in the Underworld: separation from society, despair and longing, relations only to ogres and the world of the dead.

---

155 See Hyndluljóð, Svípdagsmál, and chapter 5
156 Skírnismál, stanza 39
157 Dronke, 1997, p. 395.
158 Steinsland, 1991
159 Näsström, 1998, p. 140

With the curses, Gerðr is shown the two opposite worlds between which she may choose: the world of the dead with its devouring monsters and suffering, and the world of divine life, and love, which Freyr may offer her.[160] Also Clunies-Ross has argued that Skírnir's curse "functions to remind Gerðr of what is at stake in her refusal to cooperate."[161]

One image is particularly interesting to this study, since Gerðr, in Stanza 28, is told that she will be more famous than the guardian of gods, where she is gaping behind the fences of Hel. Thus she is imaged as a guardian of Hel – unless she lets herself be taken out of that realm.

I will repeat what seems very clear to me, at least; that the Maiden actually tricks Skírnir in to thinking that he has conquered her, when in fact she is making a tremendous demand; that Freyr achieves a state of immortality in order to get her. This will require that he undergoes the "nine nights" of descent into death followed by a resurrection that is difficult to reach and hard to endure, and which may lead to death only.

4.13: SKÍRNIR AS THE EXPERIENCED PRACTITIONER, FREYR AS THE INITIAND

I understand Skírnir's journey to be the initiatory journey of an experienced practitioner on behalf of the god – or the one who represents the god - in order to "woo the Maiden". When the Maiden has given her terms and her consent, Skírnir, carrier of the magical wand and the treasures of the gods, goes back to his master who has had the initial vision, and tells him the message. I believe that it is only then that the actual initiation experience begins, symbolized in the nine nights Freyr will have to endure before culminating in the consecrating act of Sacred Marriage.

---

160 Dronke, 1997, p. 395. Dronke perceives Gerd to symbolize the Earth who is "woken up" from the death of winter by the shining ray (Skirnir) of the Sun god (Freyr). This understanding of the myth used to be very common, but has been disputed by amongst others Gro Steinsland, 1991, and others. See appendix..
161 Clunies-Ross, 1994, p. 140

As we noted, Skírnir does not himself appear to receive any teachings, but returns hurriedly back to his lord-friend, telling him the terms of the Maiden. This is when I assume that the real trials begin: the trials of Freyr himself, the king-god. They shall last for nine whole nights, where even the first will be unbearably long. The suffering will only finish when Freyr has reached that breezeless grove of the Maiden.

It seems reasonable to assume that Freyr would have to follow a similar path to that of Skírnir's descent.

4.14: SUMMARY OF AND CONCLUSIONS TO CHAPTER 4

In this chapter, I have argued that Óðinn's trials on the world tree is directly linked to his encounter with Gunnlǫð, and that Gunnlǫð dwells in a realm that resemble that of Hel's, or more generally, a realm of death.

Steinsland has shown that there exists a multitude of pre-Christian ideas about the after-life so that our geographical assumptions which strictly place the realm of Hel here and other realms there in the manner of Snorri's descriptions may not be covering the whole of Norse conceptions about death. One image which, until Steinsland pointed it out, has been largely neglected, is the fact that death often is depicted as a sexual encounter or marriage with a supernatural lady, often identifiable as Rán or Hel, although mentioned by other names.[162]

Óðinn's descent into the death-realm of Gunnlǫð is not only connected to his nine-night's self-sacrifice, but also to the initiation into his major arts: runes, charms, esoteric knowledge, soul-flight, seiðr, and poetry (eloquence).

Through his method of learning – the descent into and the escape alive from the realm of death, he also learns a way of "conquering death", bringing back with him sacred knowledge and talents symbolized in the precious mead. He has help from the Maiden figure.

---

162 Steinsland, 1992, p. 319-332

Through comparative analysis such as that of Svava Jacobsdóttir, it is possible to link Óðinn's experience to kingship inauguration as well. However, the initiation seems to be of a more general character that would easily apply to several religious practitioners in the Norse society. I have argued that Óðinn's quest is primordial and archetypical: it creates a mythical pattern for others to follow.

In the Codex Regius, the first who apparently follows Óðinn's example is the Vanir god Freyr, who, significantly, sits down in Óðinn's own seat in order to have cosmic vision. Much like Óðinn, he peers down and detects the object of his desire: the Maiden, this time in the shape of Gerðr.

In the Óðinn-'Gunnlǫð section, I detected a structure of themes involving:

☞ A vision quest theme
☞ A vision theme
☞ A descent theme
☞ A trial theme and
☞ A Maiden theme.

I have argued that the Freyr-Gerðr story follows a very similar structural pattern and that the contents of each theme in the latter story also resemble the contents of the former to a significant degree.

The main difference between the Gunnlǫð and Gerðr stories is, to my view, the emphasis, the outcome, and the existence of a second character in Gerðr's case. The Gunnlǫð story tones down the marriage theme on behalf of the teaching theme, and Óðinn operates by himself. The marriage theme certainly exists, and we learn that Óðinn breaks his ring-oath and betrays Suttungr and Gunnlǫð in the end. The marriage or sexual union is the means by which Óðinn achieves what he is really there for: the mead of poetry, of divine knowledge. The mead appears to function as a symbol for all the arts that Óðinn learns. Emphasis in the story is on Óðinn's trials and the outcome: his becoming a sage, bringing a sacred treasure from the Underworld into the divine realm or to the "shrine of Earth".

The Gerðr story focuses much more strongly on the marriage theme. The main aim is to convince the giantess to leave her realm, marry the god and become one among the Ásyniur, the goddesses. From other sources we know that there existed a tradition in which Gerðr really became Freyr's wife and that they had a son who became the founder of a royal line. Steinsland has shown how the union represents a sacred marriage myth which helped to legitimize a royal line, and how it is significant that the marriage is between a god and a giantess, two polar forces in the universe creating something entirely new and powerful, a king figure. The myth possibly also formed a model for rituals of kingship inauguration.[163]

While the initiation of Óðinn resembles those of priests, shamans, mystics or ascetics as much as those of rulers, the initiation of Freyr, folcvaldi goða - the "gods' people-ruler"[164]- seems to point more clearly in the direction of kingship inauguration in connection to sacred marriage. But the religious practitioner is not out of the picture; he appears, in my opinion, in the character of Skírnir, who somehow "makes way" for the young god-king, and in the structural pattern that the initiation follows, which resembles that of Óðinn's to a significant degree.

Finally, something must be said about the "Maiden". Gunnlǫð and Gerðr, not to say the myths surrounding them, resemble each other closely in function. They dwell in a realm of giants that may also be identified with a realm of death.

They are strongly protected by physical obstacles and giant fathers. They are both giantesses being wedded to gods. They both have power over a precious, ancient mead, which they serve to their hero in a welcome.

They are both associated to gold (golden chair, golden treasures). Gerðr is associated to bright, illuminating shine, something we shall see that she shares with the other Maiden-figures. They are both the focal point of a similar tale of initiation.

Their stories follow much the same thematic structure. Their fates depart from each other in the way they are treated by the gods who woo them: Gunnlǫð is deprived of her "whole soul", and left weeping behind. Gerðr is, in order to kaupa friðr – buy peace - invited to stay in Ásgarðr as a goddess among goddesses, an invitation she eventually, however reluctantly, accepts.

---

163 See chapter 3.1 on Sacred Marriage
164 Skírnismál Stanza 3

The difference is puzzling but not enough to confuse our thesis. In both cases, a point is made out of the life-death-opposition:

» Óðinn could not have escaped Suttungr's deadly halls without the help of Gunnlǫð. Her realm is that of death, and through her love and gifts (and perhaps the knowledge Óðinn achieves during his quest), she provides a way for him to fly away. The frost-giants ask themselves whether Óðinn died at Suttungr's hands or whether he is (alive) among the gods: We know the answer, and it is Gunnlǫð who caused the happy outcome. As I have pointed out before, the embrace of the mistress of death did in fact mean death itself. Óðinn escaped through her help, however unwittingly she provided it.

» In the case of Gerðr, the structure takes a new turn which is to be evolved in the subsequent stories of the human initiands of the following chapters. Through Skírnir's curses, we see how Gerðr is shown the two possible turns of her fate: She may become a dweller of the Underworld, a grotesque ogress at the gates of Hel. Such a figure is in fact known from the myths elsewhere and must have been an existing tradition in the concepts of the Underworld.

» Gerðr may decide to be that, or to become a goddess, a wife of the constantly rejuvenated gods, the opposite of residence among the dead. When Gerðr is made aware of the options, she decides to take Freyr as her lover, but it is up to him to find her through a nine night's trial. Their meeting in the breezeless grove may very well represent something similar to Óðinn's flight and subsequent dwelling "among the gods": a place of no death.

5: The Great Goddess

I n this chapter, we shall explore the "Maiden-myth" of the poems Hyndluljóð [The Song of the She-Wolf] the Gróagaldr [To Grow Spell-Song] and the Fjǫlsvinnsmál [The Speech of Much Knowing]. The two latter poems are usually studied together as the so-called "Svípdagsmál" [The Speech of Swift Dawn] since they are clearly connected with each other.[165]

The poem Fjǫlsvinnsmál has been transmitted through a rather late manuscript from the 17th century, and most 20th century scholars have disregarded the poem as a late medieval poem not to be reckoned among the "real" Edda-poems but rather as a fairy tale imported from the continent, perhaps Celtic in origin.

In his study of the poem, Eldar Heide shows how the poem must be counted among the old Divine Poems and that it is an important source to Nordic mythology, even a key to the understanding of cosmology in the old, pre-Christian religion. The mythical pattern of the Fjǫlsvinnsmál is comparable to other more commonly accepted sources to Norse mythology. Heide chooses to study the Fjǫlsvinnsmál as a separate poem, the way it is presented in the source-material, since it is possible to read it as a complete lay, even though the Gróagaldr appears to be closely related.[166]

I agree with Heide that both poems are no more "fairy-tale"-like than other Edda poems, and no less pagan in origin. But I disagree with Heide when he maintains that the Gróagaldr has no function in the Fjǫlsvinnsmál Heide admits that the two poems may form part of the same story, even if they are two separate lays.[167]

---

165 In 1856, Sophus Bugge and Svein Grundtvig decided that the poems Gróagaldr and Fjǫlsvinnsmál must be understood together as a bigger poem: the Svípdagsmál -a title constructed by these scholars. This view is basically founded on how a very similar story appears in a 16th century Danish fairy tale; the Ungen Svejdal (Grundtvig, 1996(1856). Their theory is commonly accepted today. Heide, 1997, p. 12
166 Heide, 1997
167 Heide, 1997, p. 39,40

As Lotte Motz has argued earlier, the combination of the poems into a "Svípdagsmál" makes sense since the charms of Gróagaldr could appear to be describing an initiation ritual.[168] In fact, the Gróagaldr and the Fjǫlsvinnsmál together fit perfectly into the pattern of "Maiden-mythology" that we are discovering in other Edda poems, which means that they must reflect the same older mythical reality hiding behind the Gerðr-, Gunnlǫð-, Freyia- and valkyria-stories.

Even if the two poems may be read separately from each other, I find it fruitful to read both together as a "Svípdagsmál", since Fjǫlsvinnsmál without the Gróagaldr loses the initiatory vision-, vision-quest- themes and parts of the trial-theme under guidance from a "master" (in this case a female) that leads Svípdagr to the high hall of the Maiden where the ultimate trial begins.

Even when read on their own, the two poems reveal parts of the same "Maiden-mythology" that we find in the Hávamál and in the Skírnismál. Read together, the two poems as separate parts of one story follow the pattern of other "Maiden-stories" perfectly.

Menglǫð is not known from other sources than the jointed "Svípdagsmál", but she shares many characteristics with Freyia. Scholars have mainly identified her through her name, which is supposed to be derived from men – necklace, gold or treasure - and glǫð, which is supposed to be a derivation of glaðr –"bright", "clear", "light", "joyful", "happy" or "quick". [169]

Many scholars have assumed that the name indicates "the One Who takes Pleasure in Jewels."[170] Since Freyia is associated with jewels and gold, especially a certain bright necklace called the Brisíngamen – the "Fiery Necklace"[171], the name Menglǫð itself lends to the identification of the two figures.

Menglǫð, moreover, is situated behind a dangerous fence which will only open for the "right one", a feature she shares with Freyia (and, indeed, with Gerðr). Menglǫð's hall is also very beautiful, and the story about her is a love story, fitting into the pattern of our popular idea of Freyia as a goddess of love. Besides, Menglǫð is waiting and yearning for her long-lost husband, just like Freyia is - and Gunnlǫð. They all weep for the loss of their lovers.

---

168 Motz, 1975, p. 135

169 Norrøn Ordbok. Simek, 1996, p. 210

170 Simek, 1996, p. 210

171 Simek, 1996, p. 44-45. Either from brisa –"to shine", or from brísingr, "fire"

Menglǫð is surrounded by maidens, nine in number. As we know, Freyia is associated with a kind of maidens called the valkyriur, who, as we shall see in chapter 6, usually appear in a collective of nine.

As I also mentioned in chapter 3.2, the meaning of Menglǫð's name is, however, challenged by Svava Jacobsdóttir. She argues that the name could be derived from OE mengan – "to mix", and lǫð – "invitation" or "drink" (like the lǫð in Gunnlǫð). Thus the name indicates the invitation to a mixture – a drink. This is in accordance with the mead-serving goddess of the Irish sources, who often takes her name from the drink she serves.[172] In the interpretation "Invitation to a Drink" we are perhaps perceiving a tradition of a Maiden who is not only associated with, but even identified with, the precious mead. In chapter 8 we will discuss the vǫlva Gullveigr in the light of Maiden-mythology. Her name, Gull+Veigr, may be directly translated as "Gold Drink", despite numerous efforts to paraphrase the meaning of her name to fit a notion of greed for gold that simply does not present itself in any sources.

Menglǫð's goddess-hood is also challenged by Eldar Heide, who argues that her character is that of a giantess.[173]In my study, the opposition "giantess vs. goddess" is not overly problematic since the Maiden figure, as we shall argue, covers both giantess-, goddess- and valkyria-hood.

The authenticity of the Hyndluljóð has also been questioned by scholars. The poem tells of how Óttarr descends to an Underworld to learn about his "ancestry". But after being told of what may be accepted as a human, legendary ancestry, his teacher, a giantess who has much in common with a vǫlva, proceeds to reveal cosmic secrets of a visionary nature much like those of the poem Vǫluspá.

Since Óttarr has descended with the goddess in order to obtain knowledge of his ancestry, most scholars have been rather puzzled about the nature of the teachings. Larrington and Simek among many others claim that the stanzas 29-44 constitute an interpolation of an entirely different poem, namely what Snorri mentions as the Vǫluspá in skamma – "The Short Prophecy of the Vǫlva".[174]

---

172 Jacobsdóttir, 2002, p. 45

clxxiii Heide, 1997, p. 160

174 Larrington, 1996, p. 253, Simek, 1996, p. 169

However, Steinsland argues that the poem Hyndluljóð is complete in itself, and that the esoteric nature of the teachings is part of Óttarr's "ancestry" – he is actually learning that everything – gods, giants, humans, and a great Being, are his "ancestry" – that everything that appears separated and different, are in fact one.[175]

My position is similar to that of Steinsland; I believe the Stanza 29-44 form a logical part of the revelations, and that they points towards an understanding of a greater, cosmic whole from which every "lineage" in the universe descends, and in which we are all united – a secret revelation for the initiate, and a very typical one if it had been the initiation of a Mystery Religion.

In the "Svípdagsmál" and in the Hyndluljóð we are met with goddess-figures in a role very similar to that of the giantess Maidens in the previous chapter. Freyia's goddess-hood is unquestionable, she is counted among the most powerful and high-ranking ásyniur – goddesses - in Ásgarðr. However, she was not originally an ásynja [goddess].

Like Gerðr, she entered Ásgarðr from another divine tribe. Freyia's tribe is the Vanir, whose origin is unknown. Just as the perpetual enmity between the Aesir and the giants, there used to be enmity between the Aesir and the mysterious Vanir. Just as Freyr tried to "buy peace" [friðr at kaupa[176]] with Gerðr's clan, the giants, by inviting Gerðr as his wife to Ásgarðr and to subsequent goddess-hood,[177] the Aesir try to buy peace with the almost victorious Vanir through an exchange of hostages.

Among the hostages from the Vanir is Freyia and her family. Freyia teaches seiðr - the art of the vǫlur - to Óðinn and is a blótgyðja – a sacrificial priestess/goddess. The truce between Freyia's people and Óðinn's also results in the creation of the mead of poetry with its subsequent need for a quest to retrieve the mead from the giants as told in the story of Gunnlǫð.

---

175 Steinsland, 1991, p. 244-251
176 Skírnismál Stanza 19
177 Snorri counts Gerðr among the goddesses in Gylfaginning

As Näsström has shown, sources independent from that of Snorri regard Freyia as a wife or concubine of Óðinn.[178] Snorri, who neatly systematizes the divine world, regards Frigg as Óðinn's wife, while Freyia is married to "someone called Óðr". Most scholars assume that Óðr is Óðinn,[179] which is natural since the name is a combination of the word Óðr and hinn, which is the equivalent of English "the": His name, basically, means The Óðr. The "confusion" between his wife Frigg and his wife or concubine Freyia may of course be because the god, like any great king, had many wives, but we know that, at some point in history, both goddesses emerged from one and the same goddess, Frija.[180]

Snorri relates how Óðr suddenly disappeared, and that Freyia was left behind weeping, much the same way as Gunnlǫð was. Indeed, there is also a story of how Óðinn, gone traveling, left his wife Frigg for so long that she took other husbands.[181] Freyia's story does not finish with passive weeping either, for she started to travel the world wearing different shapes and names, leaving behind her tears of pure red gold everywhere she went.[182]

In fact, as Näsström has pointed out, Freyia's name is actually a title, not a name, meaning "Lady", much in the same manner that a great god may be called simply "the Lord". Through comparative analysis of features and characteristics, Näsström has shown that the great "Lady" may hide behind a large number of female deities, even norns and giantesses (see chapter 3.4).

One part of the Óðinn-Freyia relationship is particularly interesting and puzzling. We are not told how the arrangement came to be, but the Grímnismál [The Speech of the Masked One], stanza 14, reveals that Freyia, residing in the ninth world, receives the dead souls of the einherjar – the chosen dead. She decides which of the einherjar (one-harriers) shall sit in her beautiful hall of friendship, and which shall go on to Óðinn's Valhǫll to become eternal warriors in service of the gods. Significantly, she shares the einherjar with Óðinn - not the other way around. It is clearly Freyia and not Óðinn who is in control of the choice.

178 Näsström, 1998, p. 89-91
179 Simek, 1996, p. 250, Näsström, 1998, p. 90
180 Ellis-Davidson, 1998, p. 10, Näsström, 1998, p. 136, Simek, 1996, p. 94
181 Ynglinga saga 3, Gyldendal, 1944, p. 4
182 Gylfaginning (Faulkes, 1987, p. 30)

This information links Freyia to the valkyriur on one side, since they are the spirits who hover above the battle-field choosing who shall fall and taking their souls with them to Valhǫll. The Grímnismál information, which is repeated by Snorri in the Gylfaginning, makes it natural to assume that the valkyriur were as much maids of Freyia as of Óðinn, since they must have taken the souls to the goddess first.

On the other side, the information above also links Freyia to Hel, the giantess who receives the dead, and who rules in nine worlds.

Other sources also establish Freyia as a mistress of death, such as the girl of the saga who cries out that she will not eat until she "sups with Freyia", meaning that she will starve herself to death.[183]

5.1: FREYIA — LEADING THE WAY TO VALHǪLL

As remarked above, Freyia would receive dead souls, keep some for herself in her serene and beautiful halls of the ninth world, and send others on their way to Óðinn's Valhǫll – the Hall of the Chosen. Just how this happened is not known, but the Hyndluljóð may give an indication. The poem begins with a speech which sounds rather like an invocation:

1.Freyia qvaþ: „Vaki mær meyia, vaki min vina, Hyndla systir! er i helli byr; nu er rauckr rauckra, rida vit skulum til Valhallar ok til vess heilags.	1.Freyia said: "Wake, Maiden among Maidens, Wake up, my friend, She-Wolf, sister! Who lives in the rock cave: Now is the darkness of darkness itself, We ought to ride To Valhǫll And to the sacred shrines.

The goddess, Freyia, is trying to wake up her "sister", her "girlfriend", Hyndla, who lives in a rock cave. We learn that it is "the darkest of darkness itself", and that Freyia wishes to ride to Valhǫll and to the holy shrines.

---

183 Egils saga Skallagrímssonar, Lie, 1970, p.188

She continues her speech, and the sense of invocation is strengthened in the 4th stanza:

4.Þor mun hon blota,
þess mun hon bidia,
at hann æ vid þik
einart laati;
þo er honum otijtt
vid iotuns brudir.

4.To Thor she may sacrifice
and this she may pray for
that he, with you
fares gently;
although he is often hostile
to the brides of the Jǫtunn.

Freyia asks Hyndla to saddle
one of the wolves of her stables
and ride with Freyia and her
choice of steed, a great boar:

5.Nu taktu vlf þinn
einn af stalli,
læt hann renna
med runa minum."
(…)

5.Now take your wolf
one from the stable
and let him run
with my boar
(...)

Hyndla of the rock cave, the perfect image of a giantess, does wake up, but she sneers at Freyia's request. It is not a boar that Freyia is riding, it is a man in boar-shape. Her "boar" is really Óttarr, Freyia's verr [man/warrior – her lover or husband]. Even so, argues Freyia, Óttarr has always believed in goddesses, and colored red the altars of sacrifice until the rock turned to crystal:

10.Haurg hann mer gerdi
hladinn steinum
— nu er griot þat
at gleri vordit —,
raud hann i nyiu
nauta blodi,
æ trvdi Ottar
æa asyniur.

10.He made me an altar
made out of stone
Now the rocks
have turned into crystal
Red did he color it
with the blood of the
sacrifice
Ever did Óttarr
adore the goddesses.

Thus, he has behaved in a manner which deserves help and attention. His wish is to have his "heritage", namely the gold of Valland – the Land of the Dead who have been chosen by the valkyriur for Valhǫll. He has wagered this gold with a certain Angantýr [Pleasure God] and now he is in dire need of counsel about his lineage.

With this, Freyia urges Hyndla to answer who various lineages are and where they come from. The fact that Óttarr is presented as a devout worshipper of goddesses seems to convince the giantess. She and Freyia dismount from their respective steeds, the wolf and the boar, and sit down to count up Óttarr's "ancestral lineage".

THEY ARE ALL YOUR KIND, FEAR WARRIOR OF THE NARROW MIND

Hyndla starts by counting up the lineages of great men and women, of the gods, of the giants, of the Vǫlur and the Vítkir [wizards] and Seiðberandi [Pregnant with Seiðr]. Throughout her rhythmic account, she keeps asserting, like a refrain; allt er þat ætt þin, Ottar heimski! [They are all your kind, Óttarr of the narrow mind]. She constantly addresses Óttarr as heimski, which means ignorant, in the sense of "home-bound" - one who has never known more of the world that his own home.

Óttarr was a common masculine name which probably meant Fearsome Warrior, but it could potentially also mean "Fear Warrior" – as in one who conquers his fears, perhaps, or one who is also influenced by fear.

Since Óttarr is there to learn about his "lineage", we must assume that the main lesson of this revelation is that his lineage are everybody who ever lived, and that his need to specify his own is a sign of ignorance.

This is what he has to learn, if he is ever to get to Valhǫll.

Eventually, Hyndla reveals the greatest of secrets: That there is one being greater than all of those accounted for, born by nine giant maidens. This being, which we know to be Heimdall [Illuminating World" [184]], encompasses everyone else:

35.Vard einn borin i ærdaga rammaukin miok raugna kindar; niu bæru þann naddgaufgann mann iotna meyiar vid iardar þraum.	*35. One was born in the days before time immensely powerful of the rulers' kind; Nine gave birth to him that magnificent man Nine giant maidens by the edge of the Earth.*

184 Simek, 1996, p. 135

37.Hann Gialp vm bar, hann Greip vm bar, bar hann Eistla ok Eyrgiafa, hann bar Vlfrun ok Angeyia, Imdr ok Atla ok Iarnsaxa.	*37. Gjalp gave birth to him* *Greip gave birth to him* *Eistla gave birth to him* *and Eyrgiafa* *Ulfrún gave birth to him* *and Angeyia* *Imdr and Atla* *and Iarnsaxa.*
38.Sa var aukinn iardar megni, sualkaulldum sæ ok sonardreyra.	*38.He was empowered* *by the power of Earth* *by the cool, cold sea* *and the blood of the* *atonement/sacrifice.*

The nine giantesses who gave birth to this magnificent creature at the beginning of time are echoed in the story of Heimdallr as described in the Gylfaginning, where there is also a quote from an otherwise lost poem, the Heimdalargaldr, where the god is said to have been birthed by nine mothers:

Níu em ek mæðra mögr,
níu em ek systra sonr.

> *Of nine mothers I am son*
> *Of nine sisters I am son*

This myth seems related to the theme of the nine giantess daughters of Aegir and to the collectives of nine or nine by three valkyriur that we are going to meet in the next chapter. The number nine is in itself interesting, the number of nights it takes to reach Hel the number of nights it takes to complete the trials of initiation.

There is also the number of worlds which existed before the present world came into being, and the number of residing giantesses within those worlds, as is described in the Vǫluspá stanza 2. In Edda poetry, there are also mentions of nine worlds beneath Misty Hel, Hel ruling in nine worlds, and Freyia ruling the ninth world.

Finally, Hyndla reveals some of the reasons behind the end of the world which is to come and indicates a new beginning. By stanza 42, Ragnarök has come, and Hyndla reveals how the oceans are stirring up storms against heaven itself, the air is yielding, and biting snows and winds are coming, and that those who rule the world will fall

To end her revelation, she returns to the theme of the one who had been born in the beginning – Heimdallr, the Illuminating World, and this is where we see a hint of what could represent pantheistic philosophy in the background – a hint only, but not the only one as Edda poems go.

43. Vard einn borinn aullum meiri, sa var aukinn iardar megni; þann kueda stilli storaudgazstann, sif sifiadann siotum giorfaullum.	*43. One was born* *greater than all* *He was made to grow* *by the power of Earth* *It is said that he* *is the one of greatest* *power* *and that every being, all* *related* *come together in him.*

In this and stanza 38, both dealing with Heimdall's glorious birth, it is said that he was made to grow or empowered by the power of earth, the cool-cold sea and the blood of the atonement, which could also refer to sacrifice. A completely identical recipe is offered in a completely different Edda poem Guðrúnarkvíða önnur, where the princess Guðrún receives a drink of mead from her mother from a horn engraved with secret runes and spells of healing and oblivion. In the poem, Guðrún states that the drink itself was empowered by the power of earth, the cool-cold sea and the blood of the atonement – by the exact same words as the greatest divine and unifying being had been empowered, in fact:

21. Forði mer Grimildr fvll at drecka svalt oc sarlict, ne ec sacar mvnþac; þat var vm a'kit iarþar magni, svalca'ldom se oc sonar dreyra.	*21. Grimhildr brought to* *me* *a brimming drink* *Cool and bitter* *it healed all grief:* *It was empowered* *by the power of Earth* *by the cool cold sea* *and the blood of the* *atonement*
22. Voro i horni hverskyns stafir ristnir oc roþnir, raþa ec ne mattac; (…)	*22. There was in the horn* *all kinds of runes* *carved in and colored red* *I could not read them (…)*

When Hyndla has sung her song of sacred ancestry, Freyia asks Hyndla to give the "ale of memory [minnis aul[185]] to Óttarr so that he can remember her words "on the third morning" when he and Angantýr [Pleasure God] shall reckon up their lineage. Hyndla, however, refuses, saying that she wishes to sleep, and tells Freyia to run off into the night like the goat Heiðrún runs with the rams. In the next stanza, she repeats the comparison of Freyia and Heiðrún, adding that Freyia runs wildly about full of desire, and that many are those who have run about her skirts. The stanzas appear insulting, and Freyia responds that she will surround this place with the fire of troll-women [elldi of ividiu[186]] and that Hyndla will never come out unburned.

Hyndla responds that everybody wishes to save their lives, but that the ale Freyia serves to Óttarr is full of poison. Freyia has the final word, declaring that the giantess's words of bad luck shall have no effect, that Óttarr shall drink the precious drink [dyrar veigar[187]], and that all gods shall help him. Let us have another look at this apparent argument between the goddess and the giantess, going through the last stanzas first:

45. Freyia qvad:
„Ber þu minnis aul
minum gesti,
sua hann aull mune
ord at tina
þersar rædu
æа þridia morni,
þa er þeir Angantyr
ættir rekia."

45. Freyia said:
"Carry the Ale of Memory
to my guest
so that he can hold on to
all your words
of this council
on the third morning
when he must contend about
lineages
with the God of Pleasure."

46. Hyndla qvad:
„Snudu braut hedan!
sofua lystir mik,
fær þu fætt af mer
fridra kosta;
hleypr þu, edlvina!
vti æа nættum,
sem med haufrum
Heiðrun fari.

46. Hyndla said:
«Turn swiftly back where you
came from
sleep is all I want
Few fair things of value
shall you have from me
You run, noble girlfriend
outside at nights
just like, with the bucks
Heiðrún fares.

---

185 Hyndluljóð, stanza 45
186 Hyndluljóð, stanza 48
187 Hyndluljóð, stanza 50

Let us pause here to ponder the comparison between Freyia and the goat Heiðrún running with the bucks. This is normally taken to mean that Freyia was a horny and promiscuous goddess. But Heiðrún is more than a goat. Her name derives from Heiðr, which is also a common name for a vǫlva, among them the very first vǫlva in the world, as we learn in the Vǫluspá stanza 22, which we shall come back to.

The name also means "heath", both as in a meadow-like, open space or clearing within a forest landscape, and as in "heathen" [heiðningr] and "heathenism" [heiðindómr], terms attributed to the pre-Christian people in the Norse language because, it is generally thought, they believed that pagans worshipped outside on the heaths.

Since a heath tends to be bright, open clearings, the word could also poetically mean bright, open space within an otherwise dark environment (the forest), also in a more spiritual sense.

The second word that makes up this "goat's" name is rún – as in "rune". This could mean the letter, but also any kind of symbol, and is also used as a metaphor for secrets, whispers, mysteries. As such, Heiðrún is a symbol, or a mystery, of a bright, open space within darkness – which also happens to be the manner in which the hall of the Maiden with the Mead is often described – a bright, golden realm within the darkest depths of Hel.

Adding to this far more esoteric picture, the "goat" is in fact the origin and the producer of the precious mead that the valkyriur serve to the einherjar of Valhǫll. She stands on the roof of that hall, eating the leaves of Læráðr [Harmful Counsel], probably another heiti for the ash Yggdrasill.[188]

Her "bucks" may very well be the einherjar, and we must remind ourselves that the purpose of Óttarr's journey is in fact to reach Valhǫll.

---

188 Grímnismál 25 and Gylfaginning 39: en ór spenum hennar rennr mjöðr [and from her udders mead runs]

This comparison is emphasized in the next stanza too, where we also learn that she was running after Óðr (or Óðinn), something that hides another revelation; for his name means poetry, ecstasy or inspiration, and this is actually what she is said to desire, even if she appears to also have a sexual thing going with the men who, we could perhaps assume, like her verr, Óttarr, needed her aid to reach Valhǫll:

47.Rant at Odi ey þreyiandi, skutuzst þer fleiri vnd fyrirskyrtu; hleypr þu, edlvina! vti a nattum, sem med haufrum Heiðrun fari."	47. You ran after Óðr [Poetry, Ecstasy, Inspiration] always desiring it still many more have been beneath your skirts; Run, you, noble girlfriend Outside in the nights Just like with bucks Bright Opening Symbol fares.

In the last few stanzas, both the teachers, the goddess and the giantess, help revealing what each of them represent; The giantess represents death and mortality, the power of darkness and oblivion, and even if she can give Óttarr a lot of knowledge, she cannot give him the ability to remember what he learned while in a state of death (in the underworld), and all she offers is oblivion.

Freyia, on the other hand, offers the mead of memory, the ability to return to the world of the living with all the knowledge of the underworld intact. She declares that she can defeat the ogress of death, darkness and oblivion, by enclosing her within a fiery fence, just like the one we keep seeing surrounding the hall of the Maiden with the Mead.

48.Freyia qvad: „Ek slæ elldi of ividiu, sua at þu eigi kemz æa braut hedan; ------------------	48.Freyia said: «I throw a fire around the witch within wood So that you can never come out unburnt from here; ... (text missing)

Hyndla warns them of the coming apocalypse, and that many will try to survive in vain, but Freyia concludes, in the end, that Óttarr will drink the precious mead and receive the help of the gods:

49. Hyndla qvad:
Hyr se ek brenna
enn haudr loga,
verda flestir
fiorlausn þola;
ber þu Ottari
bior at hendi
eitri blandinn miok
illu heilli."

49. Hyndla said:
«I see a fire burn
and the Earth aflame
most will try to ransom their lives
when suffering
You carry to Óttarr
the beer to drink
it is much blended with poison
and ill fortune."

50. Freyia qvad:
„Ordheill þin
skal engu ræda,
þottu, brudr iotuns!
baulfui heitir;
hann skal drecka
dyrar veigar,
bid ek Ottari
aull god duga."

50.Freyia said:
"Your cursing words
shall not be ruling (this outcome)
Even if you, bride of the Jǫtunn
intend to call down the worst;
He shall drink
the precious drink
And I bid that all gods
shall help Óttarr."

5.2: STRUCTURAL ELEMENTS IN HYNDLULJÓÐ

VISION QUEST

The "vision quest theme" of the Hyndluljóð is apparent in the allusion to Óttarr's previous sacrificial activity, which led the goddess to appear and help him. We may not know what kind of effect blood sacrifice may have been expected to have on its practitioner, but it is not unlikely that it could induce a state of mind open to the supernatural powers.

This is possibly shown through the fact that Óttarr in some way or other actually becomes the sacrifice. The sacrifice is followed by his descending into the underworld in the shape of a boar. The boar was sacred to the Vanir, usually associated with Freyr. One of Freyia's names, Sýr [ow], however, also associates his sister with pigs.

The pigs were important sacrificial animals. They were considered very powerful –in the Hyndluljóð, Stanza 38, we hear that Heimdall was strengthened by the blood of the sacrificial boar, together with the power of the earth and the sea. I find it likely that Óttarr represents the sacrificial boar on its way to the realm of the dead. This element links Óttarr to Óðinn, who sacrificed himself in order to obtain the knowledge of the runes of fate, powerful spell-songs and a drink of Poetry Stir.

» **VISION**: *The vision theme must be that Óttarr's activities cause the goddess to appear, changing him into a steed for hersel*

» **DESCENT**: *The descending theme is obviously when Freyia rides Óttarr in the shape of the dying, sacrificial boar into the darkness of darkness itself, where she wakes up the maiden of the rock cave and ask for her help. The utter darkness, the sleeping giantess and the wolves that she rides are all features of the realm of the dead.*[189]

» **TRIALS**: *The trial theme is not as clear as in the previous examples. Óðinn is directly faced with giants such as Suttungr and Baugi, whom he has to overcome in cleverness, as well as a mountain which is not easy either to enter or to escape from. Skírnir has to overcome barking dogs and a fence of fire, and the threat of the giant Gýmir is alluded to.*

» *In Óttarr's case, the fence of fire is mentioned, but only as Freyia threatens to surround Hyndla with it at the end of the poem. From other sources we know that Freyia indeed was surrounded by high walls, even if it is not mentioned in this poem. The trial takes a different form: Óttarr's wish is to get to Valhǫll (Stanza 1) and to have the gold of Valland (Stanza 9), the hall of- and the land of the Chosen Dead, but the gold of that realm is being wagered with a person called Angantýr.*

Steinsland assumed that Angantýr is Óttarr's opponent as future king.[190]

---

189 See passage about Óðinn's and Hermóð's underworld journeys in chapter 4.4 , and about giantesses riding wolves in chapter 4.1

190 Steinsland, 1991, p. 256

I take a different standpoint, based on the information that
Óttarr's main aim is, in the poem, stated to be Valhǫll, not kingship.
Angan means "pleasure", and "tyr" is a word for "god". The "god of
pleasure" is Óttarr's primary opponent and challenge on his path
to the hall of the Chosen Dead and may only be overcome through
knowledge of esoteric lore that identifies Óttarr with every kind of
being in the universe, ultimately revealing that they are all one.

It is not uncommon in the history of religions for spiritual insight
and liberation to be placed in opposition to the pleasures of the
material world. Only through the knowledge of the underworld
presided over by the giantess-vǫlva, the lady of rocks and wolves,
darkness and wilderness, and, crucially, through the drink that
makes him capable of remembering what he has learned on the
"third day", may Óttarr have a chance in the wager.

> *The second trial is to obtain the knowledge from the
reluctant giantess, who is persuaded to chant her sacred lore,
but not to give him the important mead of memory.*

We are closing in on the theme of the Óðinn-Gunnlǫð story again:
how to get to the mead.

Only through the love and care of the Maiden will that be possible.
That, through sacrifice and devotion, Óttarr had already achieved.

> **MAIDEN WITH THE MEAD**
> *The "Maiden theme" surfaces in the fact that Óttarr is
Freyia's verr, which means man, lover or husband, and in
Freyia's declaration that she will offer Ottar the precious
mead, the mead of memory.*

5.3: OGRESS VERSUS GODDESS — THE LIFE AND DEATH OPPOSITION

At the end of the poem, Freyia and the giantess stand out against
each other: the giantess who, although being the very source of
sacred knowledge, can only offer destruction and forgetfulness,
promises death and accidents, whereas the goddess promises the
drink of memory and the help of all divine beings.

In fact, Freyia personifies the alternative to what Hyndla
represents, surrounding the ogress of death with a magical fire
and offering a drink that makes the hero capable of remembering
what he learned in the underworld while "dead", in the shape of the
sacrificed boar.

Like Brynhildr the valkyria tells the ogress of death to "sink" so that she may be with Sígurðr in eternity[191], Freyia puts fire to the giantess who can promise "few fair things" coming from herself [fær þu fætt af mer][192], and who only wants to sleep. The opposition between Freyia and Hyndla is also symbolized in their steeds. Hyndla rides a wolf, the wolf being, in Norse mythology, always a representative of the giant, destructive forces, the devouring, hungry animal. Freyia, however, rides a boar, the pig being the very symbol of wealth, hunger satisfied, and sacrificial power.

In this opposition, we are reminded of Gerðr's choice: life as an ogress in Hel or life as a divine bride in Ásgarðr. Freyia, it seems, represents the latter option. Steinsland has interpreted Óttarr's quest for his heritage as a part of kingship inauguration – the king must prove that he has a royal, divine and giant lineage.[193]

Although, as we have seen in chapter 4, the initiations presided over by the Maiden figure may include initiation to kingship, I believe that the "heritage" in question is of a more general religious nature, implied in the intention of going to Valhǫll or Valland stated in Stanza 1 and Stanza 9, as well as in the teachings and the challenge of Angantýr, the God of Pleasure.

Óttarr needs good lessons to know his true "heritage"- the heritage of all creatures in the universe. Here, only the knowledge of sacred inter-connectedness with all things appears sufficient to overcome the rule of pleasure. This, apparently, is necessary to claim the treasures of the Land of the Chosen Dead Ones, the alternative to extinction in death.

---

191 See chapter 7.6
192 Hyndluljóð, stanza 46
193 Steinsland, 1991, p. 256-259

Image on Bronze
Age burial lid,
Denmark

5.4: MENGLǪÐ – THE GREAT MAIDEN

...hon hér ræðr
ok ríki hefir
eign ok auðsölum.[194]
 ...She rules here
 and owns the realm
 the properties and the halls of
 abundance.

GRÓAGALDR – THE SPELL-SONG OF GROWTH

The poem Gróagaldr [Spell-Song of Growth/Incantation to Grow] begins with "the son" [sonr] standing by the gates of death invoking his long dead mother Gróa [to grow, thrive][195] who had told him to wake her up if in need:

1.Sonr kvað:
„Vaki þú, Gróa!
vaki þú, góð kona!
vek ek þik dauðra dura;
ef þú þat mant,
at þú þinn mög bæðir
til kumbldysjar koma."

1.The Son said:
"Wake up, Gróa!
Wake up, you good woman!
I wake you by the doors of death;
if you remember
That you bade your son
come to your burial cairn.

2.Móðir kvað:
„Hvat er nú ant
mínum einga syni,
hverju ertu nú bölvi borinn,
er þú þá móður kallar,
er til moldar er komin
ok ór ljóðheimum liðin?"

2.The Mother said:
«What is your trouble
my only son,
what misfortune has befallen you
that you call on your mother
who has been laid in the ground
and long since left this world of songs?

---

194 Gróagaldr stanza 7-8
195 Simek, 1996, p. 120

It is absolutely clear that we are dealing with an invocation to wake up and communicate with a dead woman, here. The dead Mother asks what ails her son, since it must be dire indeed for waking the dead.

3.Sonr kvað:
„Ljótu leikborði
skaut fyr mik hin lævísa
kona,
sú er faðmaði minn föður:
þar bað hon mik koma,
er kvæmtki veit,
móti Menglöðu."

3.The Son said:
«Difficult entanglement
she made for me, that
harm-wise woman
she who embraced my
father:
when she asked me to come
on the unknown path
to seek the maiden Menglǫð

4.Móðir kvað:
„Löng er för,
langir 'ru farvegar,
langir 'ru manna munir;
ef þat verðr,
at þú þinn vilja bíðr,
ok skeikar þá skuld at
sköpum."

4.Mother said:
«Long is the path
long it is to fare
long must the soul yearn
If it comes to be
as you intend it will
then fortune will be made
for you."

5.Sonr kvað:
„Galdra þú mér gal,
þá er góðir 'ru,
bjarg þú, móðir! megi;
á vegum allr
hygg ek at ek verða muna,
þykkjumk ek til ungr afi."

5.The Son said:
"Sing for me galdrar
they which are good
save you, Mother, your
child:
Never, I fear, will I return
home
for I think I am still too
young."

The "son" explains his mission: his stepmother has sent him on the "unknown path" to meet Menglǫð. The theme of the stepmother urging him onto the path to seek the Maiden is actually very similar to the Skírnismál story, where Skaði, who is in fact Freyr's stepmother, is the one who urges him and his servant to follow through with the vision.[196]

---

196 It is the "stepmother"-theme which has been the strongest argument for understanding "Svípdagsmál" as a "fairy-tale". However, the theme only exists in the Gróagaldr, which means that, read separately, the Fjǫlsvinnsmál has no

Gróa declares that the way is long and heavy, and that the soul will have to yearn for a long time, but if he obtains the goal of his quest, luck will follow.[197] The son asks his dead mother to chant good galdrar for him, to save her child, for he fears that he will never come back from the quest, being too young.

Gróa, then, chants nine galdrar for him. Each galdr contains advice or protective spells:

1. If he feels that he is carrying a heavy burden on his shoulders, he shall shake it off, himself leading himself: sjálfr leið þú sjálfan þik [you yourself leads you yourself], a formula that seems remarkably similar to the Hávamál stanza 138's sialfr sialfom mer [gave myself to myself].

2. If he feels insecure and unsafe, Urðr, the oldest norn, shall lead the evil away from his paths.

3.If he encounters fatally dangerous rivers, they shall turn away from his path towards Hel, and he shall walk on dry land.

4. If he meets enemies on his way, their minds shall be turned towards friendship.

5.If he is fettered and bound, Gróa's galdr shall open up any lock and loosen every knot.

6. If he encounters a storm at sea, the winds and waves shall calm down for him.

7.Cold shall not bite him.

8. A dead "Christian" woman on the misty, dark roads shall not harm him.

9. Eventually, when he encounters the great, powerful Jǫtunn, the son shall have wit and eloquence enough in his heart and his mouth to face the giant.

In the end, Gróa advises him to never himself seek bad luck, for then harm will not find him, and to remember the words of his mother - if he pays attention to her words, honor and luck will follow.

---

stepmother-theme at all. However, the stepmother theme is also to be found in the Skírnismál, a poem most accepted as a rendering of true myth.

197 Menglǫð being mentioned in the poem makes the link to Fjǫlsvinnsmál quite obvious.

FJǪLSVINNSMÁL - THE SONG OF MUCH KNOWING

1.Utan garða
hann sá upp um koma
þursa þjóðar sjöt:
„Hvat er þat flagða,
er stendr fyr forgörðum
ok hvarflar um hættan
loga?

1.Outside the settlements,
He came up to where
Flocks of thurses
dwelled;
"What is that outcast
who stands before the
courtyard
and floats/swings
around the furious
flames?

Gróagaldr ends there, and we must turn to Fjǫlsvinnsmál for the continuation.[198] The boy has, mysteriously, arrived "outside the settlements" [Utan garða] of the giants and thurses, which is likely the equivalent of Útgarðr [Outer Settlement], another word for the giant world.

Suddenly someone asks him what kind of troll he is, standing in the outer courts, moving back and forth around the "fatally dangerous fire" [hættan loga].

The one who asks is the giant Fjǫlsviðr [Very Wise/Much Knowing] undoubtedly the "wise giant" Gróa mentioned in her last charm. Fjǫl- also indicates "magically versed".[199] Much Knowing is not particularly hospitable, however, telling the boy to return along the "slippery roads" [urgar brautir].

Instead of fleeing, the boy returns the insult and demands to know who the speaker is. And the great Jǫtunn replies:

4.„Fjölsviðr ek heiti,
en ek á fróðan sefa,
þeygi em ek míns mildr
matar;
innan garða
þú kemr hér aldregi,
ok dríf þú nú vargr at
vegi."

4.»My name is much
knowing
And I own a wise soul
But nobody will call me
mild and hospitable
Within these settlements
You shall never come
So float now on your way,
you warg."

---

198 This is if we understand the Fjǫlsvinnsmál as a continuation of the Gróagaldr, as a "Svípdagsmál"
199 Simek, 1996, p. 84, Heide, 1997, p. 8. Ström, 1954, and most others, translated fjöl in the Reginsmál as "trollkunnig" —versed in magic, sorcery.

The boy, on the other hand, declares something remarkable: that he is eager to meet again the pleasure of his eyes, and that he believes he will enjoy staying in the golden hall [gullna sali]:

5.Kómumaðr kvað:
„Augna gamans
fýsir aptr fán,
hvars hann getr svást at
sjá;
garðar glóa mér þykkja
of gullna sali,
hér munda ek eðli una."

5.*The arriving man said:*
«The pleasure of my eyes
I want to see again
to see where it is the most
lovely
The settlements glow
around the golden hall
here I would enjoy my
whole self.

Much Knowing asks him who he is, and the boy replies that his name is Wind-Cold, son of Spring-Cold, son of Many-Cold. Both coolness and the wind are symbols of death. Wind-Cold asks who the lord is who has in his dominion the lands and precious halls: Much Knowing declares that it is the maiden Menglǫð who is the ruler here, as quoted above.[200] She is the daughter of the son of a certain Svafrþorinn. The name appears to be meaning "Sleep Courageous", which has been discussed in the light of a possible misspelling of a more well-known theme known from both the Edda and the sagas; the svefnþorn – a "Sleep Thorn". A sleep-thorn was used to make the valkyria Sígrdrífa sleep, and the one who used it was Óðinn.

Now follows a long dialogue between our hero Wind-Cold and the giant Much Knowing. Wind-Cold asks and Much Knowing answers, but Wind-Cold has to know how to question.

During this conversation, we learn about Menglǫð, her realm, and the trials that Wind-Cold has to overcome to be reunited with the Maiden. But each answer to what has to be done only leads to an ever more insurmountable obstacle. How to get past the barking hounds is the most difficult part, what reminds us of the Hel-hounds of the Skírnismál and the Vegtamskvíða.

1.THE GATE: First of all, the boy asks what the gate is called, which seems terrible to him, and which has been sowed among the gods. The giant replies that the gate called Þrymgjǫll, which may indicate a drumbeat-sound [Þrýmr may be derived from Þrúma – to "beat", "drum", and gjǫll; Bellow, Roar, Resounding]. She (the gate, a feminine word) was made by the sons of a certain Sólblindi [Blind to the Sun or "Sun-Blinder"].

200 Translations of name in Heide, 1997, p. 8, and in Norrøn Ordbok

2. THE FENCE OR SETTLEMENT: Secondly, the boy asks what the fence is called, adding that he (garðr- fence/settlement) is a masculine word) is a terrifying thing. The giant replies that the fence is called Gastropnir, a name that has not been determined when it comes to meaning, but which some have suggested may mean "Guest Strangler", what makes sense in the context. The dangerous fence has been made from the limbs of Leirbrímir and will stand for as long as everything lives.

This name is also obscure. Simek suggests that Brímir derives from brim, which is associated to the ocean. Brímir is also said to be the giant who owns the beer-hall [bjórsalr] in which the jǫtnar keep their drinking feasts in the Gylfaginning. Leir- may mean clay, as in the term leir-jǫtunn – a giant of clay, a being that may have been described in the story of Thor facing Hrungnir and his artificial champion made of clay; Mokkurkálfi [Mist-Calf].

3. THE HEL-HOUNDS AND WHO THEY GUARD: Thirdly, the boy asks what the dogs are called, who are barking so terribly, more than anything he has heard before. The giant replies that their names are Gífr [Greedy/Enemy] and Geri [from gerr: "greedy" or else from the verb gera; "to do" – as in the Doing One] and that they are guarding the ellifu for as long as the world exists. We recognize the dogs from the other stories of similar kind, the dogs who guard the gate to Hel.

Who are the ellifu? Mortensen Egnund translated it into Norwegian møyar – maidens, probably thinking about the maidens who actually do reside within the fences that the greed-hounds guard. The word itself could mean "eleven", but they are in fact nine maidens and one more, and one may wonder who the eleventh is? Skírnir offered exactly eleven apples to Gerðr, and there were eleven gods when Balder had died.

I cannot move further into this question, but will add that, since some names may have been misspelled (or, since they had no correct spelling systems in the beginning, just spelled in a way that is hard to recognize, there could also be a reference to ellilyf – age-medicine, as in medicine against ageing (and dying).

The goddess Iðunn, who guards the apples of eternal resurrection and thus divine immortality, is referred to in the skaldic poem Haustlǫng as Ellilyf Ása – the Age-Cure of the Gods. I think there is even the possibility of an eilífr; a "forever living", "eternal" entity, perhaps, here represented in the plural. As such, the maidens within the fence may be immortals, and somehow associated to Iðunn, the goddess who resurrects the gods to eternal life.

4. HOW TO SNEAK PAST THE HOUNDS: Fourthly, the boy asks if it is possible to sneak past the dogs when they sleep. The giant replies that the dogs of greed sleep in turns, for it had been made so that they should always be on guard.

5. HOW TO DIVERT THE HOUNDS: Fifthly, the boy asks if one could give them some food that would distract them so that one could run past them. The giant replies that there are two wing-pieces lying in Viðofnir's liðum. The name Viðofnir may mean the "Far-Shouting One"[201]. I have personally played with the possibility that it could be related to the very similar sounding, Norwegian vidåpen, which means Wide Open, or vid åpning – Wide Opening (or åpner – Opener) – but as much as such a meaning makes sense from a spiritual perspective, this notion of mine may be a result of the confusion of dealing with an ancient language that is so similar to my own that it is easy to make up meanings that may not have been there.

The word lið could possibly mean an army, but this makes little sense. There is another possible meaning for the word lið, namely a strong, alcoholic drink. Since we are going to learn more about Viðofnir shortly, we may already conclude that it is in the wing-pieces which lie in the mysterious drink of the far-sounding "rooster" who sits in the branches of the Tree of Memory, that one may find the winged food that could possibly distract the hounds of greed. Understandably, the boy resorts to a new approach.

6. THE TREE: Sixthly, the boy asks what the tree is called, which he sees in the courtyard, and which grows widely across the lands. The giant replies that it is called the Mímameiðr – the Tree of Memory. Nobody knows from where its roots have run, just as it is said about the tree on which Óðinn hung during his initiation. Nobody may know what hurts the tree, for it is neither fire nor iron. This is very much in tune with how the world tree, Yggdrasill, is generally described. The rooster sitting in his branches may be another way of saying the giant in eagle hide, as Snorri explained in the Skáldskaparmál that an eagle may be called a rooster in poetical metaphors.

---

201 Simek, 1996, p.369

7. THE SEED: The boy asks what the seed of the great tree may be used for, the tree that may not be hurt by fire or iron. The giant replies that if you throw a seed from the tree on the fire, you will heal women who are sick from pregnancy and that what has been disguised will come to light, and such is the power and authority of the tree.

8. THE BIRD IN THE TREE: The boy asks the name of the rooster that he sees sitting high in the tree, glowing all over with gold. The giant replies that his name is Viðofnir, the Far-Sounding One, and he is veðrglasi – "weather-shining" - shining high up there in the top of the Tree of Memory. The weather may be similar to the weather in the name Veðrfǫlnir [Weather-Diminisher], which is the name of the hawk who sits between the eyes of the giant in eagle hide who dwells at the top of the world tree in the world of the dead and who likes to devour corpses. The weather is also another way of saying "wind" – so there at the top of the Memory Tree sits a far-sounding bird who shines from the movement of winds and weather, mortality perhaps, as if it was an image of the mind itself.

This far-crowing "rooster" is sadly kept forever in the heavy burden of the dark Sínmara [Pale Mare]. As already mentioned, it does not matter whether the bird is a rooster, a hawk, a falcon or an eagle – all these could be used to poetically describe each other in the fluid language of Old Norse poetry. Sínmara is the giantess who is married to Surtr, the ruler of Muspellheimr, the southern primordial world of fire and poisonous gases. Incidentally, this is also from where the Sun goddess originated.

9. THE TOOL AND THE NINE LOCKS: Ninthly, now that he has identified exactly who this mysterious Viðofnir is, the part with the two wing-pieces seems more obvious, and the boy returns to his project of getting past the barking hounds. He asks if there is any weapon with which he may kill Viðofnir (thinking that he needs his wings to distract the dogs). The giant replies that there is a Lævateinn made by the cunning Loptr [Air=Loki] down beneath the nágrindr [death-gate] but that Sínmara [Pale Mare], a giantess, keeps the tool within a chest of iron, locked with nine locks. The word lævateinn means, according to Simek, "damage twig" and is a known kenning for a sword.

10. Is it Possible to Take the Tool?: Tenthly, the boy asks if there is any way of returning from a quest to retrieve the sword. The giant replies that the one who can take the twig will have what few may own and bring it to the eiri örglasis – the Healing Woman [Eir] of the Golden Crystal.

11. How to Placate the Ogress Sínmara?: Eleventhly, the boy asks if there is any way to please the pale gýgr [giantess] so that he may get the tool. The giant tells him that he has to bring her the bright scythe that may be found in the tail of the rooster Viðofnir. Only then will she willingly lend him the weapon. And this is where we begin to realize that we are going in circles, for how can you get the only weapon that may kill the rooster if you need something from that rooster to get the weapon?

12. The Hall: Twelfthly, the boy asks what the name of the hall is, the one he can see surrounded by flickering flames. The giant replies that the hall is called Hyrr [Fire (or possibly, "Mild, Kind")], and that he shall for a long time be vibrating on edges and points. But among people, there could be only favorable words about him.

13. The Dwarfs: Thirteenthly, the boys asks who had made the wondrous beauty that he could see from the divine place within the fences. The giant offers up the names of eight dwarfs and one dwarf guardian.

14. The Mountain of Medicine and the Great Maiden: Fourteenthly, the boy asks what the mountain is called, where he can see the Bride sit, the Great Maiden [Þjóðmæra], dreaming [hvat þat bjarg heitir, ver ek sé Brúði á, Þjóðmæra þruma]. The giant replies that it is called Lyfjabergr – the Mountain of Medicines, and that it has long been the comfort of the sick and the wounded. Every woman who climbs that mountain will be healed from life-long sorrows.

15. The Nine Maidens: Fifteenthly, the boy asks who the maidens are called, the ones he can see sitting by the knees of Menglǫð, all seated in happiness together. The giant replies that they are called Life and Life-Tracker, Guardian of the People, Bright One and Kind One and Mild One, and Eir [goddess of healing] and Aurboða – she who bids the aurr (to be poured over the roots of the tree?).

16. How to Worship: Sixteenth, the boy asks if these maidens will save those who make sacrifice to them [blóta þær]. The giant replies that they give salvation when they receive blót on a sacred altar, and that there is no need so great that they cannot offer release.

17. WHO MAY UNITE WITH THE MAIDEN: Seventeenth; the boy asks if there is anyone who has such fortune as to be allowed to sleep in the soft embrace of Menglǫð, upon which the giant replies that there is indeed one, called Svípdagr [Swift Dawn], who may sleep in her soft arms, for she, the sólbjarta brúðr [sun-bright bride] had been wed to him as his wife before.

18. THE REVELATION OF THE TRUE SELF: The numbers here may be significant. In the last twenty stanzas of the Hávamál, Óðinn declares that he learned nine powerful spell-songs from his uncle, and then made nine more, listing eighteen spells which all seem to culminate into his ability to keep the love of a bright golden maiden, and where the eighteenth is a hint towards a deep secret that he cannot share with anyone else but the one who holds him in her arms and who may be his sister.

What I listed as number 17 may be the eighteenth, since the questions really began with who the ruler of the halls may be (it was Menglǫð). Thus number 17 here may be the 18th question where he finally learns who he is and where he belongs. But it could also be here, in stanza 43, when the boy finally realizes that he can walk straight into the hall because he already belonged there.

Hereon follows an exchange which show that the two have always been together, but that he has been lost many times on the "wind-swept paths" (the paths of mortality?) and forgotten that he was really Svípdagr and already her wedded husband. She on the other hand had waited and waited for an eternity, sleeping and dreaming away on her sacred mountain at the root of the sacred tree, surrounded by her nine maidens.

47.Svipdagr kvað: „Svipdagr ek heiti, Sólbjart hét minn faðir, þaðan ráumk vindar kalda vegu; Urðar orði kveðr engi maðr, þótt þat sé við löst lagit."	47. Svípdagr said: «My name is Swift Dawn Sun Bright was my father The cold winds blew me away from home The words of Fate can no man dispute even if destiny seems heavy."

48.Menglöð kvað:
„Vel þú nú kominn!
hefik minn vilja beðit,
fylgja skal kveðju koss;
forkunnar sýn
mun flestan glaða,
hvars hefir við annan ást.

48. Menglǫð said:
«Well have you come!
I have had my will
The Fylgja shall offer a kiss;
The greatest joy
is to be found for those
who hold each other with
love.

49.Lengi ek sat
Lyfjabergi á,
beið ek þín dœgr ok daga;
nú þat varð,
er ek vætt hefi,
at þú ert kominn, mögr!
til minna sala.

49. Long did I sit
on the Mountain of Medicines
biding for you night and day
now it has become
as I wished for
you have returned, kinsman,
to my halls.

50.Þrár hafðar
er ek hefi til þíns gamans,
en þú til míns munar;
nú er þat satt,
er vit slíta skulum
ævi ok aldr saman."

50. Yearning we knew
And I longed for your
pleasure
And you too longed for mine
Now it is truth
That we two shall endure
Together the ages for
eternity."

5.5: THE STRUCTURAL STAGES OF "SVÍPDAGSMÁL"

• VISION QUEST: The vision quest theme is represented in the first stanza of Gróagaldr, as Svípdagr, described as the "son", invokes his mother at the doors of death [dauðra dura]. The invocation bears some resemblance to the invocation Freyia uses to wake up the sleeping giantess in the underworld. We could imagine that the "doors of death" where he performs the invocation are by the wise woman's rocky barrow cairn or burial mound [kumbldysj]. This notion of a burial mound is strengthened by the fact that Gróa declares that she is standing on an "earth-fastened stone" while she sings her charms. Sitting on a burial mound was in fact a known practice in Norse society, a part of the practice of utiseta and a means of obtaining secret knowledge from the beyond (see chapter 3.1).

- **VISION:** The vision theme manifests itself as the long dead woman rises from her grave and speaks to her son. The waking of a dead woman is known from another Edda poem, Vegtamskvíða, where Óðinn, using "charms of the Chosen Dead" [válgaldrar], wakes up a dead volva buried to the east of the gates of Hel. The east is the direction of the sunrise and new beginnings, or else the direction of the giant world – and this may be significant. The volva then reveals the meaning of Baldr's dreams of bad omens. One could imagine that a similar scene took place before the ancient volva's chanting of her prophecies in the Voluspá, since the volva in that case is said to "sink" at the end of her speech.

Similarly, the volva of Vegtamskvíða wishes to "sleep". There is indeed some similarity to Hyndla, who also is woken as she sleeps in the center of the realm of the dead, and who also states a wish to go back to sleep. Hyndla is considered a giantess, yet parts of her speech is counted as the "short Voluspá" and are indeed quite similar to the "real" Voluspá. Hyndla could be said to be both a giant representative of Hel, and a dead or sleeping volva. Gróa's joint giant- and volva- identity is strengthened by an account of Snorri's in the Gylfaginning, where a volva called Gróa chants galdrar to heal Thor's leg. This volva called Gróa is the wife of a giant. It is perhaps more than a ghost that Svípdagr is approaching.

It is possible that Svípdagr's "mother" is a volva of mythical, giant origin, like the one who were raised by giants before the beginning of time in the Voluspá. It is possible that she represents a mythic figure of many names who has been largely ignored by scholars. I am suggesting the existence in the Norse cosmology of a sleeping giantess-volva who encompassed many more characters than just Gróa: such as Hyndla, Hyrrokkin, Hel and the Volva of the Voluspá. Even if my idea of Gróa should be proven wrong, we may maintain that the vision theme is present when a creature from beyond the grave, a supernatural creature with knowledge of charms and of the way to reach Menglǫð, manifests herself and speaks to the living.

- **DESCENT:** The descending theme is present both in the Gróagaldr and in the Fjǫlsvinnsmál. Standing at the doors of death and speaking to the dead is in itself a feat of "descent" to the world of the dead. In the Fjǫlsvinnsmál, Svípdagr is discovered in the "outer settlements" or "outside the fences" [utan garða] which indicates the giant world (such as far-away Útgarðr) and, more specifically, the realm of the dead, as we shall argue in the following chapter.

- **TRIALS:** The trial theme is described in more detail in the "Svípdagsmál" than in any of the other poems. In the Gróagaldr, we learn that Svípdagr's main aim is to reach Menglǫð, just as we learned, in the Hyndluljóð that Óttarr's main aim is to reach Valhǫll. In both cases, an old wise woman of the world of the dead is approached for the purpose of seeking teaching and help. Svípdagr expresses fear, anguish and doubt, he is too young, it is too far, the stepmother who forced him onto the quest was "harm-wise" [læviss]. In fact, the stepmother theme was subtly present also in the Skírnismál, where the prose introduction declares that it was Skaði, Freyr's stepmother, who made Skírnir approach Freyr in order to help him. Skaði could be said to be "harm-wise", since her name itself means "harm".[202]

Gróa agrees with Svípdagr that the way is long and difficult and that he will have to yearn for a long time – quite like Freyr, who yearned for his beloved during nine insufferable nights. But Gróa's nine galdrar will help Svípdagr on his way. Nine powerful songs were also "given" to Óðinn by his maternal uncle before the drinking of the precious mead in Hávamál. Gróa's charms, which she "gives" to the lad, could, as Motz suggests, be describing an initiation ritual.

As we saw above, the galdrar do indicate obstacles on the way and how, both through cunning and magic, to conquer them. The charms make him ready for the big trial, namely the meeting with the giant warden and the impenetrable walls of the Maiden. During the conversation with the giant, we learn so much about the realm of the Maiden that there is not space to discuss it in detail within this study. As Eldar Heide has argued, the poem provides crucial information about the Norse cosmos. [203]

Svípdagr learns about these important secrets and about how to enter Menglǫð's hall. It turns out, through a long dialogue, that it is downright impossible, no matter what he tries to do. It is only when it occurs to the young man to ask who is so blessed that he may sleep in Menglǫð's soft embrace that the solution reveals itself. It is only the right one, the one that had already been married to the "great maiden" [þjóðmæra],[204] the one whose name is Svípdagr, who may be so blessed.

202 Norrøn Ordbok
203 Heide, 1997
204 Fjǫlsvinnsmál, Stanza 35

Once Svípdagr remembers his true identity as Menglǫð's husband and calls himself by his true name, the Maiden herself lets open the doors and receives her long lost beloved with a kiss, describing it as the kiss of the fylgja – the follower spirit. I use the word "remember" because, until then, the poems themselves do not reveal his real name. Only after having studied the realm of the Maiden, where the Mímameiðr – "tree of memory" - is situated, Wind-Cold declares himself to be Svípdagr, long "lost" on slippery roads and the winds of mortality.

In Stanza 5, Wind-Cold declares that he would like to see "again" the halls of Menglǫð, meaning that he obviously remembers them from before. Yet in the beginning of the Gróagaldr, the boy shows no signs at all of remembering that he has actually been married to the Menglǫð whom he is about the seek. An important part of Svípdagr's trial, it seems, is to remember his true identity as the husband of the Great Maiden.

• **THE MAIDEN AND THE CONSECRATION:** The Maiden theme is revealed through the marriage and love between Svípdagr and Menglǫð. The offering of a drink could be present in Menglǫð's name, if we should choose to follow Jacobsdóttir's interpretation of the name as "Invitation to a Drink". I would perhaps say an invitation to blend, or a blend-drink.

Moreover, as we will argue in the following chapter, Menglǫð is sitting at the foot of the world tree, where the three wells of the world are situated. The tree is called Mímameiðr here, the "Tree of Remembering", and alludes to the giant Mímir, who drinks from the well that contains intelligence and memory about all the worlds, that Óðinn coveted so much that he gave up one of his eyes.

One very interesting aspect of this poem is that the Maiden actually refers to herself as a Fylgja – a feminine, supernatural "follower", often functioning like a guardian spirit or as a giver of omens, and may be related to the individual "norns" that Snorri in the Gylfaginning 15 described as following their humans from birth to death;

Þar stendr salr einn fagr undir askinum við brunninn, ok ór þeim sal koma þrjár meyjar, þær er svá heita: Urðr, Verðandi, Skuld. Þessar meyjar skapa mönnum aldr. Þær köllum vér nornir. Enn eru fleiri nornir, þær er koma til hvers barns, er borit er, at skapa aldr, ok eru þessar goðkunnigar, en aðrar álfa ættar, en inar þriðju dverga ættar, svá sem hér segir:

> *There stands a hall so fair beneath the ash by the well, and from this hall come three maidens, they are called Origin, Happening and Debt. These maidens shape the ages/eras for people.*
>
> *We call them norns. And there are more norns, who come to each child who is born, and shape their lifespans, and some of these are of divine lineage, others are of elfin lineages, and there is a third type of norns who are of dwarf kind, as it is here said:*

23.Sundrbornar mjök
segi ek nornir vera,
eigu-t þær ætt saman;
sumar eru áskunngar,
sumar eru alfkunngar,
sumar dætr Dvalins."

*23. Of very diverse lineage
I say the norns have come
They do not descend from
the same clans
Some are of Áss-kind
Some are of Elf-kind
And some are the daughters
of Hibernation.*

(…) Hárr segir: "Góðar nornir ok vel ættaðar skapa góðan aldr, en þeir menn, er fyrir ósköpum verða, þá valda því illar nornir."

(...)The High One said; "Good norns from good lineages shape good fates, but those men who have misfortune in life, these are caused by bad norns."

5.6: THE REALM OF THE DEAD IN FJǪLSVINNSMÁL

6.(…)
Kómumaðr kvað:
„Vindkaldr ek heiti,
Várkaldr hét minn faðir,
þess var Fjörkaldr faðir.

6.(…)
The Arriving Man said:
"Wind-Cold is my name
Spring-Cold was my father
to him was Full-Cold
father."

The realm that Svípdagr is visiting is described in great detail, and we only have room to discuss the most essential features that may identify the realm of the dead. First of all, he has taken the name Vindkaldr – Wind-Cold – when he arrives there. Both wind and cold are typical poetical terms for death.

Menglǫð's hall is surrounded by a terrible-looking fence with a horrific gate. The gate is called Þrymgjǫll – "the Loud Resounding One" [205]- a name which immediately brings to mind the Resounding bridge and river on the way to Hel.[206] Every traveler who tries to move it will be stuck to it. The image of being stuck to something in the giants´ realm is common: In the Gylfaginning, Loki is stuck to the walls of the hall of the giant Geirrǫðr, caught and put into a chest. In the poem Haustlǫng, cited in the Skáldskaparmál, Loki finds himself stuck to the giant in eagle's disguise after trying to hit him.

In both cases, Loki is faced with (near) certain death, but is so clever that he gets out of his troubles. As we argued in chapter 4.4, the giant in eagle's disguise is a representative of death. Menglǫð's gate is made by "the three sons of Sólblindi" – the "Sunblind" – as we know, the sun is not seen in Níflheimr.[207] The symbol of death is present in the nature of that gate: a world that one gets stuck in forever when once entered, a world where there is no way out.

---

205 Simek, 1996, p. 330. From þrýmr, m. "loud noise", related to the verb þruma – to beat, drum, create rhythmic sound, and gjǫll, f., "Resounding noise"
206 See chapter 4.10
207 Vǫluspá Stanza 41

The fence is called Gastropnir, which according to Heide means "Guest-Strangler".[208] According to Simek, the - ropnir part of the word could really be – rofnir – to be torn asunder. Both meanings make sense: any "guest" in the realm of the dead may expect to die, whether they are strangled or torn asunder. That fence is made of the limbs of Leirbrímir, whose name we discussed in 5.4, and who could possibly be identified with the world giant Ymir from whose limbs the gods fashioned the world itself.[209]

If this is the case, it may follow that the fence is the fashioned, divinely ordered word itself, or at least made of the same substance. In Vegtamskvíða, a point is made of how Óðinn avoids the gates of Hel. In the story of Hermóðr in the Skáldskaparmál, a similar point is made of how Hermóðr's horse Sleipnir jumps over the gates of Hel without touching them.

The image of the death-realm is completed by the fact that two ferocious, barking dogs are guarding the gate. We recall from chapter 4.10 that barking, blood strained dogs were a feature of Hel's and of the giantess Gerðr. The dogs names are Gífr and Geri, both names meaning "Greedy".[210] Although they are dogs, their names are those of wolves and giantesses, a combination often found in connection with death.[211]

---

208 Heide, 1997, p. 8

209 Leir- means clay or something made out of clay. The concept of a leirjǫtunn – "Clay-Giant"- existed in the Norse vocabulary. Brímir probably comes from brim, n., (or brimi, n.) which means the movement of waves against land, although brimi, m., means "fire" (Simek, 1996, p.) Brimir is an alternative name for Ymir in the Vǫluspá stanzas 9 and 37; as we know, the world itself was fashioned out of the limbs of Ymir. Yet, Snorri in the Gylfaginning claims that Brímir is the name for the room where the gods hold a drinking feast. Simek, however, believes that Snorri has misinterpreted and that Brímir is the name of the giant who owns the hall where the gods drink (ibid, p.) The hall is explicitly said to be a bjórsalr –an "ale-hall", in the Vǫluspá 37. If Brímir is identical with Ymir, there is to my view no contradiction in his identity also with the great drinking hall – it is not difficult to imagine the world itself as a great banquet for the gods.

210 Simek, 1996, p. 108, 106

211 Such as the giantess riding a wolf who pushes Balder's funeral ship out to sea, another giantess riding a wolf who signals the death of Helgi Hiǫrvarðsson, or the giantess who gives birth to wolves that will destroy the world in the

These two dogs will, as long as the world last, guard the eilifi -the "eternal ones",[212] the maidens on the Mountain of Medicines. Menglǫð's grandfather is Svafrþorinn, from svafr – which is derived from sofa – to sleep, and þorinn, which means courageous, brave.[213] I find this family relation important because the valkyriur, as we shall see in the chapter 6, are connected to similar names or family relations with names indicating sleep, which, ultimately, indicates death, such as Svafnir, which is both a heiti for Óðinn and the name of one of the serpents in Hel's well – and the father of valkyriur.

As we discussed before, there have been speculations that the word could have been sleep-thorn, which is a topic in the Edda poem Sígrdrífumál, where the valkyria is stuck by a svefnþorn – a sleep thorn – and can only wake up when her human hero finds her. Finally, during the dialogue between Svípdagr and the wise giant, we learn that one woman keeps the weapon that will make it possible to enter Menglǫð's hall. Her name is Sínmara, the "pale mare" (as in nightmare)[214] , and she is the consort of Surtr [Black/Sooty] who will one day be the death of Freyr. The old "pale giantess" keeps the Lævateinn locked with nine iron locks. As Heide has suggested, Sínmara and Hel may be the same.[215]

5.7: THE REALM OF THE GIANTS IN THE FJǪLSVINNSMÁL

Inside the forbidding and well-guarded fence, there is a great tree, spreading out over the land. It is called the Mímameiðr, "the tree of Mímir". Mímir is the giant under the world tree who drinks from the well of memory and wisdom with the Gjallarhorn – thee Resounding Horn.

Vǫluspá. Einar Sveinsson (1975, p. 29-37) pointed out the fact that the dog-names belonged to wolves and giantesses.
212 Actually, the text says ellifu, which could only mean "eleven". Bugge (1867), p. 345, suggests that it must really be a form of eilifr, which means "eternal". Mortensen Egnund (1993), p. 217, translates into "møyane" – the "maidens".
213 Simek, 1996, p. 305: Simek believes that the meaning of svafr as "sleep" hardly makes sense and that it really should be Svefnthorn, "sleeping thorn". In my opinion the name as it is makes sense if understood as "Courageous Sleep(er)" insofar as sleep may be understood as "death". This will be discussed in chapter 6.
214 https://youtu.be/BR__MVshRuM
215 Heide, 1997, p. 173-174

If we remember Suttungr's association both with the realm of death and with the giant Mímir in chapter 4.4, this location of Mímir's tree is quite interesting. The tree is described in stanza 20 in a way that makes it possible to identify it with Yggdrasill - the world tree itself. Few know from what roots it has sprung, and what is eating it up slowly. Its branches stretches out across the entire world. The same kind of description is found in the Grímnismál 34 and 35, about the Yggdrasill.

The Mímameiðr has a special attribute: its seeds may be thrown on a fire, to relieve women sick during pregnancy, and in order to see what has been hidden. It is generally acknowledged that Mímameiðr is another name for Yggdrasill.[216] In the top of the Mímameiðr, a rooster is seated, all glowing with gold – in the top of Yggdrasill the bird is an eagle. In Norse poetry, there is nothing unusual about calling one thing by a different name, and the eagle in particular is a bird often named by other kinds of birds.[217]

The allusion to Mímir is very interesting. According to Snorri, the World Tree has three different roots, each reaching into a well:

1. One is situated in Hel's realm, a well infested with serpents, the origin of the rivers of the world.

2. Another is situated in the realm of giants, where the well is guarded by the giant Mímir. In that well intelligence, wisdom and memory of all the worlds is contained.

3. The third root is situated in the realm of the gods. The well at the third root is called after its guardian, Urðr, the oldest of the norns. From this well, the Urðarbrunnr, Urðr waters the tree so that it may stay eternally green. From this well, ultimately, the dew that falls into the valleys of the world is derived. By this root and this well, the maidens Urðr, Verðandi and Skuld, the three original norns, shape the lives of the living. The gods and goddesses hold court and counsel by the well of the norns, and the rainbow bridge between the worlds leads there.

---

216 Ström, 1993, p. 97, Simek, 1996, p. 216.

217 Skáldskaparmál (Faulkes, 1987, p. 137)

*The water has an obvious healing, rejuvenating, renewing
and transformative function: it keeps the World Tree from rot
and decay, and it is "so holy that all things that come into that
well go out as white as the membrane called the skin that lies
round the inside of an eggshell".[218] There are many more norns,
who have their origin first in Urðr, then in the trio of Urðr,
Verðandi and Skuld. These norns visit everybody who is born,
follow them through their lives and shape their fate.[219]*

*In the Fjǫlsvinnsmál, we are subtly presented to each of the
three realms (with their attached roots and wells with different
functions), only they are not separated from each other in
the manner Snorri describes. They seem to be aspects of each
other. We have pointed out the features of Hel and the features
of the giant world through the situation in Útgarðr, its giant
warden and the tree of Mímir.*

*Now we must turn to the world beyond the ferocious fences,
where the ferocious dogs will guard the "eternal ones" forever,
the world below the Tree of Memory.*

5.8: THE GOLDEN HALL AND THE REALM OF THE MAIDENS

5.(…) garðar glóa mér þykkja of gullna Sali (…) Fjǫlsvinnsmál	*5.(...)the settlement seems to me to be glowing from the golden Hall.*

In the Fjǫlsvinnsmál 9 and 11, the maiden's realm is said to be
"sown with the gods" [með góðum sáat][220] What is interesting
about this is that we have already learned that we are in the
Outer Settlements - the giants´ realms. This does not seem to
affect the divinity of the realm. Mengloð is described as "sun-
bright"[sólbjartr] and named as a "great maiden" [þjóðmæra]. She
is surrounded by nine maidens at the foot of the great tree. There
she sits, completely still, in utter silence.[221]

---

218 Gylfaginning 15

219 See chapter 3.1

220 Fjǫlsvinnsmál Stanza 9

221 Þruma in Stanza 35 is usually translated as "dreaming", that is, Mengloð is
dreaming. But the word actually means "to remain quiet or silent on one spot", as
Heide, 1997, p. 121 points out.

Her brightness is in accordance with that of the other Maidens: Gunnlǫð's golden throne, Gerðr's gold and arms that shine across the world, Freyia's fiery necklace and golden tears, and as we shall soon see, the immense rays and shine that unfailingly accompany the valkyriur. Luminescence, brightness and goldenness may have be common ways of describing women in a flattering manner, yet it is also very much a part of the structure of the "Maiden-mythology" and should not be overlooked.

The placing of Menglǫð and her maidens at the foot of the World Tree is important: norns, goddesses of fate, are situated at the foot of the world tree Yggdrasil. Menglǫð's hall is glowing and golden [gullna salr], situated within the Gastropnir fence, and is surrounded by flames. Its name is Hyrr – "The Shining One",[222] shivering on the tips of swords and knifes. About its beauty people may only know through its fame – indicating how unusual it is to go there – and live to tell of it. The halls of the Maidens are described similarly to the halls of goddesses and norns in the Gylfaginning:

Hárr mælti: "Í upphafi setti hann stjórnarmenn í sæti ok beiddi þá at dæma með sér örlög manna ok ráða um skipun borgarinnar.

Þat var þar, sem heitir Iðavöllur í miðri borginni. Var þat hið fyrsta þeira verk at gera hof þat, er sæti þeira tólf standa í önnur en hásætit, þat er Alföðr á.

Þat hús er bezt gert á jörðu ok mest. Allt er þat útan ok innan svá sem gull eitt. Í þeim stað kalla menn Glaðsheim. Annan sal gerðu þeir. Þat var hörgr, er gyðjurnar áttu, ok var hann allfagr. Þat hús kalla menn Vingólf.[223]

The High One said: «In the beginning of time he set ruling officials in their seats and bid them to decide together with him the fates of people. This was in the middle of the settlement, there where it is called Iðavǫllr [Returning Whirlpool/Water Spring Field].

The first thing they did was to build a temple [hóf], where, before the high seat of All-Father, there were twelve other seats made for them.

This is the largest and best house ever built on earth, both outside and within it is all like gold, this place has been called the World of Happiness. Another hall they built, it was called Altar/Shrine [hǫrgr], which the priestesses/ goddesses owned, and he was all beautiful. This house, people call Floor of Friendships.

222 Simek, 1996, p. 170
223 Gylfaginning 14

Þriðja rót asksins stendr á himni, ok undir þeiri rót er brunnr sá, er mjök er heilagr, er heitir Urðarbrunnr. Þar eiga goðin dómstað sinn. Hvern dag ríða æsir þangat upp um Bifröst. Hon heitir ok ásbrú.

(…)Margir staðir eru á himni fagrir, ok er þar allt guðlig vörn fyrir.

Þar stendr salr einn fagr undir askinum við brunninn, ok ór þeim sal koma þrjár meyjar, þær er svá heita: Urðr, Verðandi, Skuld.

Þessar meyjar skapa mönnum aldr. Þær köllum vér nornir. Enn eru fleiri nornir, þær er koma til hvers barns, er borit er, at skapa aldr, ok eru þessar goðkunnigar, en aðrar álfa ættar, en inar þriðju dverga ættar [224]

Enn er þat sagt, at nornir þær, er byggja við Urðarbrunn, taka hvern dag vatn í brunninum ok með aurinn þann, er liggr um brunninn, ok ausa upp yfir askinn, til þess at eigi skuli limar hans tréna eða fúna.

En þat vatn er svá heilagt, at allir hlutir, þeir er þar koma í brunninn, verða svá hvítir sem hinna sú, er skjall heitir, er innan liggr við eggskurn[225]

The third root of the ash stands in heaven, and beneath this root there is a well which is particularly sacred, and it is called Urðarbrunnr [the Well of Origin]. There the gods have their legal court. Every day, the Aesir ride up there over Bífrǫst [Vibrating Voice], she is also called the Divine Bridge (...) Many places standing in heaven are fair, and the gods are guarding them all.

There stands a hall so beautiful beneath the ash by the well, and from this hall come three maidens who are thus named; Origin, Happening and Debt. These maidens shape the fates of people.

We call them norns. And there are more norns, they who come to every child when it is born, to shape its lifespan, and some of these or of divine kind, others are of elfin lineage, and a third kind of dwarf lineage.

And it is said that the norns who are dwelling by the Well of Origin, every day take water from the well, and with it the aurr [mud, gravel, sand, gold, abundance] that lies by the well, and pour it over the ash, so that its branches and twigs shall never decay.

And this water is so sacred, that everything which comes into it, become so bright/ transparent as that membrane which is known to lie on the inside of an eggshell.

---

224 Gylfaginning 15
225 Gylfaginning 16

Þá mælti Gangleri: "Hverjir eru æsir, þeir er mönnum er skylt at trúa á?"
Hárr segir: "Tólf eru æsir goðkunnigir."
Þá mælti Jafnhárr: "Eigi eru ásynjurnar óhelgari, ok eigi megu þær minna."[226]

Then spoke Wandering Learner; "Who are the gods whom men are bound to believe in?"
The High One said: "Twelve are the Aesir of divine lineage."
Then spoke Equally High: "The goddesses are no less sacred, and their power is no lesser." (...)

Freyja er ágætust af ásynjum. Hon á þann bæ á himni, er Fólkvangr heitir. Ok hvar sem hon ríðr til vígs, þá á hon hálfan val, en hálfan Óðinn (...) Salr hennar Sessrúmnir, hann er mikill ok fagr[227]

Freyia is the greatest among the goddesses. She lives in that settlement in heaven, which is called People Field. And when she rides to war, then she owns half the slain, and the other half belongs to Óðinn (...) Her hall, Room for Seats, he is great and beautiful.

Óðinn unni mikit Freyju, enda var hún allra kvenna fegrst í þann tíma. Hún átti sér eina skemmu. Hún var bæði fögr ok sterk, svá at þat segja menn, at ef hurðin var aptr ok læst, at engi maðr mætti koma í skemmuna án vilja Freyju.[228]

Óðinn loved Freyia very much, for she was the most beautiful woman of her time. She owned a dwelling. She was both beautiful and strong, and people say this, that if her gate was closed and locked, no man could ever enter her dwelling unless by the will of Freyia.

Interestingly, both the Skírnismál and the Fjǫlsvinnsmál clearly reveal that even if the visitor to her realm is met by a guardian whom he must engage in word duel, it is the Maiden herself who must ask the initiand to enter her golden hall. There is a hill there called the Lyfjabergr – "the Mountain of Medicine", and there, Menglǫð sits.[229] The Mountain of Medicine may be climbed by any sick woman, and she will be healed from life-long sorrows.

---

226 Gylfaginning 20
227 Gylfaginning 24
228 Sörla þáttr eða Heðins saga ok Högna 1 (Flateyjarbók)
229 Hyfjaberg is recognized as a mistake for Lyfjabergr, "Mountain of Medicines", usually translated in Norwegian as "Lækjedomsberget" (Mountain of Healing) since, as Heide, 1997, p. 10, points out, the actual meaning of medicine in Norwegian makes it sound like it is a pharmacy.

By the knees of the dreaming lady, nine maidens sit together, and their names are Hlíf [Life], Hlífþrasa [Life-Seeker], Þjóðvarta [Guardian of the People], Bjǫrt [Bright], Blíð [Amiable], Blíðr [Mild], Fríð [Peace], Eir [Healing] and Aurboða [Bids Replenishment/Abundance/Rejuvenation[230]] These maidens will save anyone in need, if only they sacrifice to them. As I was arguing in the previous section, Fjǫlsvinnsmál presents us to each of the three worlds.

The world of the maidens and the Great Maiden by whose knees they sit is divine. It is placed at the top of a mountain, and at the same time at the foot of the World Tree. It is a place of healing, love and help. It is situated in the midst of the world of the dead, which is situated in the midst of the world of the giants. At the same time, it offers bright and loving promises.

Näsström has argued that the norn Urðr is identifiable with Freyia. Ström identifies Urðr with Hel, and Hel with Freyia.[231] Hyrr could be a representation of Freyia's beautiful after-death realm, her "Field of People" and "Hall of Friendship". That places Hyrr in the ninth of the divine realms. However, if Hyrr is rather, or at the same time, a presentation of the norns´ realm, then it is situated in the center and court of Ásgarðr, the divine realm.

In the story of Menglǫð, we, for the first time in this study, see a collective of maidens surrounding one "great Maiden". The group could represent the brúðkónur – the women accompanying the bride while she awaits the groom, and thus an emphasis on the marriage motif in the story. Yet I find in the image a striking resemblance to the valkyriur who travel in troops led by one who is more splendid than all the others. This is a link to the next chapter, where we shall discuss the valkyriur. It is also worthwhile, here, to recall the theories of Ström and Näsström of a "Great Dís" emerging from a collective of dísir, a dís identified, ultimately, as the "Lady", the Great Goddess Freyia.

---

230 Ör/Aur- from aurr – mud, sand, gravel – but also, in poetry, "gold", and the substance that the norns apply to the roots of the world tree in order to make it replenish and rejuvenate itself from all the decay that is going on, eternally resurrecting the dying universe. The word could also mean abundance.

231 Ström, 1954

Detail on standing stone, Early Viking Age,
Gotland, Sweden

Let us have a look at another listing of goddesses and their halls.

35. Frá ásynjum.
Þá mælti Gangleri:
"Hverjar eru ásynjurnar?"
Hárr segir: "Frigg er ædst.
Hon á þann bæ, er Fensalir
heita, ok er hann allvegligr.
Önnur er Sága. Hon býr
á Sökkvabekk, ok er þat
mikill stadr.
Þridja er Eir. Hon er
læknir beztr.
Fjórða er Gefjun. Hon er
mær, ok henni þjóna þær,
er meyjar andast.
Fimmta er Fulla. Hon er
enn mær ok ferr laushár ok
gullband um höfuð. Hon
berr eski Friggjar ok gætir
skóklæða hennar ok veit
launráð með henni.

Then spoke Wandering
Learner; "Who are the
goddesses?"
The High One said: "Frigg
is the greatest. She owns
that dwelling, which is
called the Bog/Moist Hall,
and it is all-beautiful.
Another is History. She
lives in the Sunken River,
and that is a great place
The third is Eir. She is the
best healer.
A fourth is Gefiun
[Provider]. She is a maiden
(unmarried) and all who die
as maidens serve her.
The fifth is Fulfilled One.
She is also a maiden, and
goes with her hair loose and
a golden band around her
head. She carries Frigg's
chest and takes care of her
shoes, and knows about all
her secret counsels.

25: About the Goddesses

Freyja er tignust með
Frigg. Hon giftist þeim
manni, er Óðr heitir. (…)
Óðr fór í braut langar
leiðir, en Freyja grætr eftir,
en tár hennar er gull rautt.

Freyja á mörg nöfn, en
sú er sök til þess, at hon
gaf sér ýmis heiti, er hon
fór með ókunnum þjóðum
at leita Óðs. Hon heitir
Mardöll ok Hörn, Gefn, Sýr.
Freyja átti Brísingamen.
Hon er ok kölluð Vanadís.

Sjaunda Sjöfn (…)
Níunda Vár, hon hlýðir
á eiða manna ok einkamál,
er veita sín á milli konur ok
karlar. Því heita þau mál
várar. Hon hefnir ok þeim,
er brigða.

Átta Lofn, hon er svá
mild ok góð til áheita, at
hon fær leyfi af Alföðr eða
Frigg til manna samgangs,
kvinna ok karla, þótt áðr
sé bannat eða þvertekit
þykki. Þat er af hennar
nafni lof kallat ok svá þat,
at hon er lofuð mjök af
mönnum.

*Freyia is the sixth; she
is the greatest alongside
Frigg. She was married to
someone named Óðr (...) He
traveled widely, and Freyia
weeps for him, and her
tears are of red gold.*

*Freyia owns many
names, and this is because
she gave herself new heiti
[nicknames] whenever she
came to people during her
search for Óðr [Poetry/
Ecstasy/Inspiration].*

*She is called Ocean
Splendor and Linen,
Provider and Sow. She
owns the Gem of Flames,
and she is called Goddess of
the Vanir.*

*The seventh is Sjöfn [Love]
(...)*

*The eight is Lofn [Law/
Permission/Appraised],
she is so mild and generous
to call on, that she gets
permission from All father
or Frigg to let people live
together, women and
men, even if their love had
been forbidden before, or
was considered illegal.
It is from her name that
we have what we call
"permission/"law", and also
because she is much praised
by people.*

Níunda Vár, hon hlýðir
á eiða manna ok einkamál,
er veita sín á milli konur
ok karlar. Því heita þau
mál várar. Hon hefnir ok
þeim, er brigða.

Tíunda Vör, hon er
vitr ok spurul, svá at engi
hlut má hana leyna. Þat er
orðtak, at kona verði vör
þess, er hon verðr vís.

Ellifta Syn, hon gætir
dura í höllinni ok lýkr
fyrir þeim, er eigi skulu
inn ganga, ok hon er
sett til varnar á þingum
fyrir þau mál, er hon vill
ósanna. Því er þat orðtak,
at syn sé fyrir sett, þá er
maðr neitar.

Tólfta Hlín, hon er
sett til gæzlu yfir þeim
mönnum, er Frigg
vill forða við háska
nökkurum. Þaðan af
er þat orðtak, at sá, er
forðast, hleinir.

Þrettánda Snotra, hon
er vitr ok látprúð. Af
hennar heiti er kallat snotr
kona eða karlmaðr, sá er
hóflátr er.

The ninth is Vár [Contract], she listens to the oaths that people swear and to the promises that women and men make between themselves; such deals are for this reasons called várar [contracts], and she takes revenge on those who betray their promises.

The tenth is Vör [Aware], she is wise and intelligent, so that nothing may be hidden from her. There is that saying, that a woman becomes vör [aware] when she becomes wise.

The eleventh is Syn [Closure]. She guards the door in the hall, and closes it to those who may not enter. And at parliament, she is set to close the cases that she does not want to come through. From this comes the saying that a case has been set to closure, when a man tries to resist her.

The twelfth is Hlín [Mild], she is set to care for those whom Frigg want to save from some danger, therefore it is said about the man who survives a danger, that he has been made mild.

The thirteenth is Snotra [Eloquent Woman], she is wise and powerfully well-spoken, after her name, a woman or a man who is very eloquent is called snótr.

Fjórtánda Gná, hana
sendir Frigg í ýmsa heima
at erendum sínum. Hon á
þann hest, er renn loft ok
lög ok heitir Hófvarpnir.
(...)
  Af Gnár nafni er svá
kallat, at þat gnæfar, er
hátt ferr.

*The fourteenth is Gná
[Hovering/Building up].
Frigg sends her out to all
the worlds on her errands.
She owns a horse who runs
through air and sea, it is
called Hófvarpnir [Hoof-
Hurler] (...) From her name,
it is called "building up to
something", whatever flies
high.*

Sól ok Bil eru talðar með
ásynjum, en sagt er fyrr
frá eðli þeira.

*Sun and Swift Moment
are counted among the
goddesses, their works have
been described before.*

5.9: SUMMARY AND CONCLUSIONS TO CHAPTER 5

....at þu ert komin, mögr!
til minna sala.[232]

*...That you have returned,
man, to my halls!*

In this chapter, I have argued that Freyia and Menglǫð could be identical with each other and moreover that, through their functions and the structure of their stories, they may be identified with the giantesses Gerðr and Gunnlǫð as represented in chapter 4.

The structure of each myth is similar to each other. It is possible to detect a pattern of themes such as 1) the Vision Quest Theme, 2), the Vision Theme, 3) a Descending Theme, 4) Trial Theme, and 5) a Maiden Theme. Each theme in each myth resembles the other themes of the other myths on a fundamental level.

The Maidens are placed in a protected spot within a realm that is identifiable as Níflhel. However, the Maidens represent an alternative to the bone-sucking monsters of Hel's extinguishing realm.

The alternative is represented by how Óðinn with the help of Gunnlǫð dug his way out of the mountain of the giants and returned to the divine realm with the precious mead inside himself, taking upon himself the features of death, eagle and serpent, and using them to escape, flying, to freedom.

---

232 Fjǫlsvinnsmál, Stanza 49

It is present in the choice to which Gerðr is presented, either to
be a wife of the gods in possession of their most sacred treasures, or
to be an ogress gaping behind the gates of Hel. It is also alluded to
in the grove that the winds do not reach – the winds, as we know,
originate in the realm of the dead, with the all-devouring eagle
Corpse Swallower.

It is present in the contrast between Hyndla, who offers poison
and forgetfulness, and Freyia, who offers love and memory which
may lead the hero to the heavenly afterlife in Valhǫll.

Finally, it is present in the contrast between Menglǫð's eternal
love on the Mountain of Medicine and in the pale giantess Sínmara,
who keeps the only weapon that could make it possible to get past
the ferocious guard dogs, locked behind nine iron locks.

Each poem is different, but, as I see it, complementary. Each fill in
gaps of information about the "Myth of the Maiden with the Mead".
Fjǫlsvinnsmál adds very much to our understanding of the Norse
cosmos. I argue that the three roots and the three wells of the World
Tree may be seen as three aspects of the same reality.

This alludes to my argument in chapter 4.5: namely that Óðinn
learns by all the three wells simultaneously. The same appears to be
the case with Svípdagr.

The poems also reveal a kind of "love and loss story" within the
myth. It could appear that Óðinn was the first to approach the
Maiden, who was then a giantess and who, after the marriage and
Óðinn's betrayal, was left behind in the giants' realm. Gunnlǫð's
weeping for Óðinn is reflected in Freyia's weeping for Óðr and
in Menglǫð's ages-old longing for her long-lost husband. Óðinn
appears to regret his treatment of Gunnlǫð, Freyr longs himself sick
for Gerðr, and Menglǫð's returning husband declares that she was
not the only one to suffer, that they have been separated by cold
winds and slippery, dark paths, all symbols that may belong to the
realm of death.

There are several indications that Svípdagr, through the workings
of the mortal realms, has forgotten his original relationship to
Menglǫð.

A theme of original union and subsequent loss and forgetfulness
seems to be present in the myth of the Maiden.

Óttarr faces the danger of forgetting everything he learned in the
Underworld unless Freyia and all the gods help him.

In Fjǫlsvinnsmál, the World Tree is called the Tree of Remembering, and Svípdagr acts as if he only has a vague memory of the golden halls in the beginning, recognizing both the Maiden and himself only at the end of the poem.

The climax of his lessons may be this fact: that he and the Maiden have always been united in their souls. We are reminded of the image of the reincarnated hero and the valkyria who is either reincarnated or only sleeps until her reborn hero finds her and wakes her up – a theme we shall discuss in the next chapter.

Monogram Drawing of Freyja and Svípdagr from Our Fathers' Godsaga by Viktor Rydberg. 1911. Public Domain

6: The Reincarnating Valkyria

36. Frá valkyrjum.

Enn eru þær aðrar,
er þjóna skulu í Valhöll,
bera drykkju ok gæta
borðbúnaðar ok ölgagna
(...)
Þessar heita valkyrjur.
Þær sendir Óðinn til
hverrar orrustu. Þær kjósa
feigð á menn ok ráða sigri.
Guðr ok Róta ok norn in
yngsta, er Skuld heitir, ríða
jafnan at kjósa val ok ráða
vígum.
Jörð, móðir Þórs, ok
Rindr, móðir Vála, eru
talðar með ásynjum.

36: Of the valkyriur
"There are still others
[among the goddesses]
whose function is to wait
in Valhǫll, serve drink and
look after the tableware
and drinking vessels.(...)
These are called
valkyriur. Odin sends
them to every battle. They
allot death to men and
govern victory.
Gunn [Battle] and
Róta [Rainstorm] and
the youngest norn, called
Skuld [Debt], always
ride to choose who shall
be slain and to govern
killings.
Earth, Thor's mother,
and Rindr, the mother of
Váli, are counted among
the goddesses."[233]

In the Gylfaginning, as quoted above, Snorri Sturluson gives the image that has had great influence on our image of the valkyriur – that of serving maids in Valhǫll and supervisors over battle. They ride to battle, choosing who shall win and who shall die, thus their title, valkyria, from valr (masculine singular: the "slain"), and kjosa – "to choose". The "slain" are the chosen dead, those whom the valkyriur chose, which is why I have often referred to them as the "chosen" or the "chosen dead" and at some point (like in the 2004 thesis) had it confused with a very similar-sounding word, val (neutral singular); which means choice or chosen.

---

233 Gylfaginning 36

Scholars generally agree that the val-part of the word valkyria refers to the masculine word valr for "the slain" and not to the neutral word for "choice" or chosen, although the valr were indeed chosen. The valkyriur are the "Choosers of the Slain, the "maidens of Óðinn", and they bring the dead souls to his warrior's paradise, Valhǫll – "Hall of the Chosen Slain" after battle. In Valhǫll, warriors are served life-renewing mead by the valkyriur, mead milked from the goat Heiðrún who stands on the roof of Valhǫll, eating from the great tree there, the Læráðr [Harm Counsel].

The way the tree is described by Snorri renders it obvious that the tree is no other than the World Tree itself, for alongside the goat Heiðrún, a stag also stands and feeds from the same tree, and its horns drip a liquid which falls right into the well of Hel, Hvergelmir [Mill/Cauldron-Eagle/Resounding], which we know to be located at one of the roots of the world tree. The mead that the valkyriur give the One-Harriers to drink is drawn directly from the tree of life itself, the very same tree that the oldest norn waters every morning. The water comes from the well that makes anyone who bathes in it come out shining bright and transparent (see chapter 5.7 about the transformative power of Urð's well).

Moreover, the goat's name means "Bright/Heath Rune"[234]. Runes [rún, feminine, plural: rúnar] were a kind of letters used by Germanic peoples, including the Vikings, but the word rún means "secret" or "hidden knowledge".[235] It seems logical that the secrets contain the hidden knowledge of destiny, since they were first inscribed by the norns, mistresses of fate.[236] Both Ström[237] and Näsström[238] regarded the norns, valkyriur and other dísir as creatures more or less identical to each other; while the norns allot fate in general, the valkyriur seem more specialized for the fate of battles. Snorri counted the youngest norn, Skuld, among the valkyriur, as quoted above. In the Hyndluljóð, the goat Heiðrún is compared to Freyia, a comparison I believe is far from irrelevant.

---

234 From heiðr as an adjective: "clear", "bright". See also discussion of said name in chapter 5.1
235 Norrøn Ordbok
236 Vǫluspá Stanza 20
237 Ström, 1954
238 Näsström, 1998, p. 177-178

The comparison is presented in the guise of an insult referring to Freyia's promiscuity. However, if we consider the fact that Heiðrún is the ultimate producer of the precious mead and the origin to the drink that rejuvenates, transforms and offers eternal resurrection and thus immortality, we realize that the "insult" provides esoteric information about Freyia that reaches far beyond moral judgement about the goddess's sexual transgressions: The goddess is compared to the goat whose name means something like "bright hidden knowledge", from whose udders flow the sacred mead of the valkyriur.

Since the "goat" feeds from the leaves of the world tree, which is watered by the Well of Origin, this mead has its ultimate beginning in the well of Urðr, whose waters will transform anyone who bathes in it into something new, shining and transparently bright, whose waters will keep the World Tree itself from rot and decay. Heiðrún is the transmitter of that mead, and Heiðrún is comparable to Freyia, and through the mead of resurrection theme, to all the ladies who appear in the form of the Maiden with the Mead. Now, Näsström has argued that Freyia may be called "the Great Valkyria"[239] , and indeed, Snorri describes how she rides to battle.[240]

In the Grímnismál, stanza 14, Freyia is described as the receiver of einherjar, the dead souls, and it is told that "she chooses the slain" every day, keeping half to herself and sending half to Óðinn. The exact words used are val hon kyss. Val and kyss (kjosa) being the same words that compose the word valkyria. As we shall see in this chapter, the valkyriur operate in a collective of maidens, but only one "Great Valkyria" stands out. It is not impossible that we are meeting Freyia in one of her many guises, and we shall see that the reincarnating valkyria fits neatly into our now well-known "Maiden-mythology". As mentioned in chapter 2.3, the different Heroic Poems are of different ages and origins, yet the editors of the Edda, perhaps basing themselves on common tradition, must have linked them together so as to form part of a very long family saga.

---

239 Ibid, p. 164
240 Gylfaginning, see appendix VI

As Alv Kragerud has argued, it seems likely that the way the editors presented the poems was in accordance with tradition. According to Kragerud, the primary motif of the Helgi poems is to convey the pre-Christian belief in reincarnation. The reincarnation theme has been largely ignored by scholars or dismissed as a mistake by the editor(s) of the Codex Regius. Kragerud, however, argues that the poems were made in order to show just how reincarnation occurs. The notes of the editor(s) function as integrating parts of the legendary material that the poems are based on. There is no reason to assume that the editors were "wrong" when they explained the poems they were writing down; on the contrary, the editor(s) belonged to a traditional chain of froði– "knowledgeable" - men and women among whom the legendary traditions behind the poems were still very much alive. There is little reason to believe that the idea of reincarnation was a late addition from the Christianized editor(s) rather than a pre-Christian concept.

Besides, Kragerud argues that the idea of reincarnation is confirmed in the poems themselves, the last stanza of the poem of Helgi Hiǫrvarðsson[241] conveys the idea that he will "come back" to the world, and the valkyria recognizes her hero in the poem of Helgi Hundingsbani. In my opinion, the theme of reincarnation is important in the poems, but more important to my thesis here is the way the poems convey an underlying "Maiden-mythology" behind these apparent sagas of love and revenge.

From my point of view, the reincarnation theme is a natural part of the theme of the Maiden with the Mead. We have seen how Svípdagr "returns" to his Maiden after having been separated for a long time due to "winds" and fate: possibly, they have been separated by the death of the former Svípdagr. How the very young Svípdagr could have been married to the Maiden a long time ago, lost on "cold and slippery paths" and "driven by the winds" – all metaphors for death(s), could perhaps be explained through the idea of reincarnation transmitted by the Heroic Poems.

---

241 Kragerud, p. 3-54

A SUMMARY OF THE MAIDEN-STORIES IN THE HEROIC POEMS

So far, we have gone through four different storylines which all follow the same pattern of initiation involving consecration by a golden-glowing maiden in the dark underworld. The giantesses Gunnlǫð and Gerðr and the goddess Freyia serve the precious mead or the mead of memory to the initiands. The Great maiden, Menglǫð, who may be a giantess since she rules the halls of Útgarðr, but who also may be a norn or a goddess, since she lives beneath the world tree, rather serves "the kiss of the Fylgja" – a hint towards a possible connection between her role as the Maiden with the Mead and the function of fylgjur – a sort of personal norn who follows her individual human through their lives. The motif of the drink-serving is not obvious, unless we accept the possibility that her very name means Blend Drink/Invitation. Now we shall present five more storylines which follow a similar pattern, but where the Maiden with the Mead turns out to be a valkyria – another sort of norn, the kind that has divine origins. Interestingly, they are usually described as being the daughters and sisters of jǫtnar – the giants.

1.HIǪRVARÐR, ATLI & SÍGRLINN

The poem Helgakviða Hiǫrvarðssonar relates the stories of King Hiǫrvarðr and of his son Helgi Hiǫrvarðsson and their relationship to supernatural women. Hiǫrvarðr hears rumors about a beautiful maiden called Sígrlinn [Victory Mild] in a far-off country and sends his earl's son Atli out to woo her for him. Atli spends a winter with the girl's father, king Svafnir [Sleep-Maker[242]] but has no luck. Later, Atli retires to a grove, where a bird speaks to him, demanding shrines, temples and sacrificial cattle in return for its help in obtaining the maiden.

---

242 Svafnir is also an Óðinsheiti and the name of one of the serpents in Hel's well.

The story proceeds with Atli taking the king up on a mountain from where they may look down into Svǎfaland [Sleep-Land]. This land is aflame, full of lanzbrvna oc ioreyki stora ["land on fire and with high smoke clouds from horses running"]. Next, Atli takes the king with him to a river's edge, where the king falls asleep.

In the middle of the night, Atli crosses the river into Svǎfaland, finds the maiden Sígrlinn accompanied by another maiden, Álof, hidden in a house guarded by a giant in eagle hide, which is "Earl Fránmarr" [Furious/Frothing Ocean] in disguise: Fránmarr iarl hafði hamaz i arnar lici oc varit þer fyr hernom með fiolkyngi ["Fránmarr Earl had assumed the likeness of an eagle and was keeping the maidens safe with his Fjǫlkyngi (great magical knowledge)"]. He is the jǫtunn father of Álof, earl to Svafnir [Sleep-Maker] and the guardian of the maidens of Sleep-Land. Atli kills the "earl" in eagle's shape and returns to Hiǫrvarðr with the maiden Sígrlinn as a bride to the king, and her friend, earl Fránmarr's daughter Álof, as his own bride.

2. HELGI, ATLI AND SVÁVA

Hiǫrvarðr's and Sígrlinn's son grows up fair-looking, but no name will stick to him, he speaks little and socializes less. He is sitting on a haugr – a (burial) mound when a company of nine valkyriur rides past:

> Hann sat a hǫ́gi, hann sa riþa valkyrior nív, oc var ein gǫfvgligvst;
>
> He sat on the burial mound, when he saw nine valkyriur ride past, and one was the greatest;

The leader of the valkyriur, Sváva [Sleeper/Floater] gives him a name, Helgi, which means "the sacred one"[243] , and incites him to seek a special sword which lies on the Sigarshólmr [Islet of Victory], all this to rule the Rǫðullsvollr [Field of Shining Light].

---

243 Larrington, 1996, p. 114

This first meeting makes Helgi intent on becoming a warrior, finding the sword that Sváva revealed to him. Sváva is said to protect him in battle. Later, Helgi kills a giant called Hróðmarr [Furious/Argument/Enmity Ocean],[244] and then another one called Hati – "Hatred". While still in Hatafjorðr, the "Fjord of Hate", the ship is threatened by an ogress, Hati's daughter with Rán, called Hrímgerðr [Frosty Enclosure]. She is one of Rán don's ocean wave daughters, eager to claim Helgi for her "lover" – which was a common, poetic way of describing death by drowning.

All the men are asleep except Atli the earl's son, who accompanies Helgi and his men. Atli, recognizing the danger she represents as she bobs up beneath the fleet, engages the death-wave ogress in a duel of words in which is revealed that Atli was castrated in the past and that only the protection of Sváva and her valkyriur are preventing the ogress from drowning the ship:

26.Hrimgerþr qvaþ:
„Hína vildo heldr, Helgi!
er reþ hafnir scoda
fyrri nott meþ firom;
Margvllin Mer
mer þotti afli bera;
her ste hon land af legi
oc festi sva yþarn flota;
hon ein þvi veldr,
er ec eigi mac
bvþlvngs monnom bana."

26. Hrímgerðr said:
«You would rather have
her, Helgi
she who was spying out
the harbor
the other night, with the
men;
The Sea-Golden Maiden
surpassed me in strength:
Here she disembarked
from the ship
and secured your vessel
She alone
is preventing me
from destroying the king's
men.

244 Hróði, m. means enmity, lack of peace, quarrel, storm. Hróðaligr – disgusting, hostile, enemy-minded. But hroðr means honorable, good fame. Marr means "ocean" (Norrøn Ordbok). In the light of Hróðmarr's giant successor Hati, I found the interpretation "un-peace" of the hroð- in his name logical: "Hate" and "Un-peace"...

27.Helgi qvaþ:
„Heyrþv nv, Hrimgerþr!
ef ec bǫti harma þer,
segþv gǫrr grami:
var sv eín vętr [=vættr],
er barg aˀþlings scipom,
ęþa foro þer fleire saman?"

27. Helgi said:
"Hear, now, Hrímgerðr
if I were to give
compensation for your
loss
tell the prince (me)
directly;
was it but one spirit
[vættr] (=valkyria)
who protected the high-
born's (my) ships
or were they many
together?"

28.Hrimgerþr qvaþ:
„Þrennar nivndir meyia,
þo reiþ ein fyr
hvit vnd hialmi męr;
marir hristvz,
stoþ af maˀnom þeirra
daˀgg i divpa dali,
hagl i hava viþo;
þaðan kǫmr meþ aˀldom ár,
alt var mer þat lęitt er ec
lęitc."

28.Hrímgerðr said:
«Three times nine
maidens
though one rode ahead:
A maiden, bright beneath
her helmet
From the manes (of their
horses)
came the dew into the
deep valleys
hail in the high forests
from here come good
fortune to men
All this I saw was terrible
to me."

As Helgi lives happily with his valkyria wife, who continues "riding air and sea", Helgi's older half-brother Heðinn meets an old giantess riding a wolf, using serpents as reins. She is said to be a fylgja – a "follower" – a spirit being who assumed a woman's shape and who functioned like a personal norn. When seen, her appearance is indicative of what sort of fate will follow, and in this case, the omen is one of doom and death (for Heðinn). The ogress asks Heðinn to accompany her, but he refuses. The ogress warns him that this refusal to walk with her (his fylgja) will have a terrible outcome for him.

Later, Helgi is killed by the Frekasteinn [the Rock of Greed].[245] He asks Sváva to marry his brother Heðinn, who loves her and who had even sworn to have her, but she flatly refuses. I agree with Kragerud that the last stanza of the poem does not reveal that Sváva accepted Heðinn as husband. On the contrary, the last stanza is Helgi's promise of returning to avenge himself.

The prose ending of the poem declares that Helgi and Sváva were reborn:

Helgi oc Svava er sagt at veri endrborin
  Helgi and Sváva are said to have been reborn.

3.HELGI HUNDINGSBANI, SINFIQTLI AND SÍGRÚN

The first and second poems of Helgi Hundingsbani relates the story of the valkyria Sígrún and Helgi, son of Sígmundr Vǫlsung. The two poems complement each other. The first poem relates how norns arrive at Helgi's birth, prophesying a great destiny for the boy. One particular norn, nipt Nera – "the kinswoman of Neri", fastened a special fate-thread northwards, bidding it to hold forever. Sígmund's son grows up a prince and harsh warrior and manages to break the "Peace of Fróði", or actually "Wisdom's Peace [Froðafríðr].

According to Snorri and the Edda poem Grǫttasǫngr [The Song of the Mill-Stone (of Fate)] the Froðafríðr – Wisdoms' Peace - was a time long ago, an era of peace and plenty, of friendship and happiness, and of wisdom, when no one stole from nor killed one another. A golden ring could lie forever in the fields without no one picking it up, so little greed was there, and no one bothered with revenge. This was under the reign of king Fróði, whose name means "wisdom".

A war was continuously waged between Helgi's family and a certain Hunding. Helgi goes in disguise to his enemies' settlement and lives there for a while in the guise of a servant woman – indeed it is remarked by passing men that the slave girl pulling the mill is unusually large, strong and fierce-eyed, and they speculate that she is really a royally born shield maiden who has had the misfortune of being taken as a slave. When Helgi notices that the enemies are noticing him and wondering about such a warlike and noble bearing in a slave girl, he escapes with enough information to be able to win the battle.

---

245 Freki: "the greedy one". Frekleikr, m., "greediness" (Norrøn Ordbok)

Helgi is busy killing and winning battles, but at some point, he sits down to rest beneath Arasteinn – the Rock of the Eagle. As we have discussed before, the eagle is a symbol of death and mortality. Suddenly, nine maidens descend from the "Mountains of Flames" and the "Fields of Heaven" while lightning and rays of fire surround them.[246]

15.Þa brá lioma
af Logafiollom,
enn af þeim liomom
leiptrir qvomo;
þa var vnd hialmom
a Himinvanga,
brynior váro þeirra
bloþi stocnar,
enn af geirom
geislar stoþo.

15. Then a light shone from the Mountain of Flames and from this radiance lightening came;
   They were beneath helmets at the Fields of Heaven
   Their armors were drenched in blood and from their spears rays were spurting.

16.Fra arliga
or vlfiþi
dǫglingr at þvi
Disir Suðrǫnar,
ef þer vildi heim
meþ hildingom
þa nótt fara;
þrymr var alma.

16.Soon enough, from the lair of the wolf the day-son asked if the Southern Red Goddesses would like to go home
   with the warriors when night fell and the weapons clang

Helgi asks them if they would like to come to him, but the leader of the valkyriur, Sígrún, declares that she has no time to lose drinking beer with men who have been busy "breaking rings" [baugbrota], a way of saying oath-breakers, when there are more important matters to attend to.

---

246 Logafell, from loga (ad.) "flaming", "burning" or loga (f.), log (n.) "torch", "light". Himinvangar: "Fields of Heaven" (Norrøn Ordbok)

Sígrún asks him to save her from her hideous suitor by killing him as well as defeating her own family, who is trying to force her into the undesired marriage. During the journey to the battle-place, Helgi and his fleet is assaulted by another wave-giantess, "Kolga's sister" and "Aegir's terrible daughter" [ógorlig Ægis dottir], but the valkyria protected them again:

30.Enn þeím sialfom
Sigrvn ofan
folcdiorf vm barg
oc fari þeirra;
snoriz ramliga
Rán or hendi
gialfrdýr konvngs
at Gnipalvndi.

30.And then came, from above
Sígrún herself
she saved the army
and their ships;
With great power she twisted
out of Rán don's hands
the sea-beasts (ships) of the king
at the Overhanging Grove

After the valkyria, just like in the previous story, saves the men from drowning, Helgi and his men venture out to a great battle against the valkyria's unwanted suitor. Like with his earlier self, Helgi is assisted – this time by his half-brother, Sinfiǫtli, who in a discourse somewhat similar to that of Atli and Hrímgerðr, leads a duel of words with one of the representatives of the enemy, in which it is revealed that Sinfiǫtli was castrated in the past, just like Atli had been. In the battle that follows, Sígrún and her "shield maidens" descend and protect their hero, who wins. This battle is held by the Frekasteinn – the Rock of Greed – exactly the place where the previous Helgi lost his battle after conquering Hatred and Furious Sea.

54. Como þar or himni
hialmvitr ofan
— óx geira gnýr —
þer er grami hlifþo;
þa qvaþ þat Sigrvn,
sárvitr flvga
— át hálo scer
af hugins barri —:

54. There came out of heaven
the helmet-bright (=valkyria)
from above
the sound of spears grew loud
they (valkyriur) protected the king:
Then said Sígrún
that wound-wise flying one
that ogresses were feasting
on the soul's food.

The second poem relates the same story in a different way. Helgi is said to be named after Helgi Hiǫrvarðsson. The first meeting between the valkyria and Helgi takes place after he has been to battle, while feasting on raw meat with his warriors. Sígrún from Sefafjǫll [Mountain of Souls] approaches on horseback, and we are told that she is Sváva reborn:

Vndan comz Helgi oc for a herscip; hann feldi Hvnding konvng oc var siþan callaþr Helgi Hvndingsbani.	*Helgi got away and went with a warship, he killed Hunding King and was since then called Helgi Hundingsbani.*
Hann la meþ her sinn i Brvnavagom oc hafþi þar strandha/gg, oc áto þar rát. Ha/gni het konvngr; hans dottir var Sigrvn, hon var valkyria oc reiþ lopt oc la/g; hon var Svava endrborin.	*He lay with his army in the Eye-Lash Waves [Brunavágom] and made a beach-camp there where they ate raw meat.* *Hǫgnir [the Thinker] was the name of a king, his daughter was Sígrún [Victory Rune], she was a valkyria and she rode air and sea; she was Sváva reincarnated.*

She asks Helgi what he is doing, and he tries to explain the bloody sight of himself and his men. Sígrún declares that she already knows, and that she has not been far away. When she saw him, she recognized him as being Helgi.[247]

Helgi and Sígrún meet a second time on the field of slain men after the battle against his arch-enemy, Hunding. After winning, Helgi is dozing off, dead tired, beneath the Arasteinn [Eagle's Rock] (like in the previous poem) when the valkyria arrives, finds him and embraces him. The eagle is a common symbol for the world of the dead.

---

247 Stanza 13; enn Ha/gna mẹr Helga kennir [The Thinker's Maiden recognizes Helgi]

Declaring her love with a kiss, she asks him to kill her unwanted suitor, and similar events take place as in the first poem. On the way, they are overtaken by a terrible thunderstorm at sea, but nine valkyriur arrive again to save the day:

Helgi samnadi þa
miclom scipaher oc for
til Frecasteins, oc fengo
i hafi ofviðri mannhętt;
þa qvomo leíptr yfir þa,
oc stoþo geislar i scipin.

Þeir sa i loptino at
valcyrior nío riþo, oc
kendo þeir Sigrv´ no;
þa lęgði storminn, oc
qvomo þeir heilir til
landz.

Helgi assembled a great fleet and went to the Rock of Greed, and on the ocean they came into a terrible storm.

Lightening flashed above them and the ships were struck by lightening rays. Then they saw in the air nine valkyriur ride, and they recognized Sígrún; then the storm abated, and they came whole to land.

The two are married, but Sígrún continues to be a valkyria riding air and sea and protecting her man in battle and from ocean storms. Finally, there is the battle at the Frekasteinn – the Rock of Greed, where the valkyria's entire jǫtunn family (and jǫtunn suitor) are killed. The valkyriur of the Edda poems are always the daughters and sisters of giants and are trying to get out of their families demands for her to marry another jǫtunn.

Sigrún's brother avenges his kin by slaying Helgi with Óðinn's spear in the Fjǫturlundr [Grove of Fetters]. He rides to Sígrún on the Sefafjǫll [Mountain of Souls] to tell her the news. Sígrún meets the dead Helgi inside his burial mound, where the two drink "the precious mead" before sleeping together in the grave. Helgi goes on to Valhǫll.

Sigrvn gecc i ha/ginn til
Helga oc qvaþ:

43„Nv em ec sva fegin
fvndi ocrom,
sem átfrekir
Oþins ha/car,
er val vito,
varmar braðir,
eþa da/gglitir
dagsbrvn siá.

46.»Vel scolom drecca
dyrar veigar,
þott mist hafim
mvnar oc landa;
scal engi maþr
angrlióþ qveþa,
þott mer a briosti
beniar líti:
nv ero Brvþir
byrgþar i ha/gi,
lofda disir
hiá oss liþnom.

Sígrún went into Helgi's
burial mound and said:

43."Now I am so happy
At our meeting
Like the all-greedy hawks
of Óðinn
when they know of slain
men
steaming hot food
or, when, drenched with
dew
they see the dawn.

"46."Well shall we drink
the precious drink
Though we have lost
both life and lands
No man should sing for me
in angry lament
Though on my breast,
wounds may be seen
Now the Bride
has entered the burial
mound
The high goddesses
are with us deceased ones.

The couple is said to be reincarnated as Helgi and Kára, who
supposedly were described in Káraljóð, a poem that is lost to us.
However, the Grípisspá identifies the valkyria Sígrdrífa as the
maiden "who has slept since Helgi died", and her hero is Helgi's
younger brother, Sígurðr, born after Helgi's death.[248]

248 Näsström, 1998, p. 164 also identifies Sígrdrífa and Brynhildr with the
former valkyriur

Throughout the stories, the valkyriur of the Helgi-poems are referred to in the following terms:
- Disir svðrǫnar – "Southern Red Goddesses"[249]
- Hialmvitr – "Helmet-bright"[250]
- Sárvitr flvga – "Wound-Wise Flying One"[251]
- In rikia męr – "The Powerful Maiden"[252]
- Hǫgna dottvr – "The Thinker's Daughter"[253]
- Svafnis dottvr – "The Sleep-Maker's Daughter"[254]
- Margvllin męr – "The Sea-Golden Maiden"[255]
- Hvit vnd hialmi męr – "Bright Beneath Helmet Maiden"[256]
- Fra Sevafiollom – "From the Mountain of Souls"[257]
- Hildr – "Battle"[258]
- Brvþr bǫgvariþ – "Bride Ring-Adorned"[259]
- grętr gvllvariþ – "The Weeping Gold-Adorned"[260]
- solbiort, svðrǫn – "The Sun-Bright, Southern Red"[261]
- Vættir – "Spirits"[262]

4. Sígurðr, Reginn & Sígrdrífa

The prose interpolation in the Poetic Edda called Frá Dauða Sinfiǫtla tells the story of Sinfiǫtli's death, and then proceeds with how Sígurðr was born. Sígurðr's father Sígmundr, who was also father to Helgi Hundingsbani and Sinfiǫtli, dies in battle with the Hundings, his late son's enemies. Sígurðr's mother marries again and Sígurðr grows up with her and his stepfather's family. The Grípisspá [The Grasping One's Prophecy] relates how the young Sígurðr approaches his maternal uncle Grípir, who "ruled countries and was wiser than all and could see the future".

---

249 Helgakviða Hundingsbana I: 16 – southern red gold is associated with the sun and with divine wisdom
250 Helgakviða Hundingsbana I: 54
251 Helgakviða Hundingsbana I: 54
252 Helgakviða Hundingsbana I:56
253 Helgakviða Hundingsbana I:56 & Helgakviða Hundingsbana II: 13
254 Helgakviða Hiǫrvarðssonar: 1
255 Helgakviða Hiǫrvarðssonar: 26
256 Helgakviða Hiǫrvarðssonar: 28
257 Helgakviða Hundingsbana II: 25, 36, 42, 45,48
258 Helgakviða Hundingsbana II: 29
259 Helgakviða Hundingsbana II: 35
260 Helgakviða Hundingsbana II: 45
261 Helgakviða Hundingsbana II: 45
262 Helgakviða Hiǫrvarðssonar 27

Grípir is persuaded to tell Sígurðr his whole fate, and the poem functions as a "synopsis" of the Sígurðr-saga. In this part of the story, we learn that there is a valkyria who has been sleeping since Helgi died, one of several subtle allusions to the lives and the valkyriur of his predecessors, and that she may be a reincarnation of Sígrlinn, Sváva and Sígrún. Likewise, Sígurðr, who is Helgi Hundingsbani's half-brother, born after the latter's death, may be a reincarnation of the Helgi characters who went before him on the same spiritual path. Grípir also offers some details on exactly what this sleeping valkyria may do for the young prince:

15. Gripir qvaþ:
„Sefr a fialli fylcis
dottir
biort i brynio eptir
bana Helga;
þv mvnt ha'ggva
hvosso sverþi, brynio
rista
meþ bana Fafnis."

15. Grípir said:
«There sleeps on the
mountain a ruler's daughter
bright in her armor, after the
death of Helgi
You shall cleave with your
sharp sword,
the armor cut
with the bane of Fafnir [=the
sword Gramr]

16.Sigvrþr qvaþ:
„Brotin er brynia,
brvþr męla tecr,
er vacnaþi víf or
svefni;
hvat mvn Snot at
heldr
viþ Sigvrþ męla,
þat er at farnaþi fylci
verþi?"

16. Sígurdr said:
«Broken is her armor, the
Bride begins to speak
the wife, awakened from
sleep
What may the Eloquent
Woman
say to Sígurdr, which will be
to the fortune of the prince?"

17.Gripir qvaþ:
„Hon mvn rikiom þer
rvnar kenna
allar þer er aldir
eignaz vildo,
oc a mannz tvngo
mæla hveria,
lyf meþ lęcning;
lifþv heill, konvngr!"

17. Grípir said:
"She will teach you the
powerful runes
all those which people can
ever want to know
and to speak every human
language
a life of healing
live you whole, King!"

Reginsmál [Reginn's Speech] relates how the young Sígurðr meets Reginn in the stables of his step-grandfather. Reginn is a dwarf, but he is wise and has a hard húgr (mind, intent, soul), and he knows about sorcery:

hann var hveriom
manne hagari oc dvergr
of voxt; hann var vitr,
grimmr oc fiolcvnnigr

...he was wiser than all men
and a dwarf of growth, he was
wise, secretive and fjǫlkunnigr
(very wise)

Reginn observes that Sígurðr chooses a special horse for himself, Grani, and as it turns out, this horse is similar to Sleipnir and able to move across the borders between the worlds and can only be ridden by someone who knows no fear. Reginn concludes that this father-less prince is very special and declares that "the web of his fate will spread through all worlds" [þrymr vm ǫll lond ǫrlogsimo].[263]

Reginn fosters Sígurðr and teaches him. He tells Sígurðr about the story of the red gold of the gods, taken from the dwarf Andvari [Breath/Spirit Guard/Alert] and now kept by the great serpent Fafnir [Embracer]. Reginn declares that the gold is his father's heritage, and asks Sígurðr to help him slay the serpent, who is Reginn's own brother. Fafnir is really a jǫtunn – a giant, and his name means "embracer". Reginn forges a sword called Gramr [Anger], which bites through anything. Sígurðr declares that he has to do his duty as a prince and son before he can go on Reginn's quest, and Reginn follows Sígurðr as he sets out to avenge his father against the Hundings.

---

263 Reginsmál stanza14

On the sea journey they are overtaken by a storm. In the midst of the storm they see a man standing quietly on a rock in the ocean. As he enters the ship, the storm quiets. The man presents himself with several names indicating that he is really the god Óðinn and gives Sígurðr important counsels. At the end of the poem, Sígurðr slays the Hundings and Reginn praises his warrior's deeds, much in the manner of a royal bard.

Fafnismál [The Embracer's Speech] relates how Sígurðr slays the great serpent Fafnir with the aid of Reginn. He moves up on the Gnítaheiðr, a place which evidently involves a heiðr – a heath, or a bright opening within the darkness, and several gnítar (f.sg: gnít), which weirdly enough means "louse eggs" – perhaps indicating something tiny and miniscule, a meaning which perhaps turns this "heath" into something more esoteric and sublime than an actual heath. There is otherwise a possible "confusion" with the Gnípahellir, which means "overhanging cave" in the Vǫluspá, by which the wolf Garmr [Greedy] barks loudly to signalize the coming of the apocalypse, but I think that the notion of a miniscule opening of brightness in the dark may actually signify something spiritual.

As the serpent dies, he reveals secrets, answers questions and gives counsel to Sígurðr. He warns him that the red gold he has taken from the serpent will be the death of him, and the young man replies that every man must fulfil his fate and die eventually, and that the important thing is not to live, but to own one's own fate. This statement leads to an interesting discourse about the norns and the judgment they will give to everyone who reaches "the other side":

10.Sigvrþr qvaþ:
„Fe raða vill fyrþa hverr
ę til ins eina dags;
þviat eino sinni
scal alda hverr
fara til heliar heþan."

10.Sígurðr said:
«Each one shall rule his own
forever until the last day;
For on one day onlys
shall every life-span
travel from here to Hel."

11.Fafnir qvaþ:
„Norna dom
þv mvnt fyr nesiom hafa
oc osvinnz apa;
i vatni þv drvcnar,
ef i vindi rǫr,
alt er feigs fo*rað."

11.Fafnir said:
«The Judgment of the norns
you will get as soon as
you reach the shore
and the fate of an
ignorant ape;
In the water you will drown
if you row in the wind
all fate is dangerous for the dying."

12. Sigvrþr qvaþ:
„Segdv mer, Fafnir!
allz þic froþan qveþa
oc vel mart vita:
hveriar 'ro þer nornir,
er naðganglar 'ro
oc kiosa mǫþr fra margom?"

12. Sígurðr said:
«Tell me this, Fafnir, since
you are said to be wise
And I really want to know:
Who are those norns
qho saves the ones in need
and chooses the mothers
for children?"

13.Fafnir qvaþ:
„Svndrbornar mioc
hygg ec at nornir se,
eigoþ þer ętt saman;
svmar ero askvngar,
svmar alfkvngar,
svmar dǫtr Dvalins."

13.Fafnir said:
«Of very diverse origins
I think the norns descent
They do not come from
one lineage;
Some are the children of the Aesir
Some are the children of elves
Some are the daughters of Hibernation."

The last of the serpent's death words declare that he has been carrying the Aegishjalmr – the Helmet of Terror, while he guarded the "red gold" of the gods, and that this "gold" has been polluted. The serpent challenges him, makes him re-think his choices and his associations. Sígurðr comes back from the slaying apparently a new and wiser man.

When Reginn tries to praise his warrior's deeds, Sígurðr replies, un-viking-like, that many men are courageous who never reddened their sword in another man's chest.

Reginn is alarmed by Sígurðr's new attitude, but, still regarding Sígurðr as his apprentice, orders him to roast the heart of Fafnir. Reginn drinks Fafnir's blood and goes to sleep while Sígurðr works with the roasting. But as he is roasting the heart, a drop of blood falls down on his finger, which Sígurðr licks, and suddenly he can understand the speech of birds.

The birds tells him that Reginn will betray him, and that he should take the gold of Fafnir and ride up to the Hindarfell – the Mountain of Obstacles[264] - where a beautiful shield maiden – a valkyria - is to be found. While it was said before that she had been sleeping since the death of Helgi Hundingsbani, she is here sleeping because Óðinn punished her with a svefnþorn [sleep-thorn] for choosing different men for Valhǫll than he wished. Sígurðr slays Reginn, gathers the treasures of the serpent on his horse's back, and rides on.

Sigvrþr hio haͬfvþ af
Regin, oc þa át hann
Fafnis hiarta oc dracc
bloþ þeirra beggia
Regins oc Fafnis. Þa
heyrþi Sigvrþr, hvar
igdvr mẹlto:

40„Bitt þv, Sigvrþr!
baͬga raͬða,
era konvnglict qviþa
morgo:
mey veit ec eina myclo
fegrsta,
gvlli gǫdda,
ef þv geta mẹttir.

*Sígurðr cut off Reginn's
head and then he ate
Fafnir's heart and drank
the blood of both Reginn
and Fafnir. Then he could
hear what the nuthatches
said:*

*40."Gather up, Sígurðr,
the red rings
It I not kingly to be afraid
I know a maiden, the
loveliest of all
endowed with gold
and you can win her."*

---

264 From hindr, n.: "Obstacle"? Turville-Petre,1975, p. 199, interpreted the meaning as the Hind-Mountain, from hind, f.: "hind".

42.Salr er
a há Hindarfialli,
allr er hann vtan eldi
sveipinn,
þann hafa horscir halir
vm gorvan
or odaccom ognar lióma.

*42. There lies a hall at the
high Mountain of
Obstacles
and he is all surrounded
by fire
Wise men made it
out of the radiant lights of
the river*

43.Veit ec a fialli
folcvitra sofa,
oc leicr yfir lindar vaþi;

Yggr stacc þorni
aþr a feldi Hörgefn, hali
er hafa vildi.

*43.I know that on the
mountain
a very knowledgeable
woman sleeps
and over her plays the
terror of women[265] :*

*Yggr stabbed her with a
thorn
for the Linen-Provider
[norn/valkyria/Freyia[266]]
chose a different man
than he wanted.*

44. Knattv, magr!
Sia mey vnd hialmi,
þa er fra vigi Vingscorni
reið;
ma-at Sigrdrifar svefni
bregþa
scioldvnga niþr fyr
scarpom norna."

*44. Young man, you shall
see
the Maiden beneath the
Helmet
She who rode Wing-Shorn
from the battle
Sígrdrífa may not break
the sleep-spell
but a princely youth, by
the norns' decree."*

---

265 Literally: the linden's terror. As Snorri pointed out, women or goddesses may
be referred to by any feminine tree-name, and lists the linden foremost.
266 Hörgefn: Linen provider. Gefn: Provider, goddess, woman, Freyiuheiti.
Hörn: Freyiuheiti, but also a word for linen, flax, which symbolizes fate.

Sígrdrífumál relates how Sígurðr rides up on the Mountain of Obstacles, where the earth trembles and flames reach up to the sky, a place few would have the courage to enter. Sígurðr, surrounded by the shine of the gold of the gods, rides through a wall of fire:

...a fiallino sa hann lios mikit, sva sem eldr brynni, oc liomaþi af til himins. Enn er hann com at, þa stoþ þar scialdborg oc vp or merki. Sigvrþr gecc i scialdborgina oc sa, at þar la maþr oc svaf meþ ollom hervapnom; hann toc fyrst hialminn af hofþi hanom, þa sa hann, at þat var kona. Brynian var fast, sem hon veri holdgróin; þa reist hann meþ Gram fra hafvþsmát bryniona igognom niþr oc sva vt igognom badar ermar. Þa toc hann brynio af henne, enn hon vacnadi oc settiz hon vp oc sa Sigvrþ oc melti:

....*On the mountain he saw a great light, as if fire was burning, and it reached up to the heavens. And when he came there, he saw a shield wall with a banner flying over it. Sígurðr went into the shield wall and saw that there lay a man there in full armor and slept with all his weapons. He first took the helmet off his head, and then he saw that it was a woman. The armor was stuck to her, as if it had grown into her flesh. Then he used the sword Anger to cleave through the armor, and so alongside both her arms. Then he could pull the armor off her, and she woke up and saw Sígurðr and spoke:*

Inside the fire-fence is a hall made of shields, and as Sígurðr enters the hall he finds a warrior in full armor. Taking off the helmet of the warrior, he realizes that the warrior is a woman. The armor has grown into her body, and Sígurðr has to cut her loose. As she wakes up, liberated from the armor, she speaks to Sígurðr and asks him to present himself. He explains who he is, and she declares that she has been sleeping for a long time, and that everybody has suffered for that reason.

Óðinn caused her deep sleep:

2.Hon qvaþ:
„Lengi ec svaf,
lengi ec sofnoþ var,
long ero lyða lę;
Oþinn þvi veldr,
er ec eigi mattac
bregða blvnnstafom."

2.She said:
"Long did I sleep
Long was my slumber
Long is the suffering of
people;
Óðinn caused this
that I could not manage
to break the spell of sleep."

She presents herself as Sígrdrífa [Victory Drift], a valkyria, and continues her tale of her disagreement with Óðinn about the fate of some warriors which led to her imprisonment. Sígurðr then asks her to teach him wisdom from all the worlds. Sígrdrífa responds, praising day, night, gods, goddesses and the holy earth, and praying for eloquence, intelligence and healing hands in life. After the prayer, she offers him the Minnisveigr – the drink of Memory, declaring that the ale is filled with power, nobility, courage, sung songs and blessing words, good galdrar and runes of pleasure:

Sigvrþr settiz niþr oc
spvrþi hana nafns. Hon
toc þa horn fvlt miaþar oc
gaf hanom Minnisveig:

Sígurðr sat down and asked
for her name. She then took
a horn full of mead and gave
him the Drink of memory:

4.„Heill dagr, heilir dags
synir,
heil nott oc nipt!
oreiþom argom
litiþ ocr þinig
oc gefit sitiondom sigr!

4."Hail Day, hail the sons of
Day
Hail Night and all her kind!
With beneficial eyes
may you look at us here
and give victory to us seated
here!

4.Heilir ęsir,
heilar asynior,
heil sia in fiolnyta Fold!
mal oc manvit
gefit ocr męrom tveim
oc lęcnishendr, meþan
lifom!"

4.Hail the gods!
Hail the goddesses!
Hail the powerful mighty
Earth!
Eloquence and wisdom
may you grant to us two
and healing hands while we
live!"

(...) Hann svarar oc biþr
hana kenna ser speki, ef
hon vissi tiþindi or ollom
heimom. Sigrdrífa qvaþ:

(...) He answers and asked
her to teach him wisdom, if
she knew tiding from all the
worlds. Sígrdrífa said:

5.„Biór fęri ec þer,
brynþings apaldr!
magni blandinn
oc megintíri;
fvllr er hann lioþa
oc licnstafa,
godra galdra
oc gamanrvna.

5." Ale I offer you,
Apple-tree of the Armor-
Parliament!
it is blended with power
and mighty glory;
He is full of songs
and runes of fortune
good galdrar
and runes of pleasure."

She proceeds to counting up all the kinds of runes that Sígurðr
needs to know and how to use them:
1. Sigrúnar [Victory runes] for victory
2. Aulrúnar [Ale runes] against trickery and mead mixed with
poison [meinblandinn mjǫðr][267]
3. Biargrúnar [Saving/Salvation runes] for healing and
midwifery
4. Brimrúnar [Ocean Wave runes] for stilling storms and
avoiding shipwrecks and drowning
5. Limrúnar [Limb runes] for healing wounds
6. Málrúnar [Eloquence runes] for eloquence and good orator,
convincing and diplomatic abilities
7. Húgrúnar [Soul/Mind/Intent runes] if you want to be wiser
than most.

---

267 A reference, perhaps, to the recurring theme of red gold and precious mead
that has been poisoned, as in the Hyndluljóð

The counting evolves into the tale of how Óðinn found the runes, where they came from, how he held the head of Mímir and spoke wise words, and how he cut the runes loose to flow into the worlds of gods, elves, the Vanir and humankind – all a reference to the first story where the god hung nine nights on the world tree and was able to take the runes up from the Well of Origin:

13.Hvgrvnar scaltv kvnna,
ef þv vilt hveriom vera
geðsvinnari gvma;
þer of réð,
þer of reist,
þer vm hugði Hroptr
af þeim legi,
er leciþ hafdi
or ha᷄si Heiddra᷄pniss
oc or horni Hoddrofnis.

13.*Soul runes you must know*
If you want to be, among many
of greater wisdom in spirit
They were interpreted
They were carved
Through the Shattered One's
[Óðinn's] soul [húgr] they ran
from that liquid which leached
from the skull of Bright Drops
and from the horn of Treasure Shatterer

14.A biargi stoþ
meþ Brimis eggiar,
hafdi ser a hofði hialm;
þa mẹlti Mims ha᷄fvþ
froþlict iþ fyrsta orð
oc sagdi sanna stafi.

14.*On the mountain he stood*
with the edge of Ocean Wave
on his head he wore a helmet
then the head of memory spoke
wisely the first word
and told true secrets.

18. Allar váro af scafnar,
þer er váro a ristnar,
oc hverfðar viþ inn helga
mioþ
oc sendar a viþa vega;
þer 'ro meþ asom,
þer 'ro meþ alfom,
svmar meþ visom vanom,
svmar hafa mennzkir
menn.

18. They [the runes] were all
shaved off
that had been carved in
and poured over with sacred
mead
and sent on the wide ways;
Some are with the Aesir
Some are with the elves
Some are with the wise
Vanir
and some are owned by
human people

19. Þat ero bocrvnar,
þat ero biargrvnar
oc allar alrvnar
oc metar meginrvnar
hveim er þer kná oviltar
oc ospilltar
ser at heillom hafa;
niottv, ef þv namt,
vnz rivfaz regin.

19. Those are book runes
those are saving runes
and all are ale-runes
and valuable runes of great
power
For those who can, without
confusing them
without destroying them
possess them for good;
Enjoy them, if you can learn
them
until the rulers are
shattered.

20. Nv scaltv kiosa,
alls þer er costr vm boþinn,
hvassa vapna hlynr!
sagn eþa þagn
hafdv þer sialfr i hvg;
all ero mein of metin."

20. Now you must choose
since the choice has been
given
you maple-tree of sharp
weapons!
My speech or my silence
you can carry in your soul
all harms are already
measured out."

In the end, Sígrdrífa asks whether Sígurðr would like "speech or silence" from her. He has a choice, but fate is still laid out for him. Sígurðr declares that he is not afraid of knowing his fate even if it is death and chooses her wise words and counsels as long as he lives. Sígrdrífa grants him eleven pieces of advice about wise behavior in life:

1. *To be blameless among his own and slow to avenge harm, even if vengeance can sometimes be good for those who are avenged, even while dead.*

2. *Secondly to never swear an oath he cannot truly keep.*

3. *Thirdly, to never argue with ignorant fools who cannot understand the impact of what they are saying.*

4. *Fourthly to not be a guest to malignant witches.*

5. *Fifthly to not be impressed by fancy appearance and beauty.*

6. *Sixthly, to not quarrel while drunk because drink steals the wit of men.*

7. *Seventhly, to fight even against enemies more powerful than yourself, which is better than just being abused.*

8. *Eighthly, to never commit adultery with other people's loved ones.*

9. *Ninthly, to bury corpses that you find on the way (surely a concern of the past), and to clean the departed and treat them with honor, biding them to sleep in bliss.*

10. *Tenthly, to never trust the oaths of known wrongdoers.*

11. *The eleventh advice of the valkyria is to be aware of his relationships to others and honor friendships.*

The poems that follow relate the events around Sígurðr's death from different angles. Only the Grípisspá (mentioned above) gives a coherent summary of why Sígurðr had to die. The story may also be found in Snorri's Skáldskaparmál and in the Vǫlsunga Saga.

Apparently, Sígurðr had sworn marriage oaths to Sígrdrífa, but as he rides down from her mountain, he forgets all his oaths and his great love for the valkyria, the way one may forget a dream when returning to ordinary, human perception. Breaking his oaths, albeit unwittingly, he is married to the beautiful Guðrún, whose mother knows more about Sígurðr's past than he now knows himself. The mother, Grimhildr, asks Sígurðr to help his brother-in-law, Gunnarr, to seek the maiden Brynhildr. It becomes clear that Brynhildr is just another name for Sígrdrífa, the valkyria who sleeps behind the flaming shield wall on the sacred mountain.

Sígurðr takes Gunnarr up onto the Mountain of Obstacles, but Gunnarr's horse refuses to enter the fire, and Sígurðr's horse, Grani, refuses to carry Gunnarr. This is when Sígurðr changes shape with Gunnarr, so that he can enter the hall of the Maiden in the shape of another man. He sleeps with Brynhildr as if she were his sister, for three nights, with an unsheathed, poisonous sword between them. Later, Brynhildr comes as a bride to king Gunnarr, but as she discovers how she has been tricked into marrying an unworthy man, her revenge is terrible, ending with Sígurðr's death. Brynhildr takes her own life.

The Edda poem Helreið Brynhildar [Brynhild's Ride to Hel] tells the tale of how Brynhildr travels the Helvegr [the Death Path] driving a wagon into Hel, where she is met by a gýgr - an ogress, who, like Hyndla before, is described as a "Bride of the Rocks/ Caves" [brúðr or steini]. The ogress, as if in a nórna dómr – a "Judgment of the Norns" - calls Brynhildr the "goddess of gold" [vár [268]gullz] from Valland and asks what she is doing in this dark realm of death, when she ought to be weaving in her own valkyria realm.

It becomes clear from the ogress's hostile words that Brynhildr is not supposed to be in that rocky realm and that she has acted wrong causing the death of men. This is certainly a puzzling remark about a valkyria, who is supposed to cause death through choosing. The only explanation for this is to reconsider our idea of the valkyria. Sígurðr is residing in Hel because of Brynhildr, and that is wrong. His relation to the valkyria should have had a different outcome, he should have been in Valhǫll or in Freyia's hall.

He even died in battle. Brynhildr defends herself by explaining the cause of her actions, laying the blame on her brother "Atli" and on the "wise king", who tricked her sisters and herself by stealing their bird hides a long time ago. It would seem that Óðinn hides behind the characters of Atli and the "wise king". At the end of her speech, she declares that she has been underestimated and that she will follow her heart, and that she will stay together with Sígurðr for all eternity. She tells the ogress to "sink", much like the vǫlva in the Vǫluspá "sinks" after her speech, as does the dead vǫlva in the Vegtamskvíða.

---

268 Vár is one of the goddesses listed by Snorri, whose name meant "Contract" – she listened to the oaths of people. Any goddess-name could be used to describe any other goddess, and their identity was known through attributes, such as here; the goldenness.

14.»Mvno við ofstríþ
allz til lengi
konor oc karlar
qvicqvir fodaz;
við scolom ocrom
aldri slíta
Sigvrþr saman.
Seycstv, gygiarkyn!"

14."For long and longer,
they must live in terrible
sorrow
men and women
who are born to live;
But we two
shall endure the ages
together
forever with Sígurðr.
Sink, you, ogress-kind!"

GUNNARR, SÍGURÐR AND ODDRÚN (AND GUÐRÚN, GRIMHILDR, BRYNHILDR & ATLI)

The Oddrúnargrátr [Edge Rune's Lament] tells the tale of how Brynhildr's "younger sister", Oddrún [Edge Rune] from Hlésey – the "wind shielded island" of Aegir - fell in love with Gunnarr after the deaths of Sígurðr and Brynhildr. The backdrop to this story is found in the several heroic poems[269] that we have omitted from the Sígurðr – story, the part after Sígurðr descended from the valkyria's mountain, before he died and what happened to his widow and her family after his death.

To sum up the story. Sígurðr rode down from the valkyria's mountain and back into the world of living human beings, forgetting some details from his transcendent experiences as he is offered marriage to a Burgund princess, Guðrún. She is not just another princess, either, she is said to be wise and able to understand the speech of birds, just like her husband, and, just like him, she has drunk of the blood of Fafnir. Her mother, Grimhildr, is able to read destiny when looking at her weave. Their marriage is very happy.

---

269 Brot af Sigurðarkviðu, Guðrúnarkviða hin fyrsta, Sigurðarkviða hin skamma, Dráp Niflunga, Guðrúnarkviða önnur, Guðrúnarkviða hin þriðja, Atlakviða hin Grœnlenzka, Atlamál hin Grœnlenzku, Guðrúnarhvöt & Hamðismál

The princess has three brothers, one of them Gunnarr, yet due to some form of matrilineal descent, it is her husband who is taken as king of the Burgunds. This is a very common theme in Edda poetry – a prince had to seek a queen elsewhere in order to become king. The brothers are not upset about this at all, and are great friends with the high king, their brother in law. But Gunnarr also wants to marry a princess, and Sígurðr agrees to help him find the valkyria on Hindarfell.

Now, Sígrdrífa [Victory Drift] has become Brynhildr [Armor Battle], but otherwise, her abode, her function and the trials she proposes are exactly the same as in the story of Sígurðr's initiation. As such, Sígurðr, having gone through the initiation before, has become a mentor to Gunnarr.

Alas, Gunnarr has too much fear in his heart to be able to ride through the high flames on the mountain, and the horse Grani refuses to take him. Sígurðr, wanting to help his brother-in-law and apprentice, now commits his one big fatal mistake; he swaps hides with Gunnarr so that the one looks exactly like the other. In the hide of Gunnarr, Sígurðr goes through the same trials a second time, pretending to be Gunnarr. When they come back from the trials, Gunnarr is offered marriage to a Hunnish princess, who is now blended in with the valkyria character Brynhildr. She is the sister of "Atli the Hun", who is of course the Edda version of the historical Attila. She marries Gunnarr, but is loathe to discover that even though she has married the oldest prince among the Burgunds, she is not going to become queen, since it is the husband of the oldest princess, Guðrún, who becomes the high king.

Feeling tricked and betrayed, and all this mixed up with the deception at the holy mountain, she plots to bring Sígurðr down and install Gunnarr as king. However, as soon as Sígurðr is dead, Brynhildr commits suicide and assumes her valkyria aspect in order to save him out of Hel, as we described before. To make a long story short, Sígurðr is killed and Gunnarr becomes king. The old king's widow (and the new king's sister), Guðrún, is so devastated by her loss that she travels into the wilderness, lives with wolves and becomes quite savage until she reaches the high hall of the maiden Thora, where there is a lake full of swans and where destiny is woven; She has reached the hall of the norns, basically. Here, she learns the art of weaving destinies.

Her mother Grimhildr and her brothers finally seek her forgiveness and offers her the precious drink, which heals her sorrows and makes her forgive her brothers for their betrayal. The drink is empowered by the power of earth, the cool cold sea and the blood of the sacrifice, the horn is engraved with secret runes of healing. This is where we see a hint towards a woman's version of the same pattern of initiation that we see in the case of gods and heroic men. Guðrún later displays not only the ability to weave fates, but also to put her arms unharmed into boiling water, and to make an entire hall full of warriors sleep, so that she can extract revenge.

Guðrún now agrees to save her brothers from the aggression of the Huns by marrying Atli the Hun, who is frequently described as if he were really Óðinn, greedy for the "red gold" of the gods that the Burgunds have now inherited – the very same red gold that the serpent Fafnir owned before Sígurðr retrieved it and carried it to his valkyria. Atli don's hall is also described exactly like Valhǫll.

During the wedding banquet, however, and now we have reached the Oddrúnargrátr, Gunnarr meets another valkyria "sister of Atli"; Oddrún [Edge Rube]. They fell in love, and, finally, Gunnarr receives the precious mead: Oddrún offered the drinking horn to Gunnarr. But her brother, Atli, opposed the match and Gunnarr could not fight them.

As Gunnarr is taken captive by her brother Atli, Gunnarr is thrown into a pit of poisonous serpents. He manages to keep the serpents back by playing on a harp with his toes (his hands are bound). The music is so beautiful that everybody who hears it has to weep, and the tones reaches far away to Hlésey - the wind shielded island of immortality owned by the ocean giant Aegir, where it is finally heard by Oddrún.

Oddrún rides the fastest she can to save her beloved, but just as she reaches the serpent pit, described exactly like the well of serpents in Hel, her brother's mother, an ogress, has taken the shape of a serpent, crawled into the pit and given Gunnarr the fatal bite.

7: THE STAGES OF INITIATION

As we have already discussed, I have detected certain thematic stages which together make up the structure of initiation within these Edda poems. I have divided these into: 1. The Vision Quest, 2. The Vision, 3. The Descent, 4. The Trial, 5. The Maiden with the Mead (Consecration). In chapter 4 and 5, we went through these stages in the four different stories: Gunnlǫð, Gerðr, Freyia and Menglǫð. Let us now take a closer look at the five valkyria stories that we have, and which follow the same structure.

7.1: THE VISION QUEST THEME

...the Great Taiga the Heart Taiga
I do climb it, I do scale it
spirit recluse, spirit recluse
my staff tingles the tender pine
Have you not seen Alan's mothers
- the ancestors of our shaman...
...born in new shape
born with miraculous power
oh mothers mine, oh mothers mine...[270]

1. ÚTISETA IN A SACRED GROVE

Sitting in a certain grove [lund nokkurn], as Atli does when he speaks to the bird, may certainly be part of a "vision quest". Groves were sacred to the Germanic peoples, often used as shrines and sanctuaries. The sanctity of the grove is ancient. Even as early as 80 A.D., the Roman historian Tacitus, whose accounts about the Germanic tribes is considered one of our most reliable Antique sources,[271] testified that groves were holy places, to which the Germans applied "the name of deities to that hidden presence which is seen only by the eye of reverence". [272]Sacrifices and rituals took place there, and no one could enter unless bound with a cord.

---

270 Siberian shaman song. A Taiga is a snowclad mountaintop. Diószegi, 1968, p. 264-265
271 Näsström, 1998, p. 17, Simek, 1996, p. 309
272 Mattingly, 1970, p.109

The grove, Tacitus asserts, is the center of their whole religion, from time immemorial. It is regarded as the cradle of the people and the dwelling place of the supreme god. Later on, Tacitus reveals how the shrine of Nerthus, Mother Earth, was situated in a grove on an island.

Groves appear quite frequently as mythical places in Edda poetry. Sitting out in a grove, especially when the result is communication with a bird who demands shrines, temples and sacrifice in order to assist in an important matter, would appear to me an obvious example of a vision quest.

2. SITTING OUT ON A BURIAL MOUND

Helgi Hiǫrvarðsson sits on a haugr – a mound - when nine valkyriur ride past, changing his fortune forever. Sitting on a burial mound was a way of gaining wisdom and inspiration in the Viking Age.[273] In the Poetic Edda, it could appear that Óðinn is sitting on a burial mound when he sings galdr to wake up a dead vǫlva in Vegtamskvíða, and that Svípdagr does the same when he invokes his dead mother in Gróagaldr. Mounds could, for example, contain elves, who would heal in return for sacrifice.[274] Burial mounds and mounds in general were places of sacrifice to powerful ghosts or elves.[275] In the Volsunga Saga, king Rerir sits on a mound when the valkyria Hljóð appears in the shape of a crow to give him an apple of fertility from Óðinn as an answer to a prayer to Frigg. In this case, Helgi receives the vision of nine supernatural maidens while sitting on a mound. He probably sat there in order to obtain a vision.

3. SITTING OUT ON A MOUNTAIN AND BY A RIVER

Atli took his king up on a mountaintop in order to see Svávaland. Sígurðr slew the serpent on a mountain and encountered the valkyria on another. Mountains are often associated with female supernatural beings. Gunnlǫð was said to dwell within the deadly rock-layer much like other giantesses such as Hyndla, the ogress in Helreið Brynhildar, and in the poem Grǫttasǫngr, two giantesses reveal how they grew nine winters within the mountain.

273 Davidsson, 1990, p. 155, Hedeager, 1999, p. 9, Solli, 2002, p., Ström, Motz,
274 Ex.: Kormáks saga, Davidsson, 1990, p. 156
275 Näsström, 2001, p. 89-91

Menglǫð sits in silence on the Mountain of Healing whereas
Sígrdrífa sleeps on the Mountain of Obstacles. Sígrlinn shows the
way to the Shining Hills, and Sigrún's dwelling is Sefafell, another
mountain (of souls), and she descends from The Mountain of
Flames. According to Motz, mountains and rocks were associated
with a kind of Germanic priesthood, as well as with the world of the
dead.[276]

In another Scandinavian tradition, the Sámi, the idea of a
Sacred Mountain was central within the lore of their shamans,
and especially connected to the residence of helping spirits. It was
also considered a dwelling for the dead.[277] In Siberian shamanism,
mountains – or the "master spirit" of the mountain - play the role
of initiating shamans.[278] It is indeed a "sacred mountain" [hélgo
fioll] that Sígurðr ascends in his quest for the serpent's gold and the
Maiden, as shown in Fafnismál stanza 26. Sváfaland, watched from
the mountaintop, belongs to a realm of death, as we shall see in
chapter 6. and is an Other World. To climb a mountain in order to
"see" such a realm must be counted as a vision quest.

Atli also takes his king to a riverside where he sleeps while Atli
crosses it. The river is a border to Sváfaland which, as already
remarked, is an Other World. In Norse Mythology, rivers frequently
function as borders between realms. In Frá Dauða Sinfiǫtla we meet
the river as a border to the world of the dead. Sleeping by a river in
order to cross it in the dark of night, entering the Other World must
be seen as a vision quest.

4. SACRIFICE

Hiǫrvarðr has to sacrifice cattle in order to obtain his goal. The
sacrifice helps Atli find his way to the Maiden. Helgi Hundingsbani
also butchers cattle, eating the meat raw when the valkyriur arrive.
We remember how Óttarr sacrificed to Freyia before descending
into the underworld – exactly in the hide of the sacrificed and
dying boar. Sacrifice may be counted as a means of obtaining the
necessary vision and power to enter the Other World.

---

276 Motz, 1983, p. 7, 87-91, 95-97, 100-104
277 Bäckman, 1975, p. 88-91, Hultkrantz, 1992 (b), p. 140, Pollan, 2002, p. 29,
Steinsland, 1992, p. 320
278 Diószegi, 1968, p. 55

5. DREAM OR MEDITATION & NEAR DEATH VISIONS

Helgi rests beneath the Arasteinn – "Eagle's Rock"- when the valkyria appears. Knowing the symbolic significance of the eagle as a force in the realm of the dead (see chapter 4. 4), we may detect the deeper meaning of such a place. Another place where Helgi meets his Maiden is while staying the night in Brunavág. Bruna means "of the edges" or "of the eyelashes", while vág means "sea" or "wave", so the name could be translated as "Edge/Eyelash Wave". Both places could signify a very special place or even state of mind where the hero is present at the borders of the Other World. These events could also be counted within the vision quest theme.

6. DRINKING SERPENT'S BLOOD

Finally, the drinking of a mythical serpent's blood in order to induce visions, as Reginn and Sígurðr (and Guðrún) do, may also be regarded as a vision quest. The serpent, who reveals knowledge about the other worlds and about fate, is obviously a powerful creature, and so is its blood and heart. Reginn falls asleep after drinking the blood, and we do not know what kind of effect it has on him. According to Ström, it was assumed that a person who could change shape or travel with the soul would be asleep or dreaming when the húgr –the "free-soul" - detached itself from the body (see chapter3.1). That the blood would have some kind of magical effect seems obvious: Sígurðr's immediate reaction is to understand bird's speech and communicate with birds who can tell him what is hidden and advise him in his actions.

7.2: THE VISION THEME

The vision theme is closely tied to the vision quest theme, and some of the visions have been alluded to in the previous chapter.

1. COMMUNICATING WITH ANIMALS: *Speaking birds may be counted as a vision, as in the cases of Atli and of Sígurðr and also of Guðrún.*

2. NINE VALKYRIUR (OR THREE BY NINE): *So is the vision from the top of a mountain into another world. Helgi Hiǫrvarðsson obtains the vision of nine valkyriur, with one more splendid than all the others, who speak to him and reveal, among other things, his name and the location of a magical sword. Helgi Hundingsbani sees three times nine maidens ride down from the heavens, surrounded by lightning and flames, their byrnies spattered with blood: "southern red goddesses", directing his future. On another occasion, the leader of these shield maidens approaches him while he is dozing off, embracing and kissing him. The number nine is recognizable from the other stories told in chapter 4 and 5:*

☞ *Óðinn's hanging on the world tree lasted nine nights according to the Hávamál. According to the Skáldskaparmál it also took him nine nights to enter Gunnlǫð's hall, and he learned nine great songs from his maternal Jǫtunn uncle.*

☞ *Freyr has to go through nine difficult nights before he can reach the breezeless grove of his bride.*

☞ *Nine is the number of galdrar sung to Svípdagr before he can enter Útgarðr, and nine were the maidens who sat by the knees of the Great Maiden.*

☞ **3.BRIGHTNESS AND FLAMES:** *In all the poems, empha-sis is laid on the immense rays, luminescence, brightness, lightening and high flames that surround the valkyriur, comparing them to the sun. Sváfaland is aflame. Sígrdrífa's hall is surrounded with flames reaching up to heaven, and her mountain shines with rays of light. They ride through air and sea, descending from the heavens. We are remind-ed of Freyr's vision of the Maiden with the arms that lights up sea and mountain, the golden chair of Gunnlǫð, Freyia's fiery necklace and golden tears, and the Shining Hall of sun bright Menglǫð. Gerðr and Menglǫð have that in common with Sígrdrífa: their residence is surrounded by a fence of fire. Gunnlǫð and Freyia are also surrounded by immense obstacles.*

7.3: THE DESCENDING THEME

Atli spends a winter with king Svafnir, Sígrlinn's father. Svafnir literally means "the One Who Puts to Sleep". Simek believes that this is a poetic way of saying "death".[279] Svafnir is one of the names of Óðinn,[280] as well as the name of one of the serpents that live in the well of Hel.[281] The Hel-serpent Svafnir and Óðinn-Svafnir, the god of the dead, contribute to the idea of king Svafnir's realm as a realm of the dead. King Svafnir and Sígrlinn's realm is called Sváfaland. Sváva may mean "the Floating Woman", but it also means "to Put to Sleep", indicating the same thing as the name of the king: death.

In "Sleep-Putting Country", Atli encounters a giant in eagle's disguise. In chapter 4.4, we discussed the symbolic significance of such a creature, identifying it with the eagle Corpse Swallower who dwells in the northernmost reaches of Hel. Sígrún dwells on Sefafjǫll. Sefa means "to calm down" or "have mercy". It could also be a genitive form of sefi, m., which is related to the húgr, m., that is, the soul, intent, will, mind, desire or thought of a person. With Christianity, the concept of the soul was assigned the word sefi.

---

279 Simek, 1996, p. 305
280 Grímnismál, Hrafnsmál and the þulur.
281 Skáldskaparmál, Faulkes, 1987, p. 137

The name of Sigrún's dwelling is either "Mount Calm Down", which would be in accordance with the above Sváva and Svafnir (calming down being associated with falling asleep), or "Mountain of Souls". Sigrún's relationship to death becomes clear when she meets Helgi in his burial mound, comparing herself to the "hungry hawks of Óðinn", and describing in detail the lovely sight of hot and bloody corpses. She talks as if she was about to devour her beloved (see 6.1.3). Sleeping in his dead arms within his burial mound further indicates death, since, in the Norse sources, death is often depicted as an embrace of the mistress of the dead.[282]

THE GREAT SERPENT

"The serpent is linked with the giants, and with the snakes that inhabit the world of death and are its symbols. Beside him we must set the fiery dragon of northern mythology, emerging from the depths of the earth, from rocks, caves, or burial mounds of the dead."
---Hilda Ellis Davidson[283]

Last but not least we must consider the great serpent that Sígurðr slays, whose blood makes it possible for him to understand the speech of birds and to cross the Mountain of Obstacles. Fafnir means "the embracer", indicating that he is coiling himself around something – in this case the gold of the gods and of the dwarf Andvari [Spirit/Breath Guard/Alerted].

Now what other great serpents do we know in the Norse mythology? Two come immediately to mind: the serpent mentioned several times already; the Niðhǫggr [Shame/Below Biter] and the Miðgarðsormr [World Serpent], also known as the Jǫrmundgandr [Great Magical Spell].[284]

---

282 Steinsland, 1992, p. 320-322
283 Davidson, 1990, p.139
284 From jörmun-(a name for Óðinn) meaning "great", and gandr, m. a name for the magic wand (cult staff) of witches and the völur, or meaning "sorcery". Simek, 1996, p. 179-180, Norrøn Ordbok

Niðhǫggr dwells in the well of Hel, Hvergelmir [Mill/Cauldron Eagle/Resounding] together with uncountable snakes, as described in the Vǫluspá:

37.Stóð fyr norðan
á Niðavöllum
salr ór gulli
Sindra ættar;
en annarr stóð
á Ókólni,
bjórsalr jötuns,
en sá Brímir heitir.

37. Stood to the north
on the Waning Plains
a hall out of gold
of the Growing Spark's
lineage:
Another stood
at the Never-Cooling:
The beer-hall of the jǫtunn
who is called Brim Wave

38.Sal sá hon standa
sólu fjarri
Náströndu á,
norðr horfa dyrr;
féllu eitrdropar
inn um ljóra,
sá er undinn salr
orma hryggjum.

38.She saw a hall standing
far from the sun
on the Shore of Corpses
To the north that door faces;
Poisonous drops fall
in through the roof-vents
That hall is woven
from the spines of serpents.

39.Sá hon þar vaða
þunga strauma
menn meinsvara
ok morðvarga
ok þanns annars
glepr eyrarúnu;
þar saug Níðhöggr
nái framgengna,
sleit vargr vera.

39. There she saw, wading
in heavy currents
oath breakers
greed-murderers
and those who by force take the confidants of others
There sucks Shame Biter
from their dead rotting bodies
and wolves tear them

We meet Niðhǫggr again in the last stanza of the same poem:

66. Þar kemr inn dimmi
dreki fljúgandi,
naðr fránn neðan
frá Niðafjöllum;
berr sér í fjöðrum
— flýgr völl yfir —
Niðhöggr nái.
Nú man hon sökkvask."

66. Then comes the dark
dragon a-flying
The shining serpent
ascending
from the Waning/Below/
Shame Hills:
In his wings he carries
corpses
he flies across the plain
Shame/Waning Biter and
his corpses
Now she (the Vǫlva) wants
to sink

We know, then, of Niðhǫggr, that he sucks the corpses in Níflheimr, and that he carries corpses in his feathers as he flies across the earth in the new world after Ragnarǫk. Of the Miðgarðsormr [World Serpent] we know a bit more. He is the brother of Hel, goddess of death, and of the great wolf Fenrir [Greed]. The serpent lies coiled around the ordered cosmos. As Heide points out, the Miðgarðsormr may appear not to be entirely destructive, in fact it might be the very bond that keeps the world together.[285]

Ellis Davidson establishes the Germanic fiery dragon as the "guardian of the burial mound", "brooding over his treasure in a megalithic stone chamber inside a burial mound".[286] The dragon in particular is associated with the graves of the dead, and Davidson points out that the fire-spitting dragon is a natural image of devouring death, swallowing up the dead body and its treasures with greedy fire. Although the dragon in Norse poetry is pictured as a great serpent, it is easy to recognize the dragon.

Both in England and Scandinavia, the dragon-serpent came to be regarded as the guardian of the grave mound, watching over its treasures. The name Niðhǫggr, she claims, means "Corpse Tearer". The serpent-dragon Fafnir, Davidson claims, is a typical example, and it has left its mark in the serpentine ornament and recurring snake-motif upon memorial stones raised over the dead. The snake as symbol of the world of the dead is as recurrent in the art as in the literature of the north.

285 Heide, 1997, p. 107
286 Davidson, 1990, p. 159. About the serpents, p. 159-162

I too believe that Fafnir [Embracer] should be seen in the light of the two great serpents, Niðhǫggr and the Miðgarðsormr. Both the World Serpent and Fafnir are pictured as coiled around something precious, the Earth and the gold of giants and gods. Fafnir meaning "Embracer" further strengthening the comparison. Both Niðhǫggr and the World Serpent are related to death, the one by its dwelling place, the other by its brotherhood to Hel. The World Serpent seems to play yet another role – that of holding the known, ordered world in one piece. When Thor tries to catch it in the Hymiskvíða, the world trembles, and even the great giant Hýmir is struck with terror, preventing the kill.

As with the eagle, the great serpents represent great cosmic figures related to the realm of death, or else the power that keeps the worlds together and apart from each other. Both figures are also crucial to the maintenance of the known world: the eagle creates the winds of the world, the serpent holds it together. Just like the eagle had to "die" so that Atli could take the maiden out of Put-to-Sleep-Country, the serpent has to "die" so that Sígurðr can find his maiden and release her from the spell of sleep. In addition, the killing of the serpent means a "killing" of the limits of the human world, represented by the serpent who with its body forms a frontier between the ordered Miðgarðr [Middle World] and the unknown Útgarðr [Outer World] thus numinous knowledge is revealed.

THE EMBRACE OF DEATH

Gro Steinsland[287] has shown how conceptions attached to the experience of death and an existence after death are rich and varied in the literature that gives us access to the pre-Christian mind. If one intends to systematize this material, one will soon realize that the variety in ideas bursts any model that takes as a starting point the existence of a cognitive connection between the various pagan perceptions of death. There is for example no logical coherence between concepts about the human body and soul on one side and the concepts of death, the grave, the death journey and the realms of death on the other side. But despite this variety in ideas that sometimes appear to be combined without any logical connection, certain motifs seem to be detectable.

---

287 Steinsland, Gro: Article in Eyvindarbók (Ed. Finn Hødnebø, Jon Gunnar Jørgensen, Else Mundal, Magnus Rindal, Vésteinn Ólason), Redaksjonen, Institutt for nordistikk og litteraturvitenskap, Universitetet i Oslo (1992)

It is usual to understand Hel as an underground collective realm of the dead for the common man and woman who lived an ordinary life. Snorri gives a gloomy depiction of this place. The death-woman, Hel, is blue-black like a corpse in half the dace, her plate is called hunger and her knife starvation[288]. We find ourselves on the giant side of the mythological person gallery. There is reason to ask whether Snorri's depiction of Hel has been influenced by medieval Christian concepts about a place of punishment after death. As we know, the Church borrowed the pagan name for the realm of death to describe Hell (In the old Scandinavian language, Helviti [Hel-punishment].

Older sources than Snorri appear to convey very different associations to Hel`s female ruler of the same name. The idea of a post-mortal retribution after death was unknown to the pre-Christian religion. It is therefore probable that the medieval Christian concept of Hell has strongly colored Snorri`s presentation of the pagan Hel.

The concept of Helgafell [Holy Mountain] is only known from the saga literature. The idea of a realm of death within the sacred mountain where all the souls of the clan gathered is a pleasant concept that appears to correspond with the collective mentality that we usually apply to the clan society. It is the fellowship around the fire and the social interaction with other clan members that is emphasize in the Helgafell-concept. The expression deyja i fjall– "to die in the mountain" was an expression used in everyday language in order to say "to die". This concept of the sacred mountain was probably quite widespread during the pagan era.

Strongly in contrast to Hel- and Helgafell- concepts is Snorri's famous depiction of Hel versus Valhǫll-concept. This latter realm of death is named after the famous hall of Óðinn where the table, the chalice and the joy of battle awaits the dead warrior. Valhǫll seems to embrace the worldview of a warrior aristocracy and gives the impression of an ideal masculine post-mortal existence. The existence in Valhalla is temporary, while awaiting the final battle of Ragnarǫk.

---

288 Gylfaginning 34

On the basis of the simple death-typology drawn here, it seems that it is a misleading to present Hel, Helgafell and Valhǫll as alternative post-mortal possibilities attached to the individual and its deeds judged ethically, just as Valhǫll is not an individual reward for a "proper" life career, is Hel not a punishment for a less glorious life. Let us look at some sources which describe a type of death-experience as an often erotic encounter with a woman who represents death.

Both from the EDDA, SKALDIC and SAGA literature there are examples of death presented as an erotic union between the dead/dying and a representative for the realm of death, usually Hel or Ran. The death experience could actually be described as a death-wedding, it is said that the dying is climbing into Ran's bed, that he is embraced by the death-woman and such like.

Why this complex of ideas usually is ignored when the Norse concepts of death is presented, can have several reasons. One explanation could be that most have regarded the connection between death and sex as a literary topos without basis in genuine pre-Christian conceptions about death. Another reason can be that the idea of a death-wedding seems macabre from the point of view of our contemporary culture.

Steinsland's work with the sources on Norse kingship ideology has strengthened her impression that there is a genuine pagan conception at the basis of the combination death and sex. From analysis of the Hieros Gamos myth (the sacred marriage), it becomes clear that the combination "wedding and death" are two mythical motifs that together create the basic pillar of Norse kingship ideology.

The Edda poem Skírnismál, which exemplify the myth about a wedding between the god and the giantess, may be seen as an image of the king's wedding and consecration as king. The ritual is based on the ancestral myth of the royal clan descending from such a marriage between a god and giantess. In the myth we find a clear combination between wedding and death. In the skaldic poem Ynglingatál, a text source dating back to before 900 AD, the combination wedding and death is repeated over and over. In verse 7, the poet describes death three times as a sexual encounter between the king and Hel, the queen of the dead. Words like gaman and leikr mean "pleasure/enjoyment" and "play", but are in their meaning inherently erotic, referring specifically to sexual play and pleasure.

The pleasure is usually on the side of the goddess of the dead, who naturally enjoys herself a hot corpse any time:

7. Kveðkat dul, nema Dyggva hrør Glitnis gnó at gamni hefr,	7.I do not deny that Dyggvi's corpse is now being enjoyed (sexually) by the Goddess of Glitnir[289] [Hel]
þvít jódís Ulfs ok Narfa konungmann kjósa skyldi;	For the steed-goddess [Hel] sister to the wolf and Narfi [Hel] chose for herself a man from among kings [King Dyggvi]
ok allvald Yngva þjóðar Loka mær of leikinn hefr.	And the great ruler of the Ynglinga lineage [King Dyggvi] Loki's maiden [Hel] took as her plaything.

In stanza 9, a woman hanging a king with his own golden mén – gem or necklace - assumes the role of death herself with kenning Loga dís – the Goddess of Flames. To "tame the cool horse of Loki" (Sígyn's husband) was another kenning for dying.

... með gollmeni Loga dís at lopti hóf, hinn 's við Taur temja skyldi svalan hest Signýjar vers.[290]	... with the golden necklace the Goddess of Flames [Hel] hoisted high him, who by the river Taur was to tame the cool horse of Sigyn's husband

---

289 Glitnir: The Shining One, known from Grímnismál 15 and Gylfaginning as the hall in which the god Forseti (god of justice and law) resides.

290 Ynglingatál 10

In stanza 32 we read:

32. Ok til þings	32. *And, to parliament*
þriðja jǫfri	*[love-making]*
Hveðrungs mær	*the third king*
ór heimi bauð,	*was invited*
þás Halfdanr,	*by Hveðrung's maiden*
sás Holtum bjó,	*[Hel]*
Norna Dóms	*from the world*
of notit hafði;	*he who lived at Holtan*
ok buðlung	*and Halfdanr then*
á Borrói	*enjoyed*
sigrhafendr	*the Judgment of the*
síðan fǫlu.	*Norns [death]*
	and, at Borre [cemetery
	in Vestfold]
	the great man
	was since buried
	by victorious men.

This Viking Age skaldic presentation of Hel as an seductive lover is in sharp contrast to medieval Snorri`s dark description, which must have be strongly influenced by Christian concepts. In the skald Thorbjörn Brúnason's ransom song from the early 11th century, we find that epli Heljar [Hel`s apples] is a kenning for death. The kenning alludes to Iðunn's apples. The apples were ancient symbols of lovemaking.

In the Edda poem Vegtamskvíða, Hel is presented as a hall decorated and well furnished for a party awaiting the arrival of Baldr to the realm of death. This gives the image of a rich húsfreyia's [lady of the house's] hall, who takes good care of her realm, and has not a trace of Snorri`s tale of hunger and misery.

Towards the end of the 900`s, the Icelandic poet Tindr Hallkelsson, described death with the kenning "the bendable branches of Gerðr's shoulders", that is, as Gerðr's (=Hel`s) supple arms. The hint to a woman's arms is always a hint to the lover's embrace and has erotic overtones. Moreover, in the same stanza, Hel is preparing a bed for the earl who was fighting on the battlefield.

The use of the names of other female characters rather than
Hel should not be seen as evidence for another identity. As Snorri
explained in his Skáldskaparmál, and what is amply testified in Old
Norse poetry, any goddess or female character could be described
in kennings by using the name or the heiti of one character,
and applying it to another, showing the "true" identity through
attributes and context.

With these examples from poetry, Steinsland believes that we
have probably moved a step closer to the Viking Age concepts of
Hel as an erotically attractive entity, and it is easier to grasp the
image of death as a loving union between the dying and the mistress
of the death-realm. This seems to be connected to death on the
battle-field or at sea. It is possible that the valkyria who takes the
dead to Valhǫll were part of the same motif, as the heroes of the
Edda are married to their valkyriur. In a poem from Holmganga-
Réfr Gestsson, the idea of death in battle as an erotic alliance is
described: "The generous warrior climbed the golden bed of the
woman, the warrior showed great virility."

Death on the sea can also be described as a sexual union between
the dying and the nine daughters of Ran. In Flateyjarbók we hear
that a crew that struggle to survive in a tempest are being tried
seduced by the daughters of Ran: "Ran's daughters tried the men,
inviting them to their embrace."

In Friðþiófs saga hin frækni, chapter 3, death by drowning is
described as a sexual encounter with the ocean giantess Rán:

Nú skal ek Ránar raunbeð troða

Now I shall enter Rán's experience-bed

It is also important to carry gold when reaching Rán:

*Nú er víst, at til Ránar skal fara (...) ok skal hverr gull hafa á
sér*

*Now it is certain that we are going to Rán (...) and each
should carry some gold with them*

Rán is also described as an "impolite woman" herding men into
her net.

(....) en Rán gætir röskum drengjum, siðlaus kona,

*(...) and Rán is herding the strong men, that impolite wom-
an*

In Sonatorrek 10, the poet Egill Skallagrimsson describes his grief after the death of his son Boðvarr. His life has been radically changed. He described his son's death journey as munvega - "the path of lust".

7.4: THE TRIAL THEME

The heroes have to overcome the monsters of the Other World. We have already touched upon the significance of "killing the serpent" which opens the way to the Maiden:

☞ Sígurðr also has the wit to obtain knowledge from the dying monster. Just like the eagle is said to be exceedingly wise, the serpent reveals cosmic secrets when it is overcome.

Atli has to kill the eagle to release the Maiden, which is the same theme as that of Sígurðr.

☞ *Helgi Hiǫrvarðsson has to defeat the giants of "Non-Peace", Hate, the ogress "Frosty Enclosure", and win a battle by the "Rock of Greed". He fails the last test, but is reborn as Helgi Hundingsbani.*

☞ *This Helgi, however, breaks the "Peace of King Wisdom" in the beginning of his career. Later, he wins the battle of the Rock of Greed. He dies by Óðinn's decree, however, but is united with his valkyria bride in the grave and is allowed to enter Valhǫll.*

Many of the "battles" could appear to have to do with proper conduct. Indeed, many of Sígrdrífa's important counsels have to do with righteous and honorable behavior, and Sígurðr has the rather "un-viking-like" realization that there is no need to kill to prove one's courage.

The two Helgi characters' tests of defeating "non-peace", "hate" and "greed" quite speaks for itself. Hrímgerðr is a daughter of Rán, the mistress of the bottom of the sea, who makes people drown. That, and her name, which means "Frosty Enclosure", certainly indicates death. Helgi, with the help of Atli, defeats what this ogress represents. He does die, but he is reborn, and later reunited with the Maiden and allowed an afterlife as a warrior for the gods. Defeating the ogress could represent an alternative to extinction in death.

There are indeed more monsters in these stories that could be discussed, but the examples just mentioned should suffice to show that the hero faces trials of proper conduct, of conquering something akin to what we today may have referred to as "inner demons", and also needs to "trick death" through following the valkyria who protects him.

7.5: THE MAIDEN WITH THE MEAD THEME

In each of the cases summarized in chapter 6.1, the hero is married to or loves the valkyria. In Helgi Hundingsbani's, Sígurðr's and Gunnarr's case, the offering of mead is mentioned. Helgi receives the "precious drink" in the grave, and apparently drinks it together with Sígrún. Sígurðr receives the "memory drink" as a prelude to Sígrdrífa's teachings about the runes, their use and their origin.

The drink is mixed with the magical powers of charms, runes and songs. It is made from the power of earth, the cool cold sea, and the blood of the atonement/sacrifice.

Sígurðr learns how to heal, how to help women in childbirth, how to calm storms, how to turn enemies into friends, how to speak eloquently, and so forth. Later he is given practical advice about how to behave, and the choice of listening to his valkyria's counsel or not. In Gunnarr's case, the drink is just mentioned as a symbol of his amorous relationship to Oddrún. The Maiden theme is prominent in all the stories, and particularly detailed and informative in the Sígrdrífumál.

7.6: Ogress versus Valkyria; the Life and Death Opposition

The ogress Hrímgerðr declares that the only thing which saves Helgi and his men from drowning is the protection of the valkyriur. Above, I argued that Hrímgerðr with her "frosty embrace" was a representative of extinction in death. The valkyria is the opposite.

In the poem of Helgi Hundingsbani, the hero's forthcoming death is announced by an encounter with an ogress riding a wolf using serpents as reins. The opposition surfaces again in the Helreið Brynhildar, where Brynhildr encounters an ogress on the way to Hel. The ogress declares that Brynhildr has nothing to do in this realm, being from Valland – the Land of the Chosen - and a "goddess of gold", and besides, that she is pursuing another woman's man. The "other woman" would, in my opinion, not necessarily mean Sígurðr's human wife, but Hel, to whom Sígurðr now belongs.

However, Brynhildr, through eloquence, argues her way into Hel, making the ogress "sink" as she declares that she will be with Sígurðr for all eternity. It could appear that Brynhildr chooses to reside in Hel with Sígurðr. But the "sinking" may be akin to when Freyia tells Hyndla to "sink" when she carries the Mead of Memory to Óttarr, winning the deal in a plot where the goal is in fact said to be Valhǫll. The sinking of the ogress and the declaration of her sinking could equally well mean that she actually saves Sígurðr from Hel.

This idea seems to be strengthened by the case of Oddrún and Gunnarr. Oddrún dwells at Hlésey, the "Wind Shielded Island"[291], where, we may guess, the winds of the eagle Corpse Swallower do not reach.

Gunnarr has always been a weak man in the spiritual sense, unable to cross the fire of the valkyria and letting another man do it for him, hiding the truth from everybody else until it leads to disaster. But his love for the valkyria is sincere and wins him the love of the "younger sister" Oddrún. However, Gunnarr is unable to conquer her vicious kinsfolk. In the poems of the Helgi [Hallowed/ Sacred] characters, we see that the valkyria's kinsmen must be regarded as the hero's enemy, just as they are in the stories of Óðinn and Freyr.

---

291 From hlér – place shielded from the wind. A dwelling of Aegir the sea-giant in Skáldskaparmál.

The jǫtnar, from whom the valkyriur of the Edda poems always descend, are representatives of the hostile world of the giants and the forces of death.

Oddrún, perhaps as a consequence of Gunnarr's failings, is far away from Gunnarr when he is thrown into the snake-pit – the perfect image of devouring death if we recall the Vǫluspá's description of Hel's snake-infested well. When Oddrún hears the beautiful strains of his music, she rides as fast as she can, but not fast enough. It is too late now; Gunnarr has become the victim of the ogress of death.

The same sad theme is touched upon in the Helgakviða Hiǫrvarðssonar. Heðinn, Helgi's brother, meets an ogress mounted on a wolf, using serpents as reins. We have seen that such an ogress is the perfect image of Hel. Steinsland has suggested that Heðinn, when he refuses to walk with the wolf-woman, refuses initiation, for initiation takes you to the depths of death itself. [292]

I agree with this view; what Heðinn is refusing when seeing the horrible creature is the company and teachings of an ogress much like Hyndla, who taught Óttarr. This is also an explanation of why – and even an argument for - the disputed fact that Sígrún refuses Heðinn and decides to wait for Helgi's reincarnation. The Maiden will only open her arms to the worthy, the initiand.

7.7: THE THREE WORLDS OF TEACHING

In chapter 4.5, I argued that Óðinn's trials on the world tree encompassed not only his learning of runes, but also his learning of galdrar by a wise giant and his union with Gunnlǫð, who offered him the precious mead of wisdom, eloquence and poetry. His journey to Mímir's well of wisdom must have been a part of the same scenario. I argued that the three wells at which he learned – the well of Mímir, the well of Urðr (the runes were, ultimately, inscribed by the norns), and the well of Hel (Gunnlǫð's realm) - are really one and the same well, or aspects of each other.

The Fjǫlsvinnsmál, as argued in chapter 5.7 to chapter 5.10, could appear to confirm this thesis, since the three worlds beneath the World Tree – the realm of giants (the giant Fjǫlsviðr and the tree of Mímir), of the dead (barking dogs), and of the gods/norns (Menglǫð and her maidens) - appear in one and the same setting, as if they were just layers wrapping themselves around each other.

292 Steinsland, 1997, p. 146

The Sígrdrífumál would appear to strengthen this thesis further. Here, the knowledge of runes is certainly combined with the offering of mead by the Maiden, and Óðinn holding Mímir's [Memory's] head is mentioned in the same stanzas that describe his discovery and liberation of the hidden runes, which are poured over with sacred mead, running like liquid through his húgr, and finally sent into all worlds (6.1.4).

7.8: THE NUMBERS NINE AND THREE

The number nine and sometimes the number three are mentioned throughout all the Maiden-stories of chapter 4, 5 and 6. The number nine is obviously important in Norse mythology and usually in connection with feminine entities. The vǫlva of Vǫluspá simultaneously remembers nine worlds and nine giantesses (or troll-women) before the present World Tree rose from the ground.

The vǫlva Hyndla relates how nine giant maidens simultaneously gave birth to Heimdallr – the "Illuminating World". Rán, the giantess ruler at the bottom of the sea, is the mother of the nine daughters of Aegir, the sea-giant. In all these cases, the number nine is certainly in connection to giantesses.

However, the number occurs also in association with valkyriur. In the poem Sólarljóð, Stanza 79, we even hear of the otherwise unknown "nine rune-carving daughters of Njǫrðr".[293] Njǫrðr is otherwise known as the father of Freyia and Freyr. He resembles Aegir insofar as both are associated with the sea and with waves, and in the fact that he does not (originally) belong to the tribe of divine Aesir.

In the Heroic Poems, the milieu is strikingly maritime. The heroes travel by and fight at sea and often fight sea monsters (such as Hróðmarr, Hati and Hrímgerðr). Perhaps this is simply reflecting the Viking Age in which the poems were created. Yet as we have mentioned in the beginning of chapter 4, the ocean itself is often imagined as a realm of death, ruled by Rán, Aegir and their nine daughters. In these stories, the valkyriur act as protective spirits who protect their chosen heroes against the onslaughts of the ogresses.

293 "Hér ´ru rúnar, er ristit hafa / Njardar dætr níu" [Here are runes which have been carved by the nine daughters of Njǫrðr], Sólarljóð, Stanza 76. The poem is a Norse, but Christian "visionary poem" (Näsström, 1998, p. 171) reflecting a transition period where pagan imagery still had a strong impact on poetry. Bugge, 1965, p. 357-370

It is interesting that the valkyria Oddrún's dwelling is Hlésey. In Skáldskaparmál, Aegir is said to live on Hlésey, and even to have the name of Hlér himself – the Wind-Shielded. One could almost get the impression that the valkyriur – usually nine in number - somehow have come to resemble the nine daughters of Aegir or a different aspect of them. The association to the sea is obvious in the poems of the valkyriur. Since Freyia, Njǫrðr's - the god of winds and waves´ - daughter, is so intimately connected to the valkyriur – specialized norns (see chapter 3.4) - it is curious that at least one poet had the notion of Njǫrðr's nine daughters, who in the Sólarljóð obviously represent norns.

The number nine in itself makes it necessary to consider whether the group of nine valkyriur is connected to the nine primeval giantesses. This is interesting to our thesis which aims at showing how the Maiden hides behind both giant and divine beings. We may look back at the Maiden Gerðr in chapter 4.10 and consider how her father, Gýmir has been identified with Aegir. As Mundal, Ström and Näsström have argued (chapter 3.4), the collective of dísir (a term covering goddesses, norns, valkyriur, fylgjur, even giantesses) and the one great Dís are identical. The number nine used to describe the collective of valkyriur – or giantesses - refers to something crucial in the mythology of the Maiden.

Within the context of Maiden-mythology, the numbers nine is repeated:

☞ *Óðinn's nine-day trial on the World Tree*
☞ *The importance of the number nine is repeated in Snorri's version of the Gunnlǫð story, where Óðinn does the work of nine thralls on the fields of the giant Baugi [The Ring].*
☞ *Óðinn's nine great songs which he learned from his uncle and another nine which he made himself (all about how to entice and keep a certain "bright Maiden"*
☞ *Freyr's nine long nights of waiting*
☞ *Svípdagr's nine galdrar which took him to the Outer World*
☞ *Menglǫð's nine maidens.*
☞ *The valkyriur, as we have seen, always appear nine in number, or, alternatively, three by nine.*

So is the number three:
☞ *Óttarr's three nights in Hel*
☞ *The three nights Sígurðr spends with Brynhildr*
☞ *Three draughts were necessary for Óðinn to fill himself up with mead from all the three cauldrons, after spending three nights with Gunnlǫð.*[294]

The *number three* repeated *three times* is the number **nine**. According to Ström, the number **nine** symbolizes the stage between life and death. The number **three** also appears in the amount of time Óttarr has to learn his lessons in the Underworld and in the number of nights Sígurðr spends with Brynhildr. The number **three** is also associated with female beings; the **three** thurse maidens who instigated the creation of humankind, and the **three norns** who carved the runes of fate in the beginning of time. It is impossible to decide exactly what the number nine means in Norse cosmology, but our study of Maiden-mythology may give us a clue as to what it means within the context of initiation.

We are starting to see that a theme of immortality in one form or another appears to be present in the Maiden stories. To look for an explanation about the nine days/nine maidens/three draughts by three nights theme, we should glance back at the idea of the nine primeval giantesses, the iviði, as worlds.

The Norse cosmos know of many worlds – realms [heimir]. The Grímnismál accounts for about twelve worlds. Snorri counts eleven, but many more worlds are mentioned here and there throughout the lore. Some of these worlds are higher even than those of the gods; they belong to the light-elves. Some of these worlds, we may assume, are not subject to the force of death: for Hel rules only in nine worlds. [295]

As the story of Hermóðr shows, the road to Hel takes nine days.

It is no coincidence that Freyia rules in the ninth world,[296] to where her chosen dead arrive.

---

294 Ström, 1954, p.84. Ström uses the poem Sólarljóð as an example, where a person sits nine days on the norna stólr –the chair of the norns- before he is taken to the realm of the dead by a horse. Ström compares this with Hermóðr traveling nine nights before he reaches the gates of Hel.
295 Gylfaginning
296 Grímnismál stanza 14

The giant Vafþrúðnir [Powerful Head-Veil] is so wise because he has been in nine worlds beneath Níflhel,[297] but cannot beat Óðinn, who knows the secret to immortality. The giant don's name itself could provide the clue to what this really means on a deeper level; for he seems to represent illusion itself. Perhaps it is only in the nine mortal worlds that illusion may exist, alongside death?

43.Vafþrvðnir qvaþ:
„Fra iotna rvnom
oc allra goða
ec kann segia satt,
þviat hvern hefi ec
heim vm komit:
nio kom ec heima,
fyr niflhel neðan,
hinig deyia or helio
halir."

43. Powerful Head-Veil said:
"About the runes of the jǫtnar
And of all the gods
I can speak truly
For I have been
in every world
To nine worlds I came
Beneath Misty Hel
Where the dead come out
from Hel."

The "ninth world" where Freyia receives the chosen dead, keeps half and sends the other half to Valhǫll, is perhaps the uppermost – or shall we say the innermost - realm where death is a rule. We have several times touched upon the idea of a realm of immortality located in the heart of darkest Hel, a theme perhaps repeated in the place Hlésey, a place of no "winds" right in the middle of giants´ ocean. There, Freyia, the Great Maiden, receives the dead, but within Maiden-mythology at least, she does not receive any dead. She receives the chosen, the worthy, and their afterlife is different from that of Hel-dwellers.

---

297 Vafþrúðnismál stanza 43

8: Masters of Initiation

Margaret Clunies Ross has argued that "myth is rarely, if ever, merely an explanation of religious usage. It has independent life even when closely associated with ritual and needs to be considered a cognitive system in its own right that has its own communicative and affective dimensions."[298] Approaching the theme of myths´ relation to ritual, Clunies criticizes the functionalist's "concentration upon the social relevance of myth to the relative neglect of intellectual and communicative aspects".[299]

I agree that myth may be read on its own and understood on its own terms without necessarily tying it up to concrete ritual behavior. In chapter 8, I will further explore some of the numinous meanings of the Maiden myths outside of the context of ritual.

However, as we saw in chapter 3.3, many scholars have been able to detect patterns or themes within Norse myths and sagas that would seem to reflect actual ritual.

In chapter 4, 5 and 6, I have shown how I perceive a single, underlying structure of themes behind several different Divine and Heroic Poems. Conclusively, I will argue that the structure follows a pattern comparable to that of a typical initiation as described in the "Encyclopedia of Religions" (chapter 3.1). In the context of initiation, Eliade here speaks of "masters of initiation", elders or religious professionals of different types who will guide and teach the neophyte. In this chapter, we will explore the teacher and helper figures that appear in the Maiden myths, asking ourselves whether these characters have counterparts in the "real" world of Norse religious practice.

If they do, their role as teachers and guides in the poems could very well reflect the role of religious practitioners during rituals or experiences of initiation.

---

298 Clunies Ross, 1994, p. 14
299 Ibid, p. 15

8.1: THE VǪLUR

In the poems Hyndluljóð and Gróagaldr, we meet three supernatural female beings. Hyndla is a giantess residing within the rock-layers of Hel, Gróa is the ghost of a woman who knows galdrar, and Freyia, we know, is a goddess often associated with love and fertility, but also with seiðr and death. However, all three of them have strong associations to the vǫlur, sg.f. vǫlva – women who are known to have roamed the Norse societies functioning as sibyls or oracles, and as practitioners of seiðr and galdrar, among other things. Not much is known about the real vǫlur, but there are numerous saga descriptions which seem relatively credible, and the association between seiðr and divination is very clear from sagas such as Eiríks Saga Rauða, Örvar Odds saga and Hrolfs saga Kráka, among others.

Snorri's Ynglinga Saga and many other sagas make it clear that vǫlur were associated with black magic as well. A vǫlva could be capable of moving beyond her body and acting in geographically distant places. One vǫlva was also known to be able to fill the bay with fish in times of dire need. The vǫlur would carry staffs, from which their title derives – Vǫl means "staff" or "wand". Simek interprets the title as "wand-bearer".[300]

A mythical vǫlva is mentioned in the Edda poem Vǫluspá [The Vǫlva's Divination] where she is associated with seiðr and gandr [magic], as well as with a sacrifice which we shall discuss in chapter 8.3 as a possible trial of initiation for the vǫlva.

The vǫlva's main art was seiðr, an art which in Örvar-Odds saga included nightly preparatory rituals and, according to Eiriks Saga Rauða, included the calling of spirits by a magical song. In Hrolfs saga Kráka, it involves deep breathing and strange facial grimaces.

The rituals described in the sagas have been discussed as examples of shamanism, a theme we touched upon in chapter 3.1. In that section, we observed that Britt Solli, using Åke Hultkrantz's definition of shamanism, argued that the séance of seiðr in Eiríks Saga Rauða could be interpreted as an example of Norse shamanism.

---

300 Simek, 1996, p. 367

Others, like Jan Peter Flood, have argued that the lack of a drum is an argument against shamanism in the Eiríks Saga ritual.[301] To this argument, I would argue that Wilmos Dioszegi observed the existence of several so-called "staffed shamans" during his ethnographical study in Siberia. The use of a staff instead of a drum was very common among female shamans, who by the help of the staff alone could enter the desired trance – a feat observed and filmed by Dioszegi himself. Male shamans would often use a staff before they acquired the drum, but some would stick to the staff most of their lives.[302] Flood's "drum argument" against shamanism in Norse society, thus, becomes irrelevant in the light of more information about "classical Siberian shamanism".

It should be said that the divination rituals of the völur may also be related to ancient traditions of oracles and oracular divinations, traditions that were central to many European cultures reaching back into the Bronze Ages.

Whether the vǫlva was a Norse version of a "staffed shaman" or and oracle, or not, she was certainly an important and respected personage in Norse society and is to be considered among the last of the Pagan practitioners in Scandinavia. These wise women were specialists in seiðr and probably in galdrar which, as Näsström and Solli have shown, are closely related to each other.[303]

Now, Freyia the goddess was the first divine teacher of seiðr, that art which, according to Snorri, contained the most power although it implied some "unmanly" behavior in the case of male practitioners.[304] This fact in itself could probably make of Freyia a vǫlva, however divine.

---

301 Solli, 2002, p. 131, and Steinsland, 1997, p. 134, assume that the völur actually had drums. But in his dissertation, Flood, 1999, p. argues that there is no evidence for this.
302 Diószegi, 1968, p. 229-241, p. 255, p. 309
303 Näsström, 2001, p. 57, Solli, 2002, p. 131
304 Ynglinga saga 7, Gyldendal 1944, p. 6

Gróa, on her side, performs galdrar, an art also associated
with seiðr and the vǫlur. Besides, a Gróa is encountered in the
Gylfaginning, where she is explicitly called a vǫlva who heals by
drawing the piece of a weapon out of a wound by singing galdrar.
In the case of Hyndla, her speech of sacred ancestry takes upon
itself eschatological dimensions much in the manner of Vǫluspá,
and is indeed called the "Short Vǫluspá" by Snorri. This title would
certainly identify Hyndla as a vǫlva.[305]

Now, the three ladies should be regarded as supernatural
creatures in the poems; however, the role they play as teachers,
advisers, and guides on the way through the Underworld would
certainly befit that of a master of initiation. It is not completely
impossible that real vǫlur played such roles in rituals and trials
of initiation. Certainly, the Hrolf Saga Kráki relates that the vǫlva
Heiðr had apprentices with her, both female and male.

8.2: ATLI, SINFIǪTLI AND SKÍRNIR

Atli is the son of king Hiǫrvarðr's earl. It is he who woos Sígrlinn
for the king, spending a winter in the realm of Svafnir. It is he
who listens to birds´ speech in the grove and carries the message
of sacrifice to the king. Again, it is he who takes the king up to
the mountaintop and to the river, from where Sváfaland may be
reached, and he who enters this realm of sleep or death while
guarding the king by the riverside at night, bringing back the
Maiden. All the actions of Atli contain the seeking of visions and
the journey into the Other World, as well as the magical ability to
understand birds´ speech.

Tacitus explained that Germanic tribes read omens in birds and
other phenomena, and that this was particularly related to sacred
groves, an art undertaken by kings or priests.[306] We may remember
that it is only after Sígurðr has come quite far in his initiation that
he may understand birds' speech, a prelude to his learning about
healing, magic and eloquence. His wife, Guðrún, also knows bird
speech, and as we have seen, she represents a woman's side to the
path of the initiation.

---

305 Steinsland, 1997, p. 135 speaks of a "volve-gyger" (völva-giantess) as an
initiator.
306 Mattingly, 1970, p. 109

It is noteworthy that Atli is the son of the earl. English "earl" and Norse "jarl" is derived from the Old Nordic word erilaR, which according to Näsström supposedly indicates "priest", "rune-master", "magician", showing the original sacral function of what should later develop into the title "earl" (jarl).[307]

In Stanza 20 of the Poem of Helgi Hiǫrvarðsson, Atli is mocked for having been castrated. This is a feature Atli shares with Sinfiǫtli, Helgi Hundingsbani's elder brother. Sinfiǫtli's role in Helgi Hundingsbani's poem is somewhat vague, but the importance of his character in the tradition is testified in the Frá Dauða Sinfiǫtla and in the Vǫlsunga Saga. The latter saga reveals that Sinfiǫtli, after proving that he can bear excruciating pains, was sent by his mother to the forest to live with his father (and mother's brother) Sígmundr Vǫlsung and share his exile.

Sinfiǫtli shows his ability to handle poisonous serpents without fear, and the father-uncle and son start living like wolves and actually changing into wolves´ shapes, howling like wolves and understanding the sounds. In the shape of wolves, they attack the men of an evil king whenever they can. In this state of being, they are able to understand the messages of weasels and ravens, and learn about healing arts from the animals.

They also have to stay in an underground dwelling when the time comes to shed the wolf-skins, which they then burn. After being restored to society, Sinfiǫtli accompanies his father-uncle when he marries and begets Helgi Hundingsbani. Both the fact that Sinfiǫtli is the child of a brother and sister, and his experiences while in "exile" in the forest, his mysterious castration and his sexual relationship to a certain Guðmundr, a man who has been both woman, mare and valkyria, make Sinfiǫtli a very marginal and special character. Although the son of a king and queen, he never appears to aspire to kingship himself.

Sinfiǫtli comes to take the role as assistant to Helgi, accompanying his younger brother and prince on his warrior's quest. He leads the initial argument of insults before the battle against Sigrún's kinsmen, the giants. During this argument it is revealed that Sinfiǫtli too, is castrated. When Sinfiǫtli dies, as related in Frá Dauða Sinfiǫtla, his father-uncle Sígmundr carries his oldest son's corpse on his back until he reaches a river -the shores of Hel- where a ferryman takes possession of the body while Sígmundr returns to the living.

---

307 Näsström, 2001, p. 69

Atli, Sinfiotli and finally Skírnir, whom we encountered in chapter 4.8 - 4.13, all share a common trait: they all master the art of venturing into the Other World. There is one character in the history of religions whose main task, according to Eliade, is the travelling into the other worlds with his soul: the shaman.

The shaman does so through so-called "techniques of ecstasy", means by which he enters a state of trance through which his soul may leave his body and fly into the other spheres of existence, such as the worlds of the dead and of the spirits.

Atli and Skírnir both have the role of "wooing the Maiden" for their royal friends: Atli woos Sígrlinn for king Hiǫrvarðr, Skírnir woos Gerðr for Freyr, the "King of Men". They both return to their lords with the messages from the Other World. In Atli's case, he finally succeeds in bringing back the Maiden for his king (and even a maiden for himself!). Sinfiotli does not woo the Maiden for Helgi Hundingsbani, but like Atli does for Helgi Hiǫrvarðsson, he accompanies his lord-brother to the world of the Maiden's kinsmen, the giants. That world could certainly also be said to be an "Other World" than the normal.

The information about castration in the past, in Sinfiotli's case undertaken by three þursa meyiar – "thurse maidens" - is puzzling and cannot be explained with any certainty. It does bring to mind, however, the idea of ergi associated with seiðr when practiced by men. Indeed, the great god of seiðr, Óðinn, calls himself Ialkr – the "Gelding", in Grímnismál stanza 49, and is also called so in the Gylfaginning.

Seiðr has often been disputed as a kind of Norse shamanism, but it has not been proven that the practitioners of seiðr were experts of soul-journeying, as Atli, Sinfiotli and Skírnir could appear to be. The "techniques of ecstasy" could easily be read into Atli's vision quest in a grove, on a mountain top or by a river at night, into Sinfiotli's shape changing, dwelling in the wilderness, learning healing from birds, and handling serpents.

It could also be perceived in Sígmundr's accompanying Sinfiotli to the shores of death, a very common task for a shaman. [308]

---

[308] Eliade, 2004, p. 205-214: "The Shaman as Psychopomp"

The activities of these three characters certainly are remindful of those of classical shamans, and, through the castration theme, we do see a possible link to their arts and the practice of seiðr. Except for the vǫlva, who cannot be proven to travel into the other worlds, it has been difficult for scholars to find any traces of "real shamans" in Norse society, a splendid argument against "shamanism" in Norse religion.

I suggest, however, that the figures of Atli, Sinfiǫtli and Skírnir reflect on a pagan practice which may be culturally unique, but which in vital ways resembles shamanism as an ethnographic umbrella term, and also resembles a more general religious office in service of royal patrons.

8.3: THE MATERNAL UNCLE

The Hávamál reveals that Óðinn was taught nine powerful charms by the "son of Bǫlþorn [Harm Thorn], Besla's father". Besla, as we know from Snorri, was Óðinn's giantess mother. That makes Bǫlþorn's son a giant, and Óðinn's maternal uncle. He is obviously well-versed in spells and connected to the journey Óðinn undertakes while hanging on the world tree. Another maternal uncle met with in the "Maiden myths" is Grípir, who is "wiser than everyone else and prescient", ruling over many lands. Sígurðr seeks his uncle for advice and divination.

As with the vǫlur and the three "Other World-experts" above, a link to seiðr may once again be suggested, since divination appears to have been one of the major purposes of seiðr. According to Näsström, seiðr is the form of divination that we meet in old Scandinavian religion.[309] The image of the maternal uncle may hold ancient symbolic implications.

Tacitus declared that most Germanic peoples considered the maternal uncle as responsible for his sister's children as the father – in some tribes the maternal uncle was even more important.[310] Sígmundr also has a role as teacher for the young Sinfiǫtli in the Volsunga Saga. He is Sinfiǫtli's father, but at the same time his maternal uncle. Sígmundr's journey to the river of death, carrying Sinfiǫtli's corpse, is certainly a very typical shamanistic feat.

---

309 *Näsström, 2001, p. 57*
310 Mattingly, 1970, p. 118

8.4: REGINN: DWARF, SMITH AND ÞULR

"...we would expect also to find examples in the literature of dwarfs acting as initiation masters, and this is in fact the case. Perhaps the most famous example in Old Norse tradition is the dwarf Reginn, foster father, educator, and initiation master for Sígurðr (...) Reginn may be seen as Sígurðr's main initiator, but, as Marold points out, there are several other figures, such as Grípir, Hníkar or Fjǫlnir, and the old man with the beard in the Volsunga saga, who advise and guide the hero through his various trials."
[311]

In Fafnismál stanza 34, Reginn is called ínn hára þulr –the "hoary þulr". A þulr is an ancient designation of a religious office, connected to the verb þylja, which means to "mumble, recite, chant".[312] The þulr is also mentioned in the Hávamál Stanza 111, where is also mentioned a þularstol – the "chair of the þulr"- placed by the well of Urðr, from where an I - person (the þulr) declares that he will recite the sacred lessons that he has heard in the Hall of the High One by the norns´ well. The main lesson that the þulr relates is the nine-night trial on the World Tree, described in I – form as if it were the þulr himself who experienced them. The possibility of the þulr being the actual initiand on the World Tree, and not Óðinn, has led some scholars to suggest that the þulr was a kind of shaman.[313]

If we dismiss this theory, the name and function of the þulr would at least reflect a bard-like sacral office: a priestly character whose task is to recite in sacral connections. Indeed, Reginn does act like a bard both in the Reginsmál Stanza 26 and in the Fafnismál Stanza 23, praising the warrior's deeds of his prince. In addition to his identity as þulr, Reginn is said to be a dwarf in the prose introduction to Reginsmál, and shown as a smith in the prose interpolation between the poem's Stanza14 and 15.

311 Grimstad, 1983, p. 195
312 Näsström, 2001, p. 70. Haugen, 1983, p. 20
313 Solli, 2002, p. 157

Lotte Motz has put forward the thesis that the dwarfs of Norse myths, as well as the smith-figures of Germanic legend, are the poetical memory of a very ancient type of priesthood connected to artisanry, craftsmanship, and grave-tombs. The dwarfs, who also are smiths, resemble such a priesthood through their functions in the stories, pictured as a race of (apparently mostly unmarried) men dwelling in rock and mounds, not seldom burial mounds, forging treasures for gods and men, thus being in the service of the divine and human ruling dynasties.

In addition, they play the role of healers and teachers, well-versed in magic and mythical lore. They frequently change shape into animals, they are the temporary keepers of the mead of poetry, and through their names, we learn that they are closely associated with chanting and reciting. They appear as sages, possessing knowledge of the past and of the future.

They fit right into the pattern of a pagan priest, being craftsmen at the same time.

The combination is, according to Motz, not at all unknown in the history of religions. The fact that the Norse word for dwarf, dvergr, does not denote a short stature, but a physical damage, and that the German word for smith, schmied, does not denote a metalworker, but a "creator", convinces Motz of her own thesis.

The "damage" alluded to in the word dvergr could refer to a mutilation during initiation, a concept reflected in the myth of Óðinn tearing out his eye for the sake of a draught of the mead of wisdom.[314] Both Motz and Kaaren Grimstad consider Reginn a typical "master of initiation" in the story of Sígurðr[315]. His role as Sígurðr's teacher and guide in the poems in which, as we have shown, the structure of themes may indicate a tale of initiation, convinces me that this is the case.

---

314 Motz, 1983, Introduction, p.1-12, p.87-121
315 Grimstad, 1983, p. 187-205

8.5: ÓÐINN

In chapter 4.6, we concluded that Óðinn as god of creation played the role of divine archetype in the many stories of his initiation. Such a divine archetype is the role model, the example, for the human beings who wish to undertake similar trials in order to learn similar lessons.

We have noted shamanistic traits in Óðinn and in his initiation, as well as in the "masters of initiation" described above. Diószegi emphasizes the role of the "shaman ancestor" in Buryat shamanism where the shaman ancestor – the first of all shamans - is in fact the main master of initiation appearing in the neophyte's dreams and visions.[316]

In the Reginsmál, Óðinn miraculously appears in the middle of the stormy ocean, counseling Sígurðr on his way. Óðinn, the god who first undertook the trials of initiation in the beginning of time, thus plays the role of a master of initiation, quite in the manner in which a shaman ancestor would direct the shaman neophyte.

---

316 Diószegi, 1968, p. 110-114

9: THE MEAD AND THE MAIDEN

48 (…)Hveriar 'ro þer
meyiar,
er liþa mar yfir,
frodgediaþar fara?"

48 (…) Who are the
maidens
who travel as one, so wise
in spirit
across the waters?"

49. Vafþrvðnir qvaþ:
„Þriar þioðár
falla þorp yfir
meyia Mꜹgþrasiss;
hamingior einar
þer er i heimi ero,
þo þer meþ iotnom
alaz."

49.The Powerful Head-Veil
said:
"Three flock-streams
fall/run across the Earth
They are the Kin-Seeker's
maidens
Hamingjur they are
who dwell in the world
although they were raised
among giants."

9.1: THE MAIDEN: ENCOMPASSING THE THREE WORLDS

Giantess, goddess and valkyria - as we have shown in the previous chapter, a "Maiden figure" offering mead to the hero after trials of initiation encompasses all three functions. The jǫtnar – a term usually translated as "giants", but which really means the "devourers", are usually understood as the enemies of the gods, representatives of the chaos before the gods ordered the world, and the ultimate destroyers of the gods.

However, as Steinsland has shown, giants, particularly giantesses, were also objects of cult and sacrifice.[317] The giantesses do play an ambiguous role in Norse mythology, being the mothers, wives, and lovers of the gods. In the Grǫttasǫngr, two giantesses called Fenia [Heath Dweller] and Menia [Necklace-Bearer][318] tell their own story. Growing up for nine winters, deep within the earth, the giantesses finally emerge, shaping the rocks and then throwing the "fast rotating rock boulder" – either meaning the Earth herself or else the millstone of fate, into the hands of humankind.

317 Steinsland, 1986, p. 212-220
318 Simek, 1996, p. 79-80, 211

The giantesses proceed to moving among the armies of men, allotting victory to some and death to others. When they come into the possession of king Fróði [Wisdom] they start "grinding" the millstone of destiny towards peace and plenty, making possible the Fróðafríðr [the Peace of Wisdom (see chapter 6:3)], until they realize that they are being abused for the sake of insane greed.

This realization, combined with the memory of their glorious past, incites the giantesses to grind once again invasion, war and un-peace, as a warning to Fróði [Wisdom] to "wake up" and listen to their ancient tales. Fenia and Menia would actually seem to play the roles of valkyriur and of norns, from the way they allot victory and death, moving among the warriors, and from the way they "grind" the fate of the world. Their giantess-hood is explicitly stated in the beginning of the poem and identifiable in their having formerly dwelled far beneath the ground.

Gunnlǫð and Gerðr also dwelled far beneath the rock layers, but Gerðr is invited out of that realm and into the divine one through marriage. As we have seen, Gunnlǫð and Gerðr could appear to be identical since both stand out as the same Maiden with the Mead character. According to the Grǫttasǫngr, as soon as the giantesses "emerge" from beneath, they become like mistresses of fate – like norns and valkyriur.

What, then, is the usual relationship between valkyriur and giants? In chapter 6.3, we saw that the valkyriur were situated in a realm of the dead before they were discovered and taken out of there by heroes such as Atli and Sígurðr. The realm is recognizable both through its names, its rulers and the symbols of "giant in eagle's disguise" and great serpent. Among other known valkyriur, there is Hljóð in the Vǫlsunga saga, the daughter of the giant Hrímnir [Frosty One]. [319]

She is also referred to as Óðinn's óskmey – "wish maiden", and in his service. In chapter 7.8, we saw that there was a certain resemblance between the collectives of valkyriur and giantesses as related to giant fathers. It could certainly appear as if the valkyriur were daughters of giants. The valkyriur also have giant "suitors". The valkyriur are often identified as a specialized type of norns. The norns, as the valkyriur, have a "questionable" past. In the Vǫluspá stanza 8, three þursa meyiar – thurse maidens (giantesses) - powerful and much knowing, emerge while the (male) gods are having fun in their recently ordered cosmos.

---

319 Simek, 1996, p. 158: "The one covered with hoar-frost". Volsunga saga 1, Byock, 1999, p.36

The arrival of the three female representatives of the older, giant world mysteriously causes the gods to create the dwarfs and the humans. As soon as the humans are created and the World Tree is presented in the poem, the theme of three maidens is repeated, only this time, the maidens are identified as norns, Urðr, Verðandi and Skuld, allotting the fate of men, carving runes into the wood.

We do not, of course, know for certain that the three giantesses of Stanza 8 are identical with the three norns of Stanza 20. In my opinion, such identification appears logical. Both events instigate major changes in the universe having to do with destiny.

In the Vafþrúðnismál stanza 49, we hear of Mǫgþrasir's [Kin-Seeker's] Maidens", owning three rivers that flow through the world. They are hamingjur and travel through the world, "even through they were born among jǫtnar".

A hamingja is considered the personified fate of a person. In modern Icelandic, it just means "fortune" or "luck" and is used to congratulate people, but going back a thousand years, the hamingja was an entity within the pagan religion and worldview. The word comes from ham-gengja, which originally referred to people who could make their hámr – their soul independent of their body – walk, yet this understanding appears to have vaned, and hamingja was understood as "fortune giver" in the late Viking age, thus closely associated with fate.[320]

Thus, the hamingja could be compared with the fylgja [f.sg: Follower] which has also, by some, been identified as the soul when it is separate from the body.[321] The most common descriptions of fylgjur, however, suggest that they are more like a kind of personal norns, like the ones that Snorri claimed would rise from the Well of Origin at the birth of a child, follow them through life and shape their lifespans, or else as a kind of guardian spirit, often seen in dreams or by people with supernatural powers. It could appear either as an animal or as a woman.[322] Else Mundal has shown that there is a fundamental difference between the animal fylgjur and the woman ones.[323]

320 Simek, 1996, p. 129
321 Simek, 1996, p. 96
322 Ström, 1985, p. 205-206
323 Mundal, 1974

The animal fylgjur appear to echo the personality and status of the human it follows, while the woman fylgjur are more like norns. The idea of a woman guardian spirit (see chapter 3.1) is combined with the idea that the fylgja and the hamingja control the person's fate. In the Gylfaginning, Snorri relates how everybody has a "norn" who is present at the individual's birth and who decides his or her fortune through life. These norns (of the individuals) "come from" the well of Urðr, the oldest norn.

Snorri apparently understood these "norns" of the individuals as aspects of the original cosmic norns. In my opinion, the norn of the individual that Snorri mentions, the hamingja and the fylgja may be overlapping concepts. The woman fylgjur may be called by many other words or words in combination with other words, and -dís [goddess] is the most common combination word in terms describing the fylgjur, next to fylgja itself.

Turville-Petre counts the valkyriur among the other dísir such as hamingjur and fylgjur as guardian spirits.[324] The valkyria, a kind of norn, certainly fits into the picture of "guardian spirit", since she follows and protects her hero and, in many ways, directs his life, as we saw in the case of the two Helgi characters, where the valkyriur appear to remind the hero of his duties and guide his way.

Turville-Petre and Ström (see chapter 3.1) have made connections between the fylgjur – dísir and the soul-concept. This is a very disputable theme,[325] but that the valkyria – dísir could be associated with the soul, in some way or other, does seem to be apparent in the theme of reincarnation where, as Kragerud showed, a big point is made of how the hero and the valkyria belong together even after death and into the next life.

A similar theme was touched upon in the story of Menglǫð.

The idea of the valkyria-Maiden as – perhaps - the hero's own soul, or at least closely associated with his soul, would certainly give us a new understanding of Maiden mythology. If that was the case, it could seem as if the point of all the trials is that the hero has to wake up the sleeping valkyria of his soul.

---

324 Turville-Petre,1975, p. 221-235. Ellis-Davidson, 1998, p. 177 believes the concept of valkyriur as guardian spirits belongs to an older tradition.
325 Else Mundal, 1974, criticizes such notions in her work on the fylgjur of Norse literature because they seem very difficult to prove on the basis of the sources themselves.

Apart from this last possibility, we are aware that there could be a very strong connection between the valkyria-norn, the fylgjur and the hamingjur. They are all associated with fate, and they could fit neatly into the picture of individuals´ norns mentioned by Snorri.

Thus, the hamingjur who are associated with the three great rivers and who "travel through the worlds", could be norns and/or valkyriur. In Vafþrúðnismál Stanza 48, the question about Mǫgþrasir's maidens is "who are the maidens who journey as one, wise in spirit, over the sea?" The valkyriur of the Heroic Poems are also described as a collective of maidens "riding air and sea". Indeed, the norns and the valkyriur are often depicted in this dynamic manner. In the Vǫluspá stanza 33, the valkyriur are seen, as they emerge for the first time in history, as "ready to ride the world". In the first poem of Helgi Hundingsbani, norns arrive at Helgi's birth and perform a dance-like, dynamic action of throwing and fastening the threads of fate. The Hárbarðsljóð stanza 18, tells of maidens who dig the ground out of the valleys, spinning threads of the sand. Among them is one, the "linen white", whom Óðinn greatly desired.

All in all, I believe that Mǫgþrasir's maidens could be identified as norns or valkyriur, and, importantly, like the valkyriur and the vǫlva of the Vǫluspá, "they were born among giants."

As the Maiden figure hides behind stories of giantesses wooed by the gods in the beginning of time, and behind stories of the later valkyriur wooed by men who were blessed by the gods, we could perhaps detect the myth of a once-giantess who became a goddess, a goddess capable of appearing in many shapes at one and the same time, spinning the fates of the individuals.

We should not forget that the valkyriur – as well as fylgjur and hamingjur - are often called dísir, a name used also of goddesses such as Freyia Vanadís. As remarked in chapter 3.4, the term dís is derived from old Indian Dhisana, a goddess who was one goddess and many goddesses at the same time. When appearing as many, their name was the dhisanas.

As Ström and Nässtrom have argued, the same type of concept is shown in the Norse tradition through the existence of a Dísarsalinn, a building used during the great ritual gathering in honor of the dísir, where the king had to be present. Although the dísir were a collective of female deities, the hall was dedicated to the one Dís, probably the "Great Goddess".

The implication of a Great Goddess, here called "the Maiden" who is a giantess in origin, opens up for many more discussions. I will here mention only two, both of which have been touched upon throughout this study.

☞ *One: the theory of the three wells that are really one, as discussed in chapters 4 and 5.*

☞ *Two: the theme of ogress versus goddess opposition. The latter leads me to a conclusion that has to do with the well-known "promiscuity" of the Great Goddess Freyia.*

9.2: THE TWO-FACED GODDESS

8.Maʹgr fann aʹmmo mioc leiþa ser, hafði haʹfda hvndrvð nío; enn aʹnnvr gecc algvllin fram brѵ́nhvít bera biorveig syni:	8.*The son found grandmother to be a horrid sight; Nine hundred heads the old woman had But another woman went forth all-golden bright browed, carrying ale-drink to her so* Hymiskvíða 8

I have earlier argued that the poems Hávamál, Fjǫlsvinnsmál and Sígrdrífumál suggest that the three wells of norns (gods), Mímir (giants) and Hel (Death) are the same, or aspects of each other. The hero learns at all the three wells simultaneously. The Maiden holds residence in Hel and is a teacher of runes (the norns), and the descent to her world is associated with Mímir's tree and well of memory.

A giant always guards the Maiden, whether he be her father or her warden. One of these giants, Suttungr, was compared to Mímir in chapter 4. The Maiden encompasses the three worlds where the hero receives sacred knowledge and sacred marriage. Since the Maiden appears to reside in Hel, or rather in a special, bright place deep in the heart of dark Hel, it is reasonable to question what kind of relation she has to the lady of the dead. Since she is a giantess of origin, it is not unlikely that she, in one aspect, is Hel.

We have shown how the Maiden is shown in opposition to an ogress of death, representing an alternative. The Skírnismál poem could give us a clue as to what exactly is the relation between the Maiden and the ogress; there, Gerðr is shown two alternative modes of existence, one as an ogress gaping behind the gates of death, deprived of the company of all but hideous ogres, another as a divine bride in possession of the most precious treasures of the gods. It is clear that the ogress and the divine bride are one and the same; Gerðr.

Of course, we know that Gerðr married Freyr and became equal with the goddesses, but it is useless, in my opinion, to read myth as if it were linear history. Gerðr is much more than a girl pressed into marriage with a god under threat of becoming an ogress. Gerðr is one of the names behind which the Maiden hides, and her marriage to Freyr should be read symbolically.

In other settings, the Maiden is married to Óðinn, to Óttarr, to Svípdagr, to Helgi, to Sígurðr, to Gunnarr - and in each case, she is shown in opposition to the ogress of death, her alternative mode of being. As Hilda Ellis-Davidson has pointed out, it is not unusual for the Great Goddess to appear both as an old hag and a beautiful maiden.[326] Svava Jacobsdóttir shows how, in the Irish sources that are equivalent to the Norse Maiden myths, the Maiden herself often appears as an old hag until the hero agrees to marry her. Through an analysis of both Irish and Indian sources, Jacobsdóttir concludes that more than kingship inauguration was involved, the idea of an immortal existence must also have been present in the myth of the mead-offering lady.[327]

The image of Hel that Snorri provides us with in the Gylfaginning 34 is extremely valuable, for he tells us that the face of the mistress of the dead is blue as death on one side, pink as life on the other:

☞ *Hon er blá hálf, en hálf með hörundarlit.*

☞ *She is half blue [death colored], and half with the color of life.*

The symbolism should be obvious; Hel is both life and death. The simplest explanation of the hero's trials in the Maiden's realm could be this: When visiting the Underworld with all its monsters and trials, the hero must "marry" the rosy-cheeked face of Hel, the Maiden, in order to return to the world alive.

---

326 Ellis-Davidson, 1998, p. 22
327 Jacobsdóttir, 2002, p. 51

The experience or ritual of marriage with the Maiden could carry in itself more implications still, such as the possibility of a hope of an alternative after-life in Óðinn's Valhǫll, where warriors are continually revived so they may serve the gods or in Freyia's friendly and serene Fólkvangr [People Field] rather than extinguishment in the dark, serpent-infested Misty Hel.

Obviously, as we have shown in the previous chapters, the marriage also included esoteric teachings that would enable the hero to function as a healer, poet, sorcerer, a religious professional and even as a king.

In the Hyndluljóð, we see that a wolf-riding giantess, whom Freyia addresses as "sister" and "girlfriend" in the beginning of the poem, is the conveyer of secrets.

In other cases, such as in the Sígrdrífumál, the bright valkyria is the teacher. There is certainly no strict border between the ogress and the Maiden – the two faces of the goddess. Their pairing and their opposition is present in all the stories in some way or other:

1. Gunnlǫð married to Óðinn versus left by Óðinn
2. Gerðr married to Freyr as an ásynja, versus as an ogress not married to Freyr
3. Freyia versus Hyndla
4. Menglǫð versus Sínmara
5. Sígrlinn married to Hiǫrvarðr versus living in Sváfaland
6. Sváva versus Hrímgerðr
7. Sígrún versus "Kolga's sister» or versus the fylgja who rides a wolf with serpent reins
8. Sígrdrífa/Brynhildr versus the "Bride of the Rock Caves"
9. Oddrún versus "Atli's mother"

9.3: THE GREAT LOVER

30. Loci qvaþ:
„Þegi þv, Freyia!
þic cann ec fvllgerva,
era þer vamma vant:
asa oc alfa,
er her inni ero,
hverr hefir þinn hór veriþ."

30.Loki said:
"Shut up, Freyia,
I can truly account
For all your failings;
Of the gods and the elves
Who are seated here
Each one has been your
lover.
---Lokasenna

Gro Steinsland has argued that the idea of death held great variety in the Norse sources.[328] One idea often ignored by scholars, who, like Snorri, prefer to order the mythic cosmos into neat geographical lines and human-like family relations ("the land of the dead here, the land of giants there, this goddess the wife of that god, this of another"), is the experience of death as an "erotic journey of pleasure".[329]

Through poetry, dying is imagined as a feast and a marriage or erotic union with the mistress of death. In women's case, it would appear to be conceived as a feast, like the girl who wanted to "sup with Freyia" in the Egils saga.

In chapter 9.2, we suggested that Hel and Freyia, or the ogress and the Maiden, are two faces of the same entity. Freyia, of course, is known as a receiver of the dead in her own right – her link to Hel is shown through the "Maiden-mythology" that we have been analyzing in this study.

Now, Freyia is often presented as "goddess of love".

This title, it seems, stems from the fact that Freyia is perceived as "promiscuous". In the Edda poem Lokasenna, she is accused of having slept with every elf and god in the hall of Aegir the sea-giant, and even with her own brother Freyr.

In the Gylfaginning, Snorri can tell us that she liked romantic poems and that she was accessible to people concerned with love. Another source, the Flateyjarbók, relates how Freyia, there the fríðla [concubine] of Óðinn, slept with four dwarfs in order to have the beautiful necklace Brisingamen [Gem/Necklace of Flames]. This information, apparently, has been enough to classify Freyia along with Aphrodite and Venus as goddess of sex and love.

---

328 Steinsland, 1992, p. 319-332
329 Ibid, p. 319

However, accusations of promiscuity are something Freyia shares with all the other goddesses in the Norse pantheon, and her roles as receiver of the dead, of being a vǫlva or a sacrificial priestess [blótgyðja] are rather more particular and prominent in her character and special to herself, than her sexuality or her romances.

Medieval Christian interpreters may have focused on the immoral behavior of the pagan goddess, and failed to realize the meaning and the depth of her loving embrace.

If we look back to the Lokasenna, we must remember that the gods are feasting in Aegir's hall. That hall is a realm of death. Aegir is the giant of the sea.

Freyia is also associated with the sea through her name Mardöll – "Illuminating Ocean". [330]

Aegir's wife is Rán, who catches the drowned ones in her net. Dying at sea was associated with a feast in Rán's and Aegir's Hall, and by "climbing Rán's bed".

When Freyia, receiver of the dead, has been the lover of every elf and Áss in that hall – a hall where the winds of death cannot reach, shielded from mortality, in fact a "hall of immortality, this is a piece of information that reaches beyond Loki's superficial accusation of promiscuity.

Let us not forget that the most detailed description we have of Freyia's relationship to a verr – one of her many "men" or lovers – is found in the Hyndluljóð (see chapter 5.1-5.3), where the relationship clearly centers around the "lover's" path towards wisdom by entering the world of the dead in the shape of a boar, which Freyia rides down into Hel, and where the primary goal for the journey is to reach Valhǫll.

Likewise, the goddess Iðunn, who is the sole reason for the eternal resurrection and thus immortality of the Aesir gods, is also referred to as Ása Leika – the One Lover of All the Gods, in the skaldic poem Haustlǫng.

---

330 Simek, 1996, p. 202 : "the one who illuminate the sea", or "who makes the sea swell"

Her embrace is death. In her role as "Maiden", she embodies
the alternative to the net of Rán and the serpents of Hel. Her love
provides her "lover" with a new beginning. And as Näsström has
argued, her person embodies all the goddesses. In that case, she
cannot be other than the lover of all the gods.

Sketch of the gold foil depiction of
idealized women from Ekerö/Helgö,
Uppland, Sweden (SHM 25075/
1101). Swedish History Museum,
G. Jansson/ CC BY 2.5 SE (a); ©
Swedish History Museum, C. Åhlin/
CC BY 2.5 SE

9.4: THE PRECIOUS MEAD

*And the Holy Spirit...took Zoroaster`s hand and filled it with
liquid all-encompassing knowledge and said "drink it". And
Zoroaster drank it, and all-encompassing wisdom was blended within Zoroaster...and he was in the Holy Spirit`s Wisdom
for seven nights.---(Zand Wahmand Yasht 3 6-12)*

*"Oh, you Golden One, I invoke your intoxication...All other
intoxications bring the violence...but Haoma`s intoxication
brings blessed justice...To you, Haoma, the just, to you who
provokes forth the Truth!"---(Yasna, Avesta, 9.17, 10.18, 11.10)*

*"Ahura Mazda the Holy Spirit, creator of just bodily existence,
took Zoroaster`s hand and poured into it liquid all-encom-
passing wisdom, and said: "Drink it"...and Zoroaster drank
it, and all-encompassing wisdom was blended into Zoroaster.
Zoroaster was within the wisdom of the Holy Spirit for seven
nights...on the seventh day, all-encompassing wisdom was
removed from him..."---(Zand Wahmand Yasht, 3 6-12)*

The Drink of Precious Mead [drykk hins dyra miaðar], the
Sacred Mead [helga mjǫðr], the Ale or Drink of Memory [minnis
aul, minnis drycc, minnis veigr], the Poetry/Ecstasy/Inspiration
Stir [Óðrerir] - thus is the drink called that the Maiden offers to
the hero. It seems possible to decode where the drink comes from,
mythically. First and foremost, the Maiden is associated with the
three wells below the World Tree.

Now, we know that Óðinn obtained a drink from the well of the
giant Mímir, the drink of memory and wisdom, by sacrificing one of
his eyes. By hanging nine days on the World Tree, he achieved the
runes, which were carved by the norns who dwell at Urðr's well, and
he received the precious drink of Poetry Stir. All evidence suggest
that he received it from Gunnlǫð in the realm of the dead.

The drink appears to be somehow connected with the three wells
and the three worlds beneath the World Tree. We do not know how,
but Gylfaginning and the Grímnismál give a clue. In the Grímnismál
stanza 36, the valkyriur are named who give ale to the einherjar –
the One-Harriers. In stanza 25, we learn that the "fair mead" that
never diminishes is milked (presumedly by the valkyriur) from a
goat called Heiðrún.

As Else Mundal has pointed out, this goat has a central function in
the continuation of life in Valhǫll and is thus very important for the
safety of the divine cosmos, whose defenders the One-Harriers are
supposed to be.[331] Standing on the roof of Valhǫll, Heiðrún (whom
we earlier identified with Freyia) eats from the tree Læráðr [Harm
Counsel] while filling a whole vat of mead every day, enough to keep
the One-Harriers eternally revived and feasting.

Next to the goat stands a stag who also feeds on the tree, and,
from its horns, drops fall down into Hvergelmir, Hel's serpent-
infested well. Since Hvergelmir is situated at the foot of the World
Tree, it becomes obvious that the tree Læráðr is the World Tree
itself, from which the goat Heiðrún eats. The mead of Heiðrún is
directly linked to the well of Hel through the stanza 25 and 26;
obviously, the eating produces the precious liquids from the goat's
udders and the strange drops from the stag's horns. The goat's mead
goes to the eternally living One- Harriers, the stag's liquid falls into
Hel. Both liquids are taken from the World Tree.

---

331 Mundal, 1992, p. 241

Now, from where is the World Tree nourished? Snorri tells us that it is nourished by the norn Urðr, who waters the tree every morning with water from her sacred well at the heart of the divine world. That well from which the tree is watered, has the effect of revival and renewal, even transformation; anyone who bathes in it comes out shining and transparently bright. The water keeps the tree from decay.

Ultimately, the mead of the One-Harriers, served by the valkyriur, is taken from that well of renewal. Something, obviously, is given back to the well of Death by the stag standing next to the goat, a symbolism too intricate to be discussed here. Turning our focus back to the goat, we are reminded that her name means something like Bright Opening/Clearing within the Darkness [heiðr] and Hidden Knowledge, Secret or Symbol [rún], and that she is compared to Freyia in the Hyndluljóð. The comparison makes sense since we have established Freyia as the Great Valkyria, the one to whom the valkyriur take the One-Harriers before the goddess allots seats in her own hall and in Óðinn's.

From this information, we learn that the mead is connected to the three wells and that it is somehow drawn from them through the leaves of the World Tree by an entity who has the shape of a goat but who could equally well be the Great Goddess.

The mead has a transformative effect and keeps the drinkers eternally alive. It is associated with "hidden knowledge". It is associated with memory and knowledge. Through the Maiden-mythology, we learn that it is strongly associated with memory of what is taught in the Other Worlds, that it conveys secrets of the cosmos, the knowledge of runes, fate, healing and poetry. As Sígrdrífa said, it is filled with good charms and runes of pleasure, manliness and power. It is offered by a goddess to a man who is her lover. The goddess may also be an aspect of his soul or his individual fate.

The mead is also described in Guðrúnarkvíða önnur stanza 23, where it is said to have been made of, or empowered by, exactly the same formula that we find in Hyndluljóð 38 and which describes what empowers the god who represents the living, sentient, watching and listening universe itself; Heimdallr [Illuminating World]. Both the mead and the universal being are empowered by the power of earth, the cool, cold sea, and the blood of the atonement [són], which was another word for sacrifice [blót].

Much more is not revealed about the nature of the mead in the poems themselves, but it is described as bright, golden, precious, sacred From chapter 3.2, we recall that Sváva Jacobsdóttir compared Snorri's version of the myth of Gunnlǫð with an Old Indian myth of Soma, sacred drink of the Vedic religion. Soma was also known as madhu ("honey") which is etymologically connected to the Norse mjǫðr – mead. In some myths, soma was in possession of the dhisanas, hypostases of the great goddess of intelligence, and "wives to the gods", which would certainly link Indian myth to Norse myth, where the mead is in possession of the dísir.

May the wives of the gods, the goddesses
connected with the All-gods
place thee on the abode of Earth
May the Dhisanas, the goddesses
connected with the All-gods
cook thee on the abode of Earth...
Do ye, O goddesses, place this sacrifice among the gods
Do ye, invoked, drink the Soma...
Ye Dhisanas, that are strong, be strengthened,
gather strength, and give me strength...
O Mother, come forth, thy unerring, watchful name
O Soma, to that of thee, O Soma, to Soma, hail![332]

A whole book (the ninth) is dedicated to soma in the Rigveda, and the hymns are many thousands of years old.[333] According to Brockington, a belief in an intoxicating beverage of the gods, a kind of honey or mead, probably goes back to the Indo-European period. Brockington also draws a parallel between the Indian legends of the eagle and Soma, the nectar-bringing eagle of Zeus, and Óðinn in eagle's shape fetching mead.

The preparation and the offering of soma was a feature of Indo-Iranian worship, known in Iran as haoma. As a deity, Soma is a sage, a poet, a seer, stimulating thoughts and inspiring hymns. As a drink, it invigorates the gods, and is conceived as conferring immortality on gods and men and is called amrta, the "draught of immortality".[334] The drink also produced ecstasy and was used by ascetics for inspiration. The ecstasy it caused could soar into the atmosphere, into the company of gods, enable one to see everything and go anywhere.[335]

332 Yayur Veda, 1.4, 4.1
333 Brockington, 1996, p. 7
334 Ibid, p. 16-17
335 Ibid, p. 16-17

In a list of universal polarities, Soma is placed against Agni alongside with "moon", "death" and the "female" as opposed to "sun", "life" and the "male".[336]Within the schools of Kundalini Yoga, Soma is placed in the topmost cakra, being the quintessence of the body, its "nectar of immortality".[337]

The initiates of Eleusis in ancient Greece had a password they needed to say before entering the temple of the Mysteries: "I have fasted, I have drunk Kykeon."[338]

In Greek mythology, the sacred drink of the gods is called Ambrosia (ἀμβροσία); it is related to Sanskrit amrita and means "immortality". It is identifiable also as Néctar (νέκταρ), which means "Overcoming Death" [from nék – "death" and tar – "overcoming"]. In Greek mythology, goddesses offer this drink to gods - and also to mortals, such as when Heracles receives the drink from Athena. And it can be used to restore youth and cleanse the body of all defilements. Just like the Norse gods, the Greek gods drank this liquid in order to achieve immortality through repeated rejuvenation. The probable origin of a ritual use of Ambrosia or Nectar is lost in myth; later Greek texts usually refer to Ambrosia as a metaphor for any delightful and cleansing liquid used in cooking, botanic works or medicine.

A drink was, however, served during the Mystery initiations of Eleusis: Kykeon [Mix, Stir]. Apparently, this drink was made from water and barley and other natural substances. Kykeon was used to break a nine day fast and provided the climax of the initiation experience, when the initiate followed in the footsteps of the divine grounder of the Mysteries: the goddess Demeter, who broke her fast after nine days of searching for her daughter, with this drink.

The Kykeon was said to be used by the sorceress Circe, who blended into it honey along with a magical potion. It has been proposed that the Kykeon used during the Mysteries, was imbued with psychoactive substances so as to provide a climax to the initiation experience. Since the drink was based on barley, it has been speculated that the drink received its particular powers from the ergot – a fungus which grows on barley, the sacred corn of Demeter.

---

336 Ibid, p. 129
337 Ibid, p. 156
338 D´Alviella, 1981

By mixing this fungus with water we will produce a mild hallucinogen not unlike LSD. The temple of Eleusis was carved and painted with images of mushrooms and poppy – the plant used to produce opium. The Minoan religion that preceded the Eleusinian mysteries also knew a poppy goddess, and there are good reasons to believe that the Minoans used an opium-blended drink to reach communion with the goddesses and the gods. (The temple of Eleusis was said to have been established by Minoan refugees after the destruction of the Minoan culture around 1400 BC).

As Michael Enright has argued, ritual drinking has its origins in an Indo-European past. The soma and the haoma and the "nectar" of Greek myths are met with again in the myth and culture of the Celts and of the Germans. According to Enright, the particulars of Germanic ritual drinking originated in the Celtic ones.

We recall that Jacobsdóttir compared Norse myth to Irish ones. Enright shows how the Celtic and Germanic traditions were connected during the Celtic Iron Age. The Celtic and Germanic sources show that ritual drinking was strongly associated with a woman and/or with a goddess, as was the case in many Old Indian myths, and often with kingship inauguration.

9.5: THE MAIDEN UNEARTHED: ARCHAEOLOGICAL EVIDENCE

Michael Enright looks to European archaeology when trying to trace the history of the Germanic "liquor ritual" with its "lady with a mead cup" at its center. Going back as far as the fifth century B.C, Enright traces burials of great, high ranking Germanic ladies buried with wine-strainer, spoon-sieves and ladles in hand. Close to these obvious liquor- serving devices are cauldrons, cups and drinking horns.

Sometimes the cauldron contains remnants of a drink, either made of barley or honey and always with a wide variety of herbs and fruits. These ladies were buried in such a way "as to suggest both her respected functions as distributor of drink as well as her high social status". Males are also buried with drinking devices, but only the women are left with spoon-sieves and devices for serving the drink – in their hands. The devices are left in their hands and in their belt alongside the keys that conveys their status as lady of the household. It becomes obvious from the rich burials that the status of great ladies was symbolized by their serving of drink.

The evidence of a "lady with a mead cup" and "liquor ritual" are trans-regional and pan-European, reaching from southern Europe to Scandinavia and lasting for at least a millennium. The control and distribution of alcoholic drink was closely linked with high-born women. Enright sees a link between the lady, the drink and "fictive kinship". This because the ladies are very often accompanied by a kind of drinking vessel called either Ringgefässe or Drillingsgefässe. The vessels are too elaborate to have ever been suitable for ordinary usage.

From inscriptions, it is clear that these were ritual vessels used for the "creation of fictive brotherhood and sisterhood".[339] The Ringgefässe design found in Germanic graves has its origin in the eastern Mediterranian, "where they have been connected with fertility cults and the idea of a mystic marriage with a goddess."[340] The Drillingsgefässe are found among many cultures throughout the world and were already being crafted in the late Neolithic. The vessels were used for liquor that would run simultaneously through three different cups and are connected to the Celto-Germanic triple mother goddesses through finds in shrines and temples dedicated to these "Mothers".

The Ringgefässe consist of three cups/vessels standing on one ring. All the cups are connected to each other so that the same liquor runs through the three vessels at the same time. It is of course a bit speculative, but I am certainly reminded of Gunnlǫð's keeping three vessels containing the same mead – that Óðinn drank from after swearing a ring-oath.

The link between the vessels to women and a "mother cult" continues into the migration period. Enright argues that the finds confirm later texts indicating that women among the Germans were regarded as "having a special responsibility for the public ritual creation of brotherhood."[341] Scholars agree that the vessels possess a pronounced religious or magical significance. Enright draws a line from the women and the vessels to a goddess cult, more specifically a cult of a prophetic goddess which emphasizes reverence for a staff-bearing prophetic goddess.[342]

---

339 Enright, p. 107
340 Ibid, p. 107
341 Ibid, p. 108
342 Ibid, p. 113

I have underlined the last words because they are extremely interesting in the light of the next chapter. Enright speaks of a "prophetic women's´ cult" which possessed the same attributes in across many regions associated with Germanic people in particular. The contours and subtleties of the cult are unclear, but the archaeological finds reveal that the connection between women and various peculiar looking staffs and containers have long traditions in southern Germany going back at least to the fifth century B.C. and perhaps into European pre-history.

The "cult staffs" accompany the ladies of the mead and the ritual vessels, as well as spinning and weaving equipment which, as Enright shows, links the woman to fate and divining. The staff, as well as the spoon-sieve and the vessel, "must (...) have had a symbolic association with leading women".[343]

The staffs are always found in women's or girls' graves, together with other objects which could easily be interpreted as magical. The links between women, staffs and cultic drinking vessels are manifold and ancient. Enright argues that the association with prophecy and the magical arts and high-ranking women was constant for more than a millennium in the Germanic world. "Neither the antiquity, continuity, intensity nor popularity of the woman/liquor/prophecy complex can now be seriously doubted".[344]

In Germanic society, he claims, the concept of aristocratic femininity was strongly correlated to the distribution of liquor. The association of women and liquor and ritual drinking has its natural explanation in the fact that brewing ale and preparing mead were the peculiar tasks of women. But the archaeological evidence also demonstrates that prophecy was a crucial part of the mead-cup motif. The links to staffs and magical objects should also lead us to ask whether the distributor of liquor was also a prophetess. Enright argues that archaeological evidence demonstrates the answer as positive.

343 Ibid, p. 113
344 Ibid, p. 125

Enright's approach is historical and sociological, trying to explain the archaeological evidence of the existence of "professional", high-ranking ladies who serve mead and carry staff and spindle whorls by their political function in society. Primarily, Enright argues that the lady had an important role within the warband where she established brotherhood and hierarchy through ritual offering of drink. The lady who stands out as a queen in late Migration period (such as the time of the Beowulf poem), has her equivalent in "prophetesses" who operated alongside kings in early Germanic society, who originated as "tribal matrons".

For my own work here, Enright's summary of archaeological finds is valuable because it shows the antiquity and popularity of the idea of a magical female and the ritual serving of mead. Enright sticks to his sociological explanation, of which he has proof, yet he admits that there are subtleties within the religion of the staff-bearing women's´ cult (and thus, the mead-serving women's) which are difficult to interpret.

Enright emphasizes the continuity, the antiquity of this wide-spread cult.

My own interpretations and conclusions about "Maiden-mythology" lead me to assume that the imagery of the Maiden with the mead in the myths somehow reflects at least some part of this "cult" (meaning a sub-religion within a greater religion, like Tantra within Hinduism).

Since I have interpreted Maiden-mythology as centered around initiation rites, I cannot agree with Enright that the only main purpose of the Lady with mead was to establish brotherhood and hierarchy in the warband.

It certainly may have been one of the purposes, while the teaching and initiation into sacred knowledge must have been another. The important thing here is that the archaeologically and materially proven, historical existence of ladies serving mead ritually in actual Germanic society would indicate that the Maiden of the myths had her human counterparts.

The other objects, such as the cult staff, the spindle-whorl related to fate and divination, and the magical objects (probably kept in pouches) indicate that she was a religious professional. There is only one woman character in the Norse sources who is definitely connected to the carrying of staffs and the art of divination and sorcery, and that is the vǫlva.

9.6: THE ULTIMATE MASTER OF INITIATION

21.Þat man hon fólkvíg
fyrst í heimi,
er Gullveigr
geirum studdu
ok í höll Hárs
hana brendu;
þrysvar brendu
þrysvar borna,
opt, ósjaldan,
þó hon enn lifir.

21. She remembers the war
The first in the world
When Gold Drink
They hoisted on spears
And in the Hall of the High
They burned her
Three times they burned
The three times born
Often, not seldom;
Yet she still lives.

22.Heiði hana hétu,
hvars til húsa kom,
völu velspá,
vitti hon ganda,
seið hon hvars hon kunni,
seið hon hugleikin,
æ var hon angan
illrar brúðar.

22.She was called Heath/
Bright/Clearing
when she came to the
settlements
the well-divining vǫlva
She knew how to make
magic [gandr]
She made seiðr wherever
she could
She made seiðr with a
passionate soul
She was always loved
By the bad brides.

In the Vǫluspá stanza 21 and 22, the first war in the world, that between Aesir and Vanir, is associated with the arrival of a vǫlva called Gullveigr and then Heiðr. She is burned three times in the hall of Óðinn and survives every time.

She proceeds to operate in society as a wandering figure performing seiðr and teaching it to the women. Somehow, this is connected with the war between the Aesir and the Vanir, a war which had as its ultimate consequence that Njǫrðr, Freyr and Freyia took up residence as gods among the Aesir, that the mead of poetry was created, and that Freyia teaches seiðr to Óðinn.

The mead of poetry is created and lost, with the subsequent quest undertaken by Óðinn in order to retrieve the mead from Gunnlǫð. Thus, our subject of the Maiden with the Mead is intimately connected with the Aesir-Vanir war and its mysterious instigator, the vǫlva Gullveigr.

Many interpretations have been presented as to the nature of Gullveigr-Heiðr. Näsström declares that Freyia herself must be hiding behind the names, and that her function here is to infiltrate the stronghold of the Aesir with witchcraft, and even if they try to kill her, she returns, continuing her destructive plan, first and foremost through demoralizing the women. Already while operating within the Aesir's fortress, the Vanir gods break down the fences of the gods, entering with their galdrar - songs of victory.

Gullveigr, Näsström decides, must mean "Gold-thirst", which shows her greed for gold, while Heiðr is simply a common name for a sorceress.[345] Clunies-Ross also identifies Gullveigr with Freyia through her role as vǫlva (practitioner of seiðr) and of sacrificial priestess. Gullveigr, Clunies-Ross argues, is sacrificed, and there is a connection between her operations before the war and her arrival at the end of it. Gullveigr and Freyia perform the same mythological functions.

The reasons for the violent treatment of Gullveigr have to do with what she represents in relation to the Aesir. The Norse cosmos is divided into polarities where male and female is one of them. The Aesir are fundamentally male, representing the ordered and reasoned world. Gullveigr is female and a master of sorcery, which makes her appear threatening to the Aesir. According to Clunies-Ross, she offers herself and her arts to the Aesir, but they will have none of it. Their stabbing her with spears is a symbolical penetration leading to death rather than the kind of penetration leading to fertility desired by Gullveigr and the Vanir.

The treatment of Gullveigr led to the war – apparently the Vanir were angry on behalf of their kinswoman.[346] According to Steinsland, Gullveigr may represent the three stages of the cosmic process of time; that she is killed three times and born three times may mean that she is present in each of the stages: the three norns by the well beneath the tree, Urd, Verðandi and Skuld, testify with their names a model of time divided into three.[347]

---

345 Näsström, 1998, p. 68, p. 91, p. 128

346 Clunies-Ross, 1994, p. 204

347 Steinsland, 1991, p. 290. Urdr is made of verda- to become, while verdandi means "becoming", and skuld marks the future form of the word.

Gullveigr IS the Golden Drink

As I see it, the problem with such interpretations as those above is that they go very far beyond what is ever actually said in the text. Snorri does not mention the Gullveigr story with a word, just as he omitted the sacrifice of Óðinn. The Gullveigr myth may, as Clunies-Ross has suggested, like the sacrifice of Óðinn simply have been "too pagan" for him. Thus, we really do not know why Gullveigr was sacrificed, stabbed and burned.

The terrible treatment of the mysterious woman has obviously made scholars puzzled and appalled, causing a need to explain why ("she was greedy, she was a witch, she threatened the male order, she demoralized the women"). Both Näsström and Clunies-Ross also seem to forget that in the Vǫluspá, it is Óðinn and not the Vanir who starts the war, which make the explanation about the Vanir waging war because they got angry about the treatment of their kinswoman rather awkward.

Steinsland's interpretation aims at a deeper understanding of the symbolism of the stanzas, but it does not explain how Gullveigr suddenly appears under a new name and operating as a religious professional, a vǫlva, just after her sacrifice.

Näsström sticks to the common notion that Gullveigr means "greed for gold", denoting the evil character of this woman, an idea which is also seen in Rudolf Simek's dictionary, where she is said to be "the personified greed for gold".

Turville-Petre was among the scholars who first presented this idea. Apparently, this is the common understanding among scholars today.[348]

However, as Simek and Clunies-Ross recognize: the literal meaning of the name is simply "Golden Drink", "Golden Intoxication", or "Gold-Power".[349] The mead of poetry or the precious mead itself is very often referred to as both golden, and as a veigr.

---

348 Simek, 1996, p. 122. Turville-Petre, 1975, p. 159. Various scholars such as Müllenhof, Krause, Nordal and Turville-Petre have explained the name as "the drunkenness of gold, hence the madness and corruption caused by this precious metal" (Clunies-Ross, 1994, p. 204)

349 Simek, 1996, p. 122, Clunies-Ross, 1994, p. 204

None of these interpretations actually denotes "greed" at all.

Gold is not always associated with greed in Norse mythology; on the contrary, the Skáldskaparmál shows that **gold is often associated with poetry and numinous wisdom**. The three possible interpretations of her name that are literal translations, not conjectures, basically identifying her as the Golden Drink, are rather in accordance with the image of the Maiden with the Mead, who is all golden, serving a mead of power.

To assume that her name indicates greed for gold is actually an assumption that has no foundation except in the scholars' wish to explain why Gullveigr "deserved" her bad treatment.

As we have argued, Gullveigr's treatment did not lead to the Vanir, her people, declaring war, but to Óðinn throwing his spear against the enemy (the Vanir) after a counsel with the other gods about who should "have the sacrifice". We do not know what sacrifice they are arguing about, but in my opinion, it is not unlikely that it is that of Gullveigr.

And this is where we should take a closer look at the sacrifice.

It is not necessary to make conjectures about what reasons lay behind the stabbing and burning of Gullveigr and who did it. The important information is right there in the poem itself. The important information is that Gullveigr defied death. She was burned to ashes three times, and reborn every time.

Gullveigr is presented as a woman who defies the lot of all mortal creatures: death.

Hoist on a spear, burned three times, she comes out alive, reborn. In my opinion, the trials undergone by Gullveigr reflect Óðinn's trials on the world tree. My idea seems strengthened by the fact that, after her trials of death, she is presented as a practitioner of seiðr in the society, or more generally, as a religious functionary, something that would logically follow any such death-trial initiation. Her new name is Heiðr, meaning "Bright One" or "Shining One".[350]

This is also in accordance to the Maiden's usual bright, beaming, golden characteristics. The results of all these events are:

☞ The arrival of the vǫlva who teaches the women who would otherwise have been "bad brides", those not fit for wifedom

☞ The arrival of Freyia and her art of seiðr

☞ The creation of the precious mead itself.

---

350 Simek, 1996, p. 135: Heiðr, f. means "light", "beaming", or "fame". The masculine noun Heiðr means "heath", "honour". The "light"-meaning semantically fits Gullveigr´s name best, according to Simek.

Gullveigr could be a goddess, or she might have become one after her trial. Gullveigr reborn as Heiðr is said to be a vǫlva - a type of office that certainly existed in the Norse society; thus, we could be seeing a person, a woman, who challenges the gods' monopoly on immortality as the first human being in the world to do so. The quest for immortality is certainly not unknown in the history of religions, and defying death is known in its most violent forms among the initiation trials of shamans and mystics all over the world. The gods, of course, are terrified; one of their creatures, a mortal, has conquered death itself. Such divine terror of human potential is known from many myths across the world, such as in the Genesis and in the Popol Vuh.

Or, since the gods are not immortal, but only owe their eternal resurrection and rejuvenation to the grace of the goddess Iðunn, as theme surely testified in one of our oldest mythological source, the Haustlǫng, she may have been the first among them to walk the path towards immortality. Gullveigr could then be seen as an equally supernatural creature as the gods from the start. The gods and giants of Norse cosmology are, after all, not eternally immortal, although they stay young for eons due to the apples of the goddess Iðunn.

Gullveigr shows an art that Óðinn coveted, the art of changing fate – the ultimate date; the art of conquering death. The art is closely connected to seiðr, which not only encompassed divination as a foretelling of the future, but also functioned as operative divination – where the future, fate itself, could be altered.[351] Fate, ultimately, is death for all mortals. Seiðr in its most advanced aspect could have been a means to change that ultimate fate.

This would more easily explain Óðinn's subsequent action of throwing a spear against the Vanir, thus starting the war. Óðinn's throwing a spear at someone is an action that represents a "kind of magical power the god possessed that would dedicate those warriors to himself as future inhabitants of Valhǫll."[352]

He wanted Gullveigr and her associates to come to Ásgarðr.

The war led to the trio of Njǫrðr, Freyr and Freyia entering the Aesir's world, and Óðinn got what he wanted: Freyia's teachings of seiðr and the creation of the precious mead.

---

351 Näsström, 2001, p. 62, argues that seidr and divination could be active and "operative" – where the practitioner could realize his or her desires through divine help if she/he had sufficient magical power.
352 Clunies-Ross, 1994, p. 206

When Clunies-Ross argues that Gullveigr was killed because the Aesir did not want the sorcery she represented, she must have ignored the fact that Óðinn himself caused the war that led to the possibility of his learning exactly what Gullveigr represented, and that he eagerly enough learned it and taught it to the other gods, who must have been quite interested, too.

Thus, the "aggression" against Gullveigr emerges in a different light.

We do not have to look for "aggressors", nor for their reasons.

The "they" who stab and burn her could be just like the "they" who did not give the stabbed and hanged Óðinn drink nor food – "they" could be those who assisted the initiand in her and his trials.

That it happens in the hall of the High One indicates that Óðinn observes the trial – and desires the same abilities. Both Óðinn's and Gullveigr's death-trials and sacrifices lead to their becoming operating professionals: Gullveigr becomes a wandering vǫlva performing seiðr and teaching the women, Óðinn becomes a much-sought sage whose words and actions lead to more words and more actions, and who teaches the priests.

In her study on Sumerian mythology around the sacred marriage of the Great Goddess, Anita Hammer points out that, while the older Sumerian religion knows of a female "culture hero", namely Inanna, who undertakes a journey to the realm of the dead and other tasks that shape culture, later Greek and Teutonic mythologies only know of male "culture heroes".[353]

This is the common conception, and scholars have argued how the Norse ordered, human and divine world is conceived of as male in essence, whereas the world of giants is female in its essence. This would explain why the "culture hero" is always a male - the representative of "this side" is usually male - while the representative of the "other side" is a female.[354]

However, it could appear as if Óðinn, Freyr and all the heroes had their predecessor when it comes to trials of initiation and the conquest of death.

And she was not a male.

---

353 Hammer, 1999, p. 83
354 Clunies-Ross,1994, p. 128-129, Heide, 1997, p.

9.7: SALVATION AND THE ELEUSINIAN MYSTERIES

We have often touched upon the theme of resurrection from death in this work, or, by another word, salvation. Many may think that "salvation" is a Christian concept, but this concept existed by the very same terms many centuries before Christ, mostly associated with the classical Mystery Cults.

Concepts of salvation and alternative, blissful afterlives abound in ancient, Pagan religions, preceding the Christian concept of salvation by many centuries. Classical sources speak of ancient Greek concepts that appear to have similarities to Old Norse concepts, as we shall see.

According to the Greek story-teller Homer, who lived some time during the ninth century BC, the blissful afterlife realm was called the Elysian fields or Elysium, and had a particular geographical location here in Earth, described as a place where heroes and other mortals belonged.

Later sources describe the place as an afterlife for the blessed, the righteous, those chosen by the gods, where they could live a blessed and happy life indulging in their favorite pastimes. The poet Hesiod [7th century BC] described Elysium as the "Isles of the Blessed" and as the "Fortunate Isles", whereas Pindar [522-443 BC] spoke of a single island. Elysium is sometimes described as an island, or as various isles, but also as a plain or as fields. All describe the place as one of bliss, beauty, peace, pleasure and of music, art and inspiration. Many describe it as a place where good people are rewarded after death.

The Roman poet Virgil [70 BC-19 BC] claimed that there were two paths where souls go after death:

"Here comes the place which cleaves our way in two: Thy road, the right, towards Pluto´s dwelling goes, and leads us to Elysium. But the left Speeds sinful souls to doom, and is their path to Tartarus the accursed." [Aeneid].

In the same work [the Aeneid], Virgil describes Elysium in further detail:

"In no fixed place the happy souls reside. In groves we live, and lie on mossy beds. By crystal streams that murmur through the meads...all the shining fields below. They wind the hill, and through the blissful meadows go."

The Classical concepts of Elysium were intimately connected to the Classical Mysteries. The Greek word mysteria simply means "to initiate" – and the Mysteries were schools of initiation, sometimes called "cults" (Mystery cults) or "religions" (Mystery Religions). The oldest, known European Mystery School was situated in Eleusis near the city-state of Athens. The city-state itself supported the Temple economically.

The Temple of Eleusis originated in a very ancient, cultic center of goddess worship primarily devoted to Demeter, the mother goddess, and her daughter Persephone, the corn maiden. Archaeological finds show that the iconography of the goddesses and their symbolic attributes (the sow, the mare, the serpent, the cow, the hallucinogenic mushroom and the poppy, among other things) reach back thousands of years into prehistoric times around the area of Eleusis.

Yet, the Temple and the Mysteries were said to have been introduced by emigrants from Crete, survivors of the catastrophe that destroyed the Minoan empire during the 15th century AD. Like the labyrinthine temple of Knossos in Crete had once been a thriving center of pilgrimage for Bronze Age Europe, Eleusis became a similar center of religious pilgrimage for the next two thousand years, until it was destroyed by Christian invaders (Goths, actually) in 392 AD.

Between the 15th century BC and the 4th century AD, approximately two thousand people from all over the Classical world were initiated every year during the annual nine-day festival of Demeter at Eleusis. Both genders and all classes – even slaves – were admitted and could participate in the Mysteries, which also had three stages, one higher and more secret than the other. Most people were content with the first stage, where most of the procedures were quite public, except for the personal revelations that were supposed to happen during the climax of the initiation ritual.

An ancient myth of how Demeter searched for her daughter, who had been abducted by Hades, the Lord of the Underworld, provided the great myth of the Mystery, where the initiate would walk in the footsteps of Demeter for nine days and nights, fasting and submitting to various trials. It was said that the myth was a disguise for deep spiritual truths that could only be revealed to the initiate and which would not be truly understood by those who had not experienced the initiation.

The true meaning of the myth would be revealed step-by-step to the initiate during the re-enactment. After the initiation, the reborn initiate would perceive the world, life, fate and death, in a different manner, having become purified and reached a higher state of awareness and knowledge. The initiate would now be able to know a different fate in death – a fate that would lead their soul to Elysium rather than to dark Hades. As such, the Mysteries provided a Pagan kind of salvation.

According to Goblet D´Alviella[355] the theology of the Mysteries went through different stages. He based the theory of the stages on the written evidence: the degree to which it is possible to prove that a concept existed at a particular time. I would say that the only thing the written evidence proves is that we have the first written evidence for a concept at a certain time – it is entirely possible that the concepts themselves existed a long time before they were written down, or that similar concepts were written down in texts that are now lost to us.

The earliest evidence we have for a concept of resurrection and rebirth during initiation is dated to the 9th century BC, where the highest purpose of the initiation at Eleusis was a kind of salvation where the initiate could look forward to a blessed and bright existence after death. During the 6th century BC, we have the earliest evidence that the cult of Dionysus, earlier a cult open to women only, was integrated into the Eleusinian Mysteries.

At the same time, we find evidence of the so-called "Orphic Doctrine" as an important part of the Mystery revelations. The Orphic Doctrine was a Pantheist doctrine teaching that all gods and goddesses are but aspects of the great Supreme Being, called the Universal Life, the Universal Being, the Supreme Spirit or the All-Soul. The individual souls of people are temporary, separate parts of the original All-Soul.

At Eleusis, the goddesses Demeter and Persephone, as well as the god Dionysus, are all mythological expressions of the All-Soul, the Ultimate Being. This Pantheist revelation was at the heart and core of the secret teachings that would be integrated into the soul and knowledge of the initiate during the initiation. It was no less than a school of salvation, where salvation involved the union of the individual soul with the Universal All-Soul.

---

355 Goblet D´Alviella (1981): The Mysteries of Eleusis – the Secret Rites and Rituals of the Classical Greek Mystery Tradition

THE CRYSTAL FIELDS

Þórr qvaþ:
21.«Segðv mer þat,
Alvíss!
oll of rauc fira
voromc, dvergr! at vitir:
hve þat logn heitir,
er liggia scal,
heimi hveriom i?»

Þórr spoke:
21."Tell me now, All-Wise!
about everything in life:
I expect, dwarf, that you
know:
what is that Tranquility called
that shall lie
within every world?"

Alvíss qvaþ:
22«Logn heitir meþ
monnom,
enn Logi meþ goðom,
kalla Vindslot vanir,
Ofhlý iotnar,
alfar Dagseva,
kalla dvergar Dags
Vero.»

All-Wise spoke:
22"Tranquillity it is called
among humans
Quenching among gods
Wind-less among Vanir
Death-Air with the giants
Day-Ceasing among elves
Day-Peace among dwarfs."

---Allvìsmàl, st. 21-22, Poetic Edda

Old Norse equivalents of the Elysian fields actually abound. There is the golden hall of the goddess, and there is Valhǫll, both places where resurrection take place. They may be identified with or perhaps be points of entry into the shining fields of immortality that appear in other terms such as the Glasisvellir, meaning the Shining Fields. These fields are also encountered in the Helgi poems, then called the Rǫðullsvollr, which means the same.

There are also other concepts in Norse mythology such as the Ódainsakr, literally the "Field of the Immortals", as well as the Iðavǫllr, a field where the "streams return to source" – in fact the place where the gods once met in order to create the cosmic order, and where the children of the gods will meet again after the end of this world.

Ásgarðr, the World of the Aesir, is another divine afterlife, where the center is the Well of Origin, from which a soul will come out transparently bright and shining. Another description is Gimli, which means "Fire-Shielded", and Glitnir, "Glittering", as Snorri described them:

"One place is called Wide Perception [Breidablik], and no fairer place is there. Also there is one called Glittering [Glitnir], and its walls and columns and pillars are of red gold (...) There is also a place called Seat of the Choice [Valaskialf].

That place is Óðin´s (...) and is there in this hall that the Seat of Openings [Hlíðskiǫlf] is, the throne of that name. And when All-Father sits on that throne he can see out over all the world.

At the southernmost end of heaven is the hall which is fairest of all and brighter than the Sun, and it is called Shimmering [Gimli]. It shall stand when both heaven and Earth have passed away, and in that place shall live good and righteous people for ever and ever."

When the present world-story is finished, the gods and the illuminated Light elves will gather at the Wind-Shielded Island of Immortality, the Hlésey, where they will gather and drink the precious mead of memory, and memorize the history of the world, the sacred story.

9.8: THE GREAT GODDESS OF MYSTERY RELIGIONS

The Greek-Roman civilization represented two thousand years of Mysteries. Not only the Mysteries of Eleusis: Various schools and cults flourished all over the Hellenistic and Roman empires. One school that became immensely popular, almost to the point of becoming more popular than the Eleusinian, was the Mysteries of Isis. Isis began as an Egyptian goddess known as Aset.

In the Hellenistic and Roman empires, she became known as Isis, and her adherents identified her as the ultimate face of the great Universal All-Soul. All Mystery initiates recognized all deities as aspects of the Supreme Being and were inspired by other Mystery schools, so that it is difficult to see any actual differences between the theology of Isis and the theology of Demeter.

Sometime around 180 BC, an Algerian-Roman poet and priest of Isis known as Apuleius wrote a novel called The Golden Ass or Metamorphoses, where the Mystery initiation is described in as much detail as the Mysteries could allow. Some things would not be revealed to the uninitiated, but Apuleius let slip that what could not be said directly would be said in symbol and metaphor – through mythical and poetical language.

When I read Apuleius' work for the first time, I was struck by the immense similarity in structure and content between the Mysteries of Isis and the initiations described in the Poetic Edda.

To sum up the journey of our Edda heroes and gods: The initiation always began with a Vision Quest, where the hero would seek a vision of the bright golden maiden of the Underworld through some kind of ritual or meditative activity. The Vision follows, where the hero would usually see or hear of the golden lady. She, or those who talk of her, would point out the path that he must follow. Then follows a Descent, where the hero moves into the Underworld.

There he is faced with various trials, which I have called the Trial Theme. The Consecration involves the embrace of the goddess and the imparting of her wisdom, often symbolized by the precious mead. Then there is a Resurrection, where the initiate returns to the world, often with a new name or new profession (such as king or sage). Often, he lives life with the guidance of the golden goddess, until he dies – when he experiences Salvation through the love of the goddess.

The exact same structure is described in Apuleius's initiation journey. The hero, Lucius, seeks a vision by ritually immersing himself seven times in the ocean during the night of a full moon. The ritual cleansing is accompanied by intense prayer. The Quest is followed by a Vision, where the goddess reveals herself before him through the night sky and the full moon: He learns that she is the primary mover of the universe and the true identity behind all goddesses, and the mother of all gods.

Just like in the Norse myths, the goddess then points out the direction that young Lucius must take next – seeking the Mysteries of Isis. Only then will Lucius [Light] be able to restore his human shape, much like Helgi must seek the path of initiation in order to earn his true name, Helgi [The Sacred One].

Lucius seeks the Mysteries, and after initial preparations and guidance from an ancient priest of Isis (who, incidentally, is actually called Mithras, sharing name with a deity whose Mystery cult is generally assumed to have been an entire cult altogether), he is allowed to take the initiation, which is described as a voluntary death and a descent into the Underworld:

"I approached the borders of death, I put my foot on the doorsteps of Persephone, I travelled through all the elements and returned, I saw the sun by midnight, shining in a white light, I came close to the gods of the higher and lower regions, and worshipped them in their closeness...
Both the keys to the gates of the Underworld, as well as the guarantee of Salvation were in the hands of the Goddess; The Initiation itself was like a voluntary death and a gracious salvation."

The philosopher Plutarch described the experience of dying and compared the experience of the soul at death with the experiences of the initiates during a Mystery initiation: The soul wanders around in tiring circles, on scary roads through absolute darkness that lead nowhere; and then, just before the final end to all cruelties the soul experiences panic, perspiration and trembling.

Then a wonderful light approaches the soul, it is met by clean spheres and fields that welcomes the soul with sacred words and sacred sights, and there the initiate will, now in its most perfect form, free of bondage, wander about, crowned with laurel, celebrating great festivals with others of sacred, pure souls. After such an experience, Plutarch concludes, the initiate will look at the uninitiated with new eyes and see all their impurity.

The revelations of the Underworld are described in symbol and metaphors, and one central theme is highly recognizable from Norse initiation myths: the concept of the light within the darkness, the "sun by midnight", and the appearance of the gracious, savior goddess just as the darkness of death descends upon the soul. In Apuleius´ account, the Savior Goddess declares that she will forever provide guidance in life for her initiate, and that she will save and deliver his soul after death, exactly in the manner of the valkyriur of the heroic Eddas:

"You shall live blessed in this world, you shall live in honor through my guidance and my protection, and when, after your given life-span, you descend into the Underworld, you shall see me there, shining."

Apuleius also happens to be one of our best sources to ancient Pantheism, when he describes the revelation that Lucius has when the goddess appears before him during that full moon night.:

BOOK XI:1-4: (...) *Wishing to purge myself I ran at once to the sea to bathe, plunging my head seven times under the waves since divine Pythagoras declared that number especially fitting for religious rites. Then, my face wet with tears, I prayed to the Great Goddess: 'Queen of Heaven, whether you are known as bountiful Ceres [Demeter], the primal harvest mother, who, delighted at finding your daughter Proserpine again, abolished our primitive woodland diet, showed us sweet nourishment, and now dwell at Eleusis; or heavenly Venus, who at the founding of the world joined the sexes by creating Love, propagating the human race in endless generation, and worshipped now in the sea-girt sanctuary of Paphos; or Diana, Apollo's sister, you who relieve the pangs of countless childbirths with your soothing remedies, venerated now at Ephesus; or dread Proserpine herself, she of the night-cries, who triple-faced combats the assault of spirits shutting them from earth above, who wanders the many sacred groves, propitiated by a host of rites; oh, light of woman, illuminating every city, nourishing the glad seed with your misty radiance, shedding that light whose power varies with the passage of the sun; in whatever aspect, by whatever name, with whatever ceremony we should invoke you, have mercy on me in the depths of my distress, grant good fortune, give me peace and rest after cruel tribulation.*

Let the toil, the dangers I've endured suffice. Rid me of this foul four-footed form, restore me to the sight of my own people; make me the Lucius I once was. Or if I may not live, if I have offended some deity who hounds me with inexorable savagery, grant me the gift of death.'

*When I had poured out my prayers, ending them in
pitiful lamentation, my fainting spirit sank back, once more
engulfed in sleep. I had scarcely closed my eyes when a divine
apparition appeared, rising from the depths of the sea, her
face worthy to be adored by the gods themselves. Slowly she
rose, till her whole body was in view, shaking herself free of
the brine to stand before me, a radiant vision. If the poverty
of human speech allows me, if the goddess herself grants
me a wealth of verbal inspiration, I shall try to describe her
marvelous beauty to you (...)*

BOOK XI:5-6 : *'Behold, Lucius, here I am, moved by your
prayer, I, mother of all Nature and mistress of the elements,
first-born of the ages and greatest of powers divine, queen
of the dead, and queen of the immortals, all gods and
goddesses in a single form; who with a gesture commands
heaven's glittering summit, the wholesome ocean breezes,
the underworld's mournful silence; whose sole divinity is
worshipped in differing forms, with varying rites, under many
names, by all the world.*

*There, at Pessinus, the Phrygians, first-born of men, call
me Cybele, Mother of the Gods; in Attica, a people sprung
from their own soil name me Cecropian Minerva; in sea-girt
Cyprus I am Paphian Venus; Dictynna-Diana to the Cretan
archers; Stygian Proserpine to the three-tongued Sicilians; at
Eleusis, ancient Ceres; Juno to some, to others Bellona, Hecate,
Rhamnusia; while the races of both Ethiopians, first to be lit
at dawn by the risen Sun's divine rays, and the Egyptians too,
deep in arcane lore, worship me with my own rites, and call
me by my true name, royal Isis. I am here in pity for your
misfortunes, I am here as friend and helper. Weep no more,
end your lamentations. Banish sorrow. With my aid, your day
of salvation is at hand...*[356]

Isis, here, is clearly identified as the great pantheist One behind
all the others, among them behind the goddesses of other Mystery
religions, such as that of Demeter in Eleusis. Isis as Creator and
Savior made her the greatest competition to Christianity towards
the end of the Pagan era. By then she was the most popular deity of
all, offering her worshippers salvation, healing miracles and a deep
religious experience of unity with the divine.

---

356 https://www.poetryintranslation.com/PITBR/Latin/TheGoldenAssXI.
php#anchor_Toc353982290

When Bishop Cyril argued his successful doctrine of Virgin Mary at Ephesus, 431 AD, he was struggling hard against the faith in Isis and the popular Gnostic belief that Mary and Isis shared the same basic characteristics - and that they were ultimately the same. As R.E. Witts describes it in his work Isis in the Graeco-Roman World (1971): *"A bitter struggle had to be fought before the Greek-Roman world at last accepted Jesus instead of Isis."*

THE STRUCTURE OF STAGES IN LUCIUS' INITIATION

1.VISION QUEST: *Lucius seeks the beach on a full moon night, submerging himself in the ocean seven times while praying to the goddess*

2. VISION: *The goddess appears, reveals how she is the true face behind all the gods and goddesses together, and the ruler of the universe. She speaks to him and tells him to seek initiation with her priests. As soon as he seeks initiation, he will return to his original, human form.*

3. DESCENT: *Lucius seeks the temple of Isis and goes through apprenticeship before being initiated into the Mysteries of Isis: He goes through Hades (the world of the dead) and sees the light of the goddess shining in the dark like a sun at midnight, like a light in the darkness.*

4. TRIALS/TEACHINGS: *He encounters obstacles along the way and is taught, but the teachings are secret, and he may not reveal them.*

5.CONSECRATION/TEACHING (MAIDEN THEME): *The goddess has mercy on his soul and offers resurrection.*

6. RETURNS WITH A NEW ROLE: *Lucius, enlightened, becomes a priest of Isis and lives his whole life under her guidance and protection.*

7. DEATH/RESURRECTION/SALVATION: *Lucius will be free from death and oblivion in Hades and spend eternity in Elysium among the gods.*

The number nine is not present in the story of Lucius, but it is known that nine was the number of nights that the initiates of Eleusis had to spend for their initiations. As you may see, I have here added two stages to the original staging of the structure; the return with a new role in society or a new spiritual status, and living with the guidance of the goddess for the rest of his life, as well as the death and resurrection or salvation theme.

Let us have another look at the structure of stages in the Edda myths of initiation, to see if these extra stages involving a new state of being and a promise of salvation.

1.The Initiation of Óðinn

☞ *Vision Quest/Ritual Death/Techniques of Ecstasy: Hangs, is stabbed, fasting, enduring «the Nine Nights»*
☞ *Vision: «Peers down»*
☞ *Descent: «Wind-swept». Enters a «mountain» of «clashing rocks», serpent and eagle symbol, a giantess = Typical Death Symbolism). Enters the realm of the norns in order to pick up the runes of fate. Enters the realm of giants in order to receive powerful spell-songs (or a drink from the Well of Memory.*
☞ *Trials/Teachings: Must overcome the giants and the giantess of the underworld through cunning, eloquence, and power*
☞ *Consecration/Teachings (Maiden): (in the Three Worlds beneath the Tree).Gets a drink of the precious mead from the giantess in the Underworld. Gets the runes of fate from the norns by the Well of Origin. Gets the powerful spell-songs from giant uncle by the Well of Memory - AND learns the art of Seiðr from Freyia*
☞ *Return with a new title/knowledge/professional status: "Falls back there" - Becomes a Reciting Sage, wise, eloquent, full of great magical knowledge, a seiðr-man, "comes among gods", has conquered death*
☞ *Death/Resurrection: Immortality through annual resurrection by being served the apples of Iðunn, the goddess of eternal resurrection.*

2. The Initiation of Freyr/Skírnir

☞ *Vision Quest/Techniques of Ecstasy/ Ritual Death: Freyr sits in Óðinn's seat – The Opening Shelf – and «looks into all the worlds»*
☞ *Vision: Sees a maiden in the underworld whose arms illuminate the worl*
☞ *Descent to the Underworld/Otherworld: Skírnir, Freyr´s servant, obviously enters the world of the dead (dark paths,*
☞ *Trials/Teachings: Must ride past barking Hel-Hounds. Faces a herdsman guardian who sits out on a haugr (burial mound). Proves his eloquence, magical power and wit against the giantess Gerðr*
☞ *Consecration/Teachings: A drink of precious mead and the gift of knowing how Freyr can reach the Maiden in a «breezeless» (=immortal) grove - after enduring The Nine Nights.*
☞ *Return with a new Status/Knowledge/Title: Returns with the message of The Nine Nights. Has received divine gifts from Freyr which enable him to move between worlds and survive jǫtunn attacks.*
☞ *Death/Resurrection: Reaches Immortality in «Breezeless» (Death-less) Grove in union with the Mead-serving Maiden.*

3. THE INITIATION OF ÓTTARR

☞ Vision Quest/ «Techniques of Ecstasy» / Ritual Death: Óttarr ("Fearsome/Fear Warrior") sacrifices a boar to the goddesses and colors the altar red with blood
☞ Vision: The altar turns into crystal and the goddess Freyia appears
☞ Descent into the Underworld/Otherworld: Freyia merges Óttarr´s spirit with that of the dying, sacrificed boar – her typical «steed» (when not driving cats or flying in a hawk´s hide).The goddess rides Óttarr the Boar down into the darkness of darkness itself, the Underworld, where they meet a wolf-riding giantess of the rock caves.
☞ Trials/Teachings: Freyia must convince Hyndla («She-Wolf») to reveal her knowledge to Óttarr, who needs to know about his lineage. The main argument is that they will be able to take him to Valhalla. Óttarr learns that all the lineages of humans, giants, gods, the Earth and the entire Universe are related – «They are all your kind, Óttarr of the narrow mind».

☞ Consecration/Teachings: Óttarr receives the Precious Mead so that he can remember what he learned.
☞ Return with New Role/Knowledge: Óttarr can demonstrate his esoteric knowledge about his universal «lineage»
☞ Death/Resurrection: Óttarr is guided to Valhalla by the goddess and the giantess together.

4. THE INITIATION OF ATLI AND HIǪRVARÐR

☞ *Vision Quests / Techniques of Ecstasy: Atli sits out in a sacred grove. Atli spends six months in the Land of Sleep. Atli & Hiǫrvarðr sit out on the top of a sacred mountain. Atli & Hiǫrvarðr sit out to dream by a riverVision: Atli understands the speech of birds (grove), they tell him of a golden maiden held captive in the Land of Sleep (Sváfaland) Atli & Hjörvardr see into the Land of Sleep from the mountaintop*
☞ *Descent into the Underworld/Otherworld: Atli spends six months in the Land of Sleep. Atli crosses the river while Hiǫrvarðr sleeps and enters the Land of Sleep.*
☞ *Trials/Teachings: Atli must conquer the Giant in Eagle Hide (=Death) and find two «maidens» that the eagle had held captive, and frees them*
☞ *Consecration (Maiden): Atli and Hiǫrvarðr marry the supernatural maidens.*
☞ *Return/New Status: Hiǫrvarðr becomes king. Atli becomes a seið-man or a Fjǫlkyngis-man.*

5. THE INITIATION OF HELGI HIǪRVARÐSSON

☞ *Vision Quest/Techniques of Ecstasy / Ritual Death: The unnamed prince sits out on a haugr – a burial mound – seeking a name for himself.*
☞ *Vision: Nine valkyriur ride by. The foremost among them is Sváva (The Sleeper) from Sefafell (Soul Mountain). She speaks to the prince, gives him the name Helgi, and demands that he goes on a quest to seek her hand in marriage.*
☞ *Descent into the Underworld/Otherworld: Atli (who earlier went on this journey) mentors Helgi as he enters the Hatafjorðr (Fjord of Hatred) in the giant world.*

☞ *Trials/Teachings: Helgi slays Hati (Hatred) and Hróðmarr (Furious Sea). While resting, they are accosted by a giant-ess of the ocean depths who wants to clasp them in her cold embrace (death). Atli keeps her entertained with eloquence and wit and magical power until the valkyriur arrive to save them.*

☞ *Consecration/Teachings (Maiden): Gets a name. Helgi can marry the valkyria Sváva. She continues to «ride the air and sea» and be a valkyria even after marriage. She protects him and guides him all his life.*

☞ *Return/New Title/Profession/Knowledge: Helgi becomes King, and lives his whole life under the guidance of the valkyria.*

☞ *Death/Resurrection: Helgi dies by the Rock of Greed. His valkyria joins him and they are both reincarnated.*

6. THE INITIATION OF HELGI HUNDINGSBANI

☞ *Vision Quest: I: Helgi dozes off after a battle, sleeping by the Rock of the Eagle (=Death). II: Helgi and his men eat raw meat and cover themselves with blood*

☞ *Vision: I&II: The Valkyria Sígrún appears and reminds Helgi of his previous life and his true quest now.*

☞ *Descent into the Underworld/Otherworld: Must enter the realms of the giants (with mentor Sinfiǫtli)*

☞ *Trials/Teachings: Must fight giants similar to previous life and prove eloquence, wit and magical power (with mentor) and retrieve his legacy. Must win the Battle of Greed that he lost in previous life.*

☞ *Consecration/Teachings (Maiden): Marries the valkyria. She continues to ride air and sea.*

☞ *Return/New Title/ Profession/ Status/ Knowledge: Be-comes king. Is always protected and guided by the valkyria.*

☞ *Death/Resurrection: His valkyria bride comes into his grave, shares the precious mead, and he can go to Valhǫll.*

7. The Initiation of Sígurðr

☞ Vision Quest: Ascends Holy Mountain. Quest for «Red Gold». Drinks serpent´s blood.

☞ Vision: Understands the speech of birds. The birds speak to him of a Maiden who has slept since the death of his half-brother Helgi Hundingsbani. She will teach him, but he must wake her up.

☞ Descent into the Underworld/Otherworld: Ascent to serpent´s lair, where the Red Gold and the Helmet of Terror are found. An ascent to the top of the mountain where the valkyria sleeps.

☞ Trials/Teachings: Must fight serpent. Must fearlessly cross high flames and break the sleeping valkyria free from her armor, when she wakes up.

☞ Consecration/Teachings (Maiden): Serpent offers advice. The valkyria, awake, offers the precious Mead of Memory. She teaches him about the runes, about healing, language and many other things

☞ Return to Society with a New Role: Becomes King and Sage, is Married

☞ Death/Salvation: The valkyria drives into Hel and saves him (his soul) from the ogress, to be together in peace for all eternity.

8. The Failed Initiation of Gunnarr (two attempts)

☞ *Vision Quest: A) Gunnarr rides the holy mountain. B) Gunnarr seeks the groves and listens to bird speech*

☞ *Vision: A) Sees the flickering flames that surround the valkyria. B) Sees his own, imminent death*

☞ *Descent into Underworld/Otherworld: A) Is too fearful to cross the flickering flames, deceives with help from mentor. B) Fearlessly moves towards his certain death*

☞ *Trials/Teachings: A) Fails to learn. B) Keeps the snakes of death at bay with his music, music that reaches all the way to the Wind-Shielded (Immortal) Island*

☞ *Consecration/Teachings (Maiden): A) Deceptive marriage with valkyria. B) True but clandestine union with valkyria who offers mead*

☞ Return to Society/New Role, New Knowledge: A) Becomes king (deceptively)/ B)Becomes wise (but dies)
☞ Death/Resurrection: Valkyria tries to save him from the snake-pit, but comes too late, Gunnarr is taken by the ogress of death.

9. THE INITIATION OF SVÍPDAGR

☞ Vision Quest/Techniques of Ecstasy: Sits on haugr (Burial Mound) and invokes his dead mother Gróa, who was a vǫlva.
☞ Vision: The dead vǫlva wakes and sings nine galdrar that take him into the Otherworld
☞ Descent into Underworld/Otherworld: Arrives, "floating", in Útgarðr (Outer World), the land of giants.
☞ Trials/Teachings: Must show his wit, eloquence and bravery to a giant who finally teaches him everything he wants to know about this realm, and how to reach the golden hall of the Great Maiden, Menglǫð (menga=to blend/mix (a drink) + lǫð =invitation), who rules the Outer World and the golden realm of the Tree of Memory and the Mountain of Medicines. Nine Maidens.
☞ Consecration/Teachings (Maiden): The fylgja (Menglǫð) gives him the kiss. He learns that he has always belonged with her but had forgotten about their true union because he was so many times lost on the "windy paths" – his mortality.
☞ Return: The return is to the arms of the Great Maiden at the Mountain of Medicine and the Tree of Memory, and to the memory of his own true self.
☞ Death/Resurrection: While others must strive, live and die, Svípdagr and Menglǫð may dwell in peace together for all eternity.

10. THE INITIATION OF THE DIVINE VǪLVA GULLVEIGR-HEIÐR (FREYIA)

☞ Vision Quest/Techniques of Ecstasy/Ritual Death: Is stabbed (like Óðinn) and burned (he is hanged)
☞ Vision: Not known, but must have seen how to conquer death
☞ Descent: Dies three times, is resurrected three times
☞ Trials: Burned three times, conquers death three times, is reborn three times (3 by 3 – the "Nine Nights"?)

☞ Consecrations/Teachings: Resurrects from death - knows/ learns how to conquer death

☞ Return/New Status: Takes a new name, Heiðr, becomes a vǫlva and a teacher of seiðr, travels the world performing and teaching her powerful arts of galdrar, gandr & seiðr – Fjǫlkyngi (great magical knowledge. * *(Freyia teaches seiðr to Óðinn and the Aesir, she too is a vǫlva)

☞ Death/Resurrection: Is eternally resurrected, lives forever

A WOMAN'S PATH (GUÐRÚN)

☞ Vision Quest/Descent: Guðrún leaves her family and enters the wild forests, suffers, lives with wolves

☞ Vision: Guðrún sees the Hall of the Southern Goddesses and finds her «friend», the valkyria Thora. She lives by a well described like the Well of Origin.

☞ Trials/Teachings: Guðrún lives in this hall and learns how to literally weave fate.

☞ Consecration/Teachings: Guðrún is approached by her family offering apologies and compensation. Her mother offers her a powerful drink of mead, containing the ingredients that gave life to the universe. The drink heals her pain.

☞ Return/New Role: Is married to a king. Knows a lot of magic, runes, potions. Can fight with sword.

☞ Death: Unknown, but it is said that she tried to drown herself but could not die. She becomes the celebrated destroyer of the Hunnish Empire and queen among the Goths for her third and last marriage.

9.9: UPPSALA – A MYSTERY RELIGION IN THE NORTH?

Mercury is the deity whom they chiefly worship, and on certain days they deem it right to sacrifice to him even with human victims. Hercules and Mars they appease with more lawful offerings. Some of the Suevi also sacrifice to Isis. Of the occasion and origin of this foreign rite I have discovered nothing, but that the image, which is fashioned like a light galley, indicates an imported worship.--Germania, Tacitus [357]

When Romans were to describe the religious customs and beliefs of other peoples, they tended to assume that, since the gods were real, then they must naturally be known among all people, and the only reason why they have different names and sometimes different attributes, is because people spoke different languages and knew different parts of the lore.

The god Wodan- Óðinn, for example, was simply translated as, and identified with, the Roman god Mercury, that wing-footed messenger of the gods, because the Romans saw a likeness that was sufficient for them. Likewise, the god Thor was identified as their divine hero Hercules, although he could sometimes be identified with Jupiter/Zevs because of the thunderbolt-wielding. Some early, Germanic version of Njǫrðr was Neptune, and Tiwaz/Týr, god of war, became Roman Mars.

And then, Tacitus observed, there was a Germanic version of Isis, the Great Goddess of the Mysteries. Aside from letting us know that her worship appeared to have been imported from somewhere else, he does not further explain exactly how the Germanic tribes worshipped a goddess from Egypt and the Roman Empire, and of course, the most reasonable explanation is that there was a native goddess whose functions and attributes and cult of worship was so clearly similar to that of Isis, that he thought it was perfectly fine to identify the two. After all, Isis was the great being behind all other gods and goddesses, so a great deal fluidity when it came to identities was not a problem.

---

357 Complete Works of Tacitus. Tacitus. Alfred John Church. William Jackson Brodribb. Lisa Cerrato. edited for Perseus. New York. : Random House, Inc. Random House, Inc. reprinted 1942. http://www.perseus.tufts.edu/hopper/text?doc=Perseus%3Atext%3A1999.02.0083%3Achapter%3D9

To emphasize the point here; when he spoke of Isis, he was probably just putting a Roman name to a native goddess, the same way he applied Roman names like Mercury and Hercules and Mars to native gods. It does not mean that the goddess Isis was actually worshipped by Germanic peoples. The thing is, Tacitus could have chosen among countless Roman goddess names. He could have said Venus, or Juno, or Ceres – but he said Isis.

Since he was a Roman living during the age of Mysteries, I am absolutely certain that his association to Isis was because he thought that there was a Goddess of Mysteries – as in a Goddess of Initiations and Salvation – among the Germanic peoples. Old Norse myths show several interesting similarities to the myths of Classical Mystery schools, especially to those dedicated to the oldest of goddesses; Demeter from Eleusis, Greece, and Isis from North Africa.

References to castration of initiates in Old Norse myths (particularly the character Sinfiǫtli in the Helgi Hundingsbani poems, and the name Ialkr [Castrate] for Óðinn), may even bring to mind the Mysteries of Cybele/Kubaba, a goddess also known as Magna Mater [Great Mother] by the Romans, who adopted her religion as their own. The latter goddess was depicted flanked by two felines or drawn in a chariot by two great cats in an iconography which had persisted since the early Neolithic ages. It is interesting indeed that in the Gylfaginning, Snorri claimed that Freyia was drawn in a chariot by two large cats during Baldr´s funeral.

The Old Norse myths show a basic structure and a focus on themes that are strikingly similar to those of ancient Mystery schools, particularly to the initiation structure of the Mysteries of Isis that was revealed by Apuleius during the 2nd century BC. In my opinion, it is highly probable that Scandinavia had a Mystery school of its own. It may have been very old indeed: There are indications that the Mystery schools were already flourishing during the Bronze Ages in the Mediterranean areas – and we know with certainty that Scandinavia had an old and strong connection to this part of the world during that era. However, an Old Norse Mystery school may also have been one adopted from a Classical school, and then adapted to Old Norse cultural and mythological context.

This kind of flexibility would have been typical of the Mystery schools which professed that the Great Goddess showed herself with different names and different shapes among different people and in different languages – yet was ultimately always the same. Interestingly, Snorri claimed (in Gylfaginning) that Freyia was a goddess who took upon herself a new name and a new shape wherever she came among different people.

Like the goddesses of the Mystery schools, she was searching for a lost beloved, an allegory for the All-soul´s search for its own wholeness, shattered into billions of individual souls. The importance of the initiation lore and the resurrection theme in Old Norse myths is so crucial and central that in my opinion, it must have originated in a school of thought that was well established and powerful – powerful enough to shape the mythology of an entire culture.

If one such school existed, it would have had at least one powerful center – a publicly or nationally sponsored temple complex and center of pilgrimage like that of Eleusis in Greece.

Indeed, there was one place that in my opinion could possibly have nurtured such a center: The Temple of Uppsala in Sweden.

Old Uppsala is situated a few kilometers north of the modern city of Uppsala in Sweden. It is famous for having been a large Pagan cultic center and for its three great burial mounds that are aligned and oriented towards where the sun sets on certain dates.

Every year – or else every ninth year – of this the sources seem to waver, a great festival happened at Uppsala in honor of the many goddesses: the Dísaþing – "The Parliament of the Goddesses".

There was a temple of the one Dís there [Dísarsalr], the one Goddess that may have served as a focal point for this ritual. It was a grand, public event and the kings and the chiefs were expected to partake in the ritual. We know very little of the ritual itself except that it included a sacrifice and that the king was expected to consecrate the site by riding around the Temple of the Goddess

A dísting is still held in Sweden at Old Uppsala to this day, an annual market named after the Pagan Dísaþing – Parliament of the Goddesses. While the only aspect of this event to survive into our day is the market that was certainly also held during Pagan days, this market once took place with a great political and religious backdrop.

Here, the Viking Age aristocracy would meet to hold a national parliament dedicated to the goddesses, just like the gods of the myths held parliament at the Well of Origin, the abode of the fate-goddesses. The Assembly of the Swedes was held in conjunction with the Dísablót - the Sacrifice to the Goddesses, and there were celebrations and a grand public fair or market associated with it – the latter tradition surviving unto this day.

Snorri describes the custom in his Heimskringla from 1225 AD:

"In Sweden, it was the old custom, as long as heathenism prevailed, that the chief sacrifice took place in Goe month at Uppsala. Then sacrifice was offered for peace and victory to the king; and thither came people from all parts of Sweden. All the Assemblies of the Swedes, also, were held there, and markets, and meetings for buying, which continued for a week; and after Christianity was introduced into Sweden, the Assemblies and fairs were held there as before. After Christianity had taken root in Sweden, and the kings would no longer dwell in Uppsala, the market-time was moved to Candlemas, and it has since continued so, and it lasts only three days."

As to the three burial mounds, we do not know exactly how old they are or what purpose they served, but their alignment and orientation towards important ritual dates are the same as the orientation of other Swedish passage graves, and the tradition of this alignment of mounds dates back to at least 3300 BC. There was a well-developed and prosperous society around the Uppsala Mounds during the early Iron Ages, at least, since time immemorial, the kings had their estate here and the Swedes gathered here to worship. There is a long-lived myth about the three mounds containing the remains of Pagan gods, and the East mound was said to be Óðin´s mound, while the West Mound was Þórr's, and the middle mound belonged to Freyr. This is of course not historically correct, but makes sense in a mythical landscape.

Snorri wrote that Freyr had built the Temple of Uppsala as his abode. Freyr was the most important deity in Sweden, and said to be the ancestor of the royal lines there:

"Freyr built a great temple at Upsal, made it his chief seat, and gave it all his taxes, his lands, and goods. Then began the Upsal domains, which have remained ever since. But after Freyr was buried under a cairn at Uppsala, many chiefs raised cairns, as commonly as stones, to the memory of their relatives."--

Snorri´s older contemporary, the Danish scholar Saxo Grammaticus, confirms the mythical notion that Freyr was said to have established the center at Uppsala:

"Also Freyr, the regent of the gods, took his abode not far from Uppsala, where he exchanged for a ghastly and infamous sin-offering the old custom of prayer by sacrifice, which had been used by so many ages and generations. For he paid to the gods abominable offerings, by beginning to slaughter human victims."

Saxo was, as one may notice, less than favorably inclined towards the Pagan gods. He continues to tell the story of the hero Starkaðr, who came to Uppsala and was appalled:

"...because when stationed at Uppsala, at the time of the sacrifices, he was disgusted by the effeminate gestures and the clapping of the mimes on the stage, and by the unmanly clatter of bells."

As disgusted as Saxo was, we may read something valuable from his information – that there was a mime-stage at Uppsala. The mime stage means that it is possible that myths were played – re-enacted – as in what could have been Mystery Plays. The actors or the participants appear to have been playing music, dancing or moving in a way that to an outsider of the New School of continental, Christianized machismo were "effeminate" and "unmanly".

This could perhaps be seen in light of how certain gender-nonconforming aspects may have been a part of initiation rituals. As I argued in my other work The Seed of Yggdrasill, where I delve into other types of initiation myths as well, divine and human initiates like Þórr, Helgi and Óðinn, at least, would don the garments of women and pretend to be serving maids, witches or even brides in order to reach their spiritual goals.

In a culture that was relatively gender-polarized, this may have represented a powerful and mind-altering transgression of gender roles that was designed to perhaps humiliate, perhaps to challenge the self-importance of the initiate, or else done in order to access some power that had to do with femininity and the womb.

THE GOLDEN HALL OF THE MAIDEN

Adam of Bremen, a German chronicler of the 11th century, wrote an account of the temple at Uppsala, based on other accounts by witnesses that were there when Uppsala was still a Pagan center:

"At this point I shall say a few words about the religious beliefs of the Swedes. That nation has a magnificent temple, which is called Uppsala...In this temple, built entirely of gold; the people worship the statues of three gods.

A general festival for all the provinces of Sweden is customarily held at Uppsala every nine years. Participation in this festival is required of everyone....those who have already adopted Christianity buy themselves off from these ceremonies. The sacrifice is as follows: of every kind of male creature, nine victims are offered...Their bodies, moreover, are hanged in a grove which is adjacent to the temple. This grove is so sacred to the people that the separate trees in it are believed to be holy because of the death...of the sacrificial victims.

There even dogs and horses hang beside human beings...The incantations, however, which are usually sung in the performance of a libation of this kind are numerous and disgraceful, and it is better not to speak of them.

Near that temple is a very large tree with widespread branches which are always green, both in winter and summer. What kind of tree it is nobody knows. There is also a spring there where the Pagans are accustomed to perform sacrifices and to immerse a human being alive. As long as his body is not found, the request of the people will be fulfilled. A golden chain encircles the temple and hangs over the gables of the building.

Those who approach see its gleam from afar because the shrine, which is located on a plain, is encircled by mountains so situated as to give the effect of a theatre. For nine days feasts and sacrifices of the kind are celebrated. Every day they sacrifice one human being in addition to other animals, so that in nine days there are 72 victims which are sacrificed. This sacrifice takes place about the time of the vernal equinox."

We do not know if these accounts are exactly true, since they are all written by Christian outsiders, who had never actually observed the temple or the rituals themselves. However, through these filters several elements from the mythology emerge. Firstly, the temple site is connected to the worship of the many Dísir and the one Dís. The Dísir is a word that covers all the numerous female powers, whether they are giantesses, goddesses, Valkyries or norns. In the myths, we have seen that the role of the consecrating Maiden with the Mead, who takes the initiates into her sacred embrace, may be played by a giantess, a goddess, a valkyria or a Norn. They all come together in the one great Dís, Freyia, "The Lady Sovereign".

Moreover, the temple is said to be all golden, surrounded by a golden chain that glimmers and shines and might be seen from afar. This is exactly how the Hall of the Maiden is described in the myths. It is also standing on a plain surrounded by mountains. In the myths we have seen how the heroes ascend mountains in order to see into the great land. We learn about the Resplendent Fields, the Crystal Fields and so forth.

People travel far and wide to get to the temple, just as the initiates have to travel long distances to get to the Golden Hall. The rituals last for nine days and nights, just as the initiation lasts for the same duration of time. There is a grove dedicated to a sacred tree and a lake which can only resemble the World Tree or the Tree of Memory and the Well of Origin. Both the Hávamál and the Fjǫlsvinnsmál emphasize the presence of a sacred tree – in the latter poem, the Tree of Memory is growing out of the halls of the Maiden.

HÁVAMÁL – THE HIGH ONE'S SPEECH: AFTER THE INITIATION

111.Mál er at þylia
þvlar stóli a
Vrþar brvnni at;
sa ec oc þagþac,
sa ec oc hugþac,
hlydda ec a manna mál;
of rvnar heyrda ec dœma,
ne vm rádom þa'gðo
Hava ha'llo at,
Háva hollo i,
heyrda ec segia sva:

111. It is time to speak
from the Seat of the Reciting Sage
by the Well of Origin
I saw and was silent
I saw and I contemplated
I listened to the speech of people
Of runes I heard speak
and they did not withhold their counsels
at the High Hall
in the High Hall
I heard them speak like this:

142. Rvnar mvnt þv finna
oc raðna stafi,
mioc stóra stafi,
mioc stinna stafi,
er fáþi Fimbvlþvlr
oc gorðo ginnregin
oc reist Hroptr ra'gna.

142. Runes you shall find
and the interpreted symbol
Very powerful symbols
Very potent symbols
that were colored by the Great Reciter
and made by the holy powers
and carved by the Shattered One among the Gods

143. Oþinn meþ asom
enn fyr alfom Dainn,
Dvalinn oc dvergom fyr,
Asvidr iotnom fyr,
ec reist sialfr svmar.

143. Óðinn with the gods
and for the elves, the Dead One
Hibernation for the dwarfs
Divine Wood for the jǫtnar
I myself carved some (runes)

144. Veiztv hve rista scal?
veiztv hve raþa scal?
veiztv hve fá scal?
veiztv hve freista scal?
veiztv hve bidia scal?
veiztv hve blóta scal?
veiztv hve senda scal?
veiztv hve soa scal?

145. Betra er obeþit
enn se ofblotiþ,
ęy ser til gildis giof;
betra er osennt
enn se ofsóit.
Sva Þvndr vm reist
fyr þioþa raⳋc,
þar hann vp vm reis
er hann aptr of kom.

146. Lioþ ec þaⳋ kann,
er kannat þioðans kona
oc mannzcis maⳋgr;
hialp heitir eitt,
enn þat þer hialpa mvn
viþ saⳋcom oc sorgom
oc svtom gorvollom.

147. Þat kann ec annat,
er þvrfo yta synir
þeir er vilia lęcnar liva:

[Text missing]

148. Þat kann ec þriþia,
ef mer verþr þaⳋrf micil
haptz viþ mina
heiptmaⳋgo:
eggiar ec deyfi
minna andscota,
bitaþ þeim vapn ne veler.

144. *Do you know how to carve?*
Do you know how to interpret?
Do you know how to color?
Do you know how to test?
Do you know how to ask?
Do you know how to sacrifice?
Do you know how to send?
Do you know how to atone?

145. *Better not to ask*
than to sacrifice too much
a gift expects a gift in return
Better not to send
than to atone too much
Thus Thin Mist [Óðinn] carved it
before the peoples emerged
when he ascended
when he returned back

146. *I know a song*
not even known to the ruler's wife
nor to the children of men:
"Help" one is called
and it will help you
against allegations and sorrows
and misery of any kind.

147. *I know a second*
which humanity needs
those who want to live as healers:

[Text missing]

148. *I know a third*
which is of great use to me
to make fetters against my enemies
The edges I blunt
for my enemies
neither weapons nor clubs will bite

149. Þat kann ec et fiorþa,
ef mer fyrðar bera
band at boglimom:
sva ec gel,
at ec ganga ma,
sprettr mer af fótom
fiotvrr,
en af handom hapt.

149. I know a fourth
If I am bound
with chains upon my limbs
I sing thus
that I may go free
Fetters spring from my feet
and chains from my hands

150. Þat kann ec it fimta,
ef ec se af fári scotinn
fleín i folci vaða:
flygra hann sva stint,
at ec stardvigac,
ef ec hann siónom of sec.

150. I know a fifth
if I see, shooting
a malicious dart against
people
It cannot fly faster
than that I can stop it
if I see it with my eyes.

151. Þat kann ec et setta,
ef mic serir þegn
a rótom rás viðar,
oc þann hal
er mic heipta qveþr,
þann eta meín heldr enn
mic.

15. I know a sixth,
If a man wounds me
with the roots of the sap of
the woods
At that one who wished me
harm
I turn it against him, rather
than me.

152. Þat kann ec it
siaunda,
ef ec se havan loga
sal vm sessmargom:
brennrat sva breit,
at ec hanom biargigac,
þann kann ec galdr at gala

152. I know a seventh
If I see the high flames
Burning the halls of my
friends:
It cannot burn harder
Than that I can quench it
I know the spell-songs to
chant.

153. Þat kann ec iþ átta,
er allom er
nytsamlict at nema:
hvars hatr vex
meþ hildings sonom,
þat ma ec bota brát.

153. I know an eight
which is, for anyone
very useful to learn:
Where hatred grows
among the sons of warriors
I can quickly make truce.

154. Þat kann ec iþ
níunda,
ef mic naуþr vm stendr
at biarga fari míno a floti:
vind ec kyrri
vagi á
oc svefic allan sе.

154. I know a ninth
if I am in need
to protect my ship at sea
The wind I quiet
and lull the waves
and make the ocean
peaceful

155. Þat kann ec iþ tíunda,
ef ec se tvnriþor
leica lopti a:
ec sva vinc,
at þеr villar fara
sinna heim hama,
sinna heim hvga.

155. I know a tenth
if I see court-riders
(malicious spirits)
play around in the air:
I can make it so
that they get lost
from their own hides
from their own souls

156. Þat kann ec iþ ellipta,
ef ec scal til orrosto
leiþa langvini:
vndir randir ec gel,
enn þeir meþ ríki fara
heilir hildar til,
heilir hildi fra,
coma þeir heilir hvaþan.

156. I know an eleventh
if I am going to battle
to lead my long-term
friends
I chant beneath the shield
and they travel with power
whole to the battle
whole from the battle
they come whole wherever
they go.

157. Þat kann ec iþ tolpta,
ef ec se a tre vppi
vafa virgilná:
sva ec rist
oc i rуnom fác,
at sa gengr gvmi
oc mеlir viþ mic.

157. I know a twelfth
if I see, high in a tree
a dangling, hanged corpse
I carve this
and color the runes
so that the corpse walks
and speaks to me.

158.Þat kann ec iþ
þrettánda,
ef ec scal þegn vngan
verpa vatni á:
mvnaþ hann falla,
þótt hann i folc komi,
hnígra sa halr fyr hiorom.

158. I know a thirteenth
if I am to name a youth
and pour over him the
water
He will not fall
if he comes to a battle
nor will he sink before
swords

159. Þat kann ec iþ
fiugrtánda,
ef ec scal fyrða liþi
telia tiva fyr:
asa oc alfa
ec kann allra skil,
fár kann osnotr sva.

160. Þat kann ec iþ
fimtánda,
er gól Þioðreyrir
dvergr fyr Dellings
dvrom;
afl gol hann asom,
enn alfom frama,
hyggio Hroptaty.

161. Þat kann ec iþ
sextánda,
ef ec vil ins svinna mans
hafa ged oc alt oc gaman:
hvgi ec hverfi
huítarmri kono
oc sny ec hennar a/llom
séfa

162. Þat kann ec iþ
siautiánda,
at mic mvn seint firraz
eþ manvga man.
Lioþa þessa
mvn þv, Loddfafnir!
lengi vanr vera,
þo se þer goð ef þv getr,
nyt ef þv nemr,
þa/rf ef þv þiggr.

159. I know a fourteenth
if I have to reckon up
and count the gods before
men
Gods and elves
I can recognize all
few of no eloquence will
know

160. I know the fifteenth
which was sung by People-
Mover
a dwarf before the doors of
Fame
He sang power to the gods
and before the elves
and wisdom to the
Shattered God.

161. I know a sixteenth
if I want to have the wise
maiden
to have her heart and
pleasure:
Her intent I turn
of that bright-armed wife
and I turn her entire soul

162. I know a seventeenth
So that late will she leave
me
That I will not lose the
young maiden
These songs
You must, Fate-Embracer
Long be without
It would be good for you if
you get them
Enjoy them if you learn
them
Good for you to keep them.

163. Þat kann ec iþ
átiánda,
er ec æva kennig
mey ne mannz kono,
— alt er betra
er einn vm kann,
þat fylgir lioða locom, —
nema þeirri einni,
er mic armi verr
eþa min systir se.

163. I know the eighteenth
which I shall never teach
not to maiden nor man's
wife
All that is good
is known only to one
This is the end of the songs:
Only to her
who holds me in her arms
or may my sister be.

164. Nv ero Hava mál
qveðin
Háva haɾllo i
allþaɾrf yta sonom,
oþaɾrf iotna sonom;
heill sa er qvað!
heill sa er kann!
nióti sa er nam!
heilir þeirs hlyddo!

164. Now has been sung
the Speech of the High One
in the Hall of the High One
of great use to the children
of men
of no use to the children of
jǫtnar
Whole the one who sang it!
Whole the one who knows
it!
Enjoy it the one who
learned!
Whole the ones who heard!

SUMMARY AND CONCLUSIONS

Throughout this study, I have argued the existence of a "Maiden mythology" hidden behind the texts of the Poetic Edda. "Maiden mythology" is revealed through a common structure of themes, a pattern that may be traced in widely different poems from the Hávamál to the Heroic Poems. The center of this mythology is the "Maiden", a supernatural young woman who receives a god or hero in her hall and offers him a cup or a horn of "precious mead", a "drink of memory". The offering is accompanied by a marriage between the Maiden and the hero.

Before being granted the drink and the embrace of the Maiden, however, the hero has to undergo some fierce trials beginning with vision quests, visions, and a descent into the realm of the dead. In chapter 3.1, I explained the term "initiation", basing myself on Eliade's "Encyclopedia of Religion". Whether the initiation be part of a "puberty rite" or an initiation into a secret society or a mystical vocation (such as shamanism), the initiation usually includes isolation from society, secret revelation, and a ritual death followed by resurrection or rebirth. As Schjødt has pointed out, it is important that the one undergoing these trials actually receives a new position in society or cult after that, in order to call it an "initiation".

In Maiden mythology, the hero descends into the underworld, receives secret revelations, and returns to the living. Several of the poems, such as the Hávamál and the Hyndluljóð, indicate that the hero experienced a very severe "ritual death" involving the sacrifice of himself. Many of the poems, particularly the Hávamál and the poems of Sígurðr also indicate that the hero returned from the trials a sage, a poet, a healer, even a king. It appears that the Maiden-mythology reflects the typical basics of initiation rituals into a sacred office.

I have frequently touched upon the kind of initiation ritual that is revealed, without arriving at any certain conclusions. The indications in the myths are varied at best. My main aim, as stated in the Introduction, is not to decide what the hero is initiand into, but to prove that the pattern, the structure of themes, exists, and thus, a "Maiden mythology" reflecting initiation.

Our study has, however, made it possible to get a vague idea about the nature of the initiations, and I have pointed out significant similarities not only with shamanism or royal inauguration through sacred marriage, but also to ancient Mystery religions. We may still see these myths as products of a religious tradition unique to pre-Christian Scandinavia, yet one that may have drawn from many different traditions which are related to and thus similar to other world traditions of the kind just mentioned.

Firstly, the initiation is centered around the Maiden figure, whom we have identified as the Great Goddess. The initiation culminates in marriage.

Since the Maiden is a goddess or other supernatural entity, we are talking about a sacred marriage, a Hieros Gamos as defined in chapter 3.1. Sacred Marriage is closely connected to kingship inauguration in many ancient cultures, and was known in Scandinavia during the Bronze Age, probably an idea imported from the great civilizations of the south such as the Sumerian, where sacred marriage was the central ritual of the religion. In Scandinavia, sacred marriage appears to have had a new "boom" from around the fifth century A.D, when the Germanic tribes started to constitute little kingdoms.

From comparative sources such as the Sumerian and the Irish, the sacred marriage of the king and the goddess had to do with the consecration of a king by the Great Goddess of the land: only through her authorization may a king enter his sacred office.

From the studies of Steinsland, it seems clear that sacred marriage was closely connected to kingship and it would seem as if the king had to undergo trials of initiation before claiming the throne.

However, I have frequently referred to the nature of the teachings in "Maiden mythology" and had to conclude that the myths of the Maiden seem to cover a lot more than kingship initiation.

The art of healing, poetry, galdr, seiðr, magic, sorcery and journeys into the Underworld were hardly the unique domain of the king in Norse nor in Germanic society. In chapter 8, I showed that so-called "masters of initiation" were present at the trials, and that they could be identified with actual religious professionals operating in Scandinavia and Germania in pre-Christian times. These masters could not have been ignorant about the trials and teachings of the neophyte; on the contrary, we would assume that they were experts. They would become experts only by going through the same kind of trials beforehand.

In some cases, these experts would appear to be working in the service of kings, such as Atli, Sinfiǫtli and Skírnir. The relationship between kingship and the Maiden is visible in the Heroic Poems, where the heroes are royal princes. The focus in the Heroic Poetry is not so much on kingship, however, as on the continuity of the relationship between the hero and the valkyria through lives and deaths. The theme could very well be about the journey of the soul through different lives, as Kragerud suggested, and, as I suggested, about the valkyria perhaps being the actual divine, immortal soul of the hero. This does not out rule the importance of kingship and sacred marriage, but it could show that the union with the Maiden is a far broader and more universal theme than that of kingship.

Looking back to "masters of initiation" such as the Atli figure, we will recall that Atli not only brings a Maiden back to the king, but also a Maiden for himself. Atli is certainly not a king, but an earl's son, "earl" being the echo of an ancient religious office. Thus, the marriage to a Maiden from the Other World is not restricted to kings. Atli's expertise has to do with journeying in the Other World, journeys that begin with vision quests and visions of a thoroughly ecstatic character. We should not ignore the ecstatic nature of the heroes´ experiences.

The vision quests and visions followed by journeys to a different realm, a realm of giants and of the forces of death, are vividly described and I, at least, do not get the impression that these are descriptions of organized, routinized ritual. I am convinced that, if these myths reflect actual practice, that practice must have been of a highly ecstatic character. The ecstasy is not induced only among royal candidates. It would rather appear to have been part of the religious practice of Old Norse cult, performed by professionals – the initiand. I have pointed out the likeness to shamanism, yet it is impossible to decide whether we are dealing with shamanism in its strictest, classical sense or something that only resembles it in greater or lesser degree.

Shamanism was certainly known and even used by the Norse population, who lived very close to the shamanistic Sámi, whom they apparently approached for help in magical matters. In chapter 8.5, I pointed out the likeness of Óðinn's role as divine archetype and the role of Siberian "ancestral shamans".

Óðinn is certainly the most shaman-like character in the Norse sources, if we should believe Snorri's descriptions of the god in the Ynglinga saga. I have touched upon the subject of shamanism in the Norse sources quite often, because I believe it is too prominent to be ignored, particularly in the context of Maiden-mythology.

As far as I have been able to investigate, the classical shamans' relations to great female divinities is a subject rather more prominent than Eliade ever suspected, but this is a subject which reach beyond the scope of this thesis. In any case, shamanism in some way appears to have had some influence on Norse mythology, whether it be because there were shamans in Norse society, practitioners who resembled classical shamans to some degree, or perhaps the influences were only remnants of a distant past.

In the Encyclopedia of Religions, Eliade gives the impression that many scholars believe shamanistic rituals and tribal initiations were the structural and mythical origins of different kind of ritual behavior such as the type detected in Antique mystery cults. In this second edition of my original thesis, I have put greater emphasis on this possible resemblance.

While shamanism certainly could involve marriage to supernatural beings, such a union is also known from Mystery religions. Such religions also involved a "journey" (how ritualized or how personally experienced we do not know) through the Underworld, leading to a mystic union with the primary deity, very often the Great Goddess.

This kind of initiation also involved esoteric teachings, and one of its central ideas had to do with overcoming death: how to earn a blessed existence after death. The emphasis on the life-death opposition in the Maiden mythology (as seen in the ogress-Maiden polarity) could in fact resemble mystery religions. We know for a fact that Germanic religions were influenced by Celtic and (often through them) other Indo-European religions such as the Greek and the Mediterranean ones, so that a link to Antique mystery religion would not be an impossibility. Michael Enright has pointed out that the emerging Germanic warrior tribes were greatly influenced by Celtic culture and religion at the end of the Celtic Iron Age (which started from about 500 B.C.).

Enright shows that the ideology of the lady with a mead cup and the German liquor ritual was borrowed from the Celtic upper classes when Germanic tribes evolved their own class hierarchy. The Celts again were certainly influenced by Mediterranean culture through mercenaries and merchants. This period is the same that saw a wide variety of mystery cults in the Mediterranean. In fact, the way the Maiden mythology is conveyed certainly indicates a degree of secrecy and "mystery": it has to be deciphered through intricate symbols and is never explained or presented in complete. All in all, Maiden mythology is not restricted to covering consecration of kingship. It appears that the Maiden will teach anyone who seeks her through the realm of death and who has the power to withstand that realm.

As to the idea that Maiden mythology reflects cultic practice, we have the archaeological evidence pointed out by Enright, as referred to in chapter 9.5. The Maiden with the Mead had her living counterpart in the world of Germanic tribal society. She was a woman holding a spoon sieve or other equipment for the ladling and serving of mead, and she was buried with cauldrons which designs were often of great antiquity and elaboration, and of obvious cultic purpose. She was also buried with jewelry showing her high rank, equipment for spinning and weaving which was forever associated with divination and fate-magic in the Germanic world.

Finally, she would often have a staff which was exclusively for women of her rank, identified as a "cult staff" by the archaeologists, as well as objects that she had carried in a pouch in her belt. She has been found in burial sites from before the birth of Christ up to the last pagan strongholds in Scandinavia. Her cult was old and of great continuity and popularity. Her grave always holds a special position in the burial site, showing her as a revered and important person: in one site she is at the center with all the other graves laid in a half-moon formation around her. The finds strongly suggest a religious function, and Enright identifies the women as the "prophetesses" who held such authority in early Germanic societies. He also sees the connection between them and a goddess cult. According to Enright, the queens offering mead in later medieval literature were their descendants.

Michael Enright has argued that the (non-religious) literary evidence shows that the living Mead-Lady's main function was to establish brotherhood and social positions through a ritual in the king's hall. This would appear to be true and reminds me of the idea of Freyia "arranging seats in the hall". The arrangement of seats was important in Norse and Germanic society, showing the exact social position of each individual.

Freyia's arrangement of seats takes place, however, in an afterlife-realm. Extending our idea of the living Mead-Lady to the supernatural Maiden figure, we see that the Maiden, first and foremost, initiands and consecrates. Perhaps, reflecting how the living Mead- Lady established the social positions of men within a warband by the chieftain's table, the Maiden established the spiritual (and thus social, religious) position of the neophyte.

Regarding the possibility of an actual ritual setting behind the Maiden mythology, the women's´ staffs could perhaps indicate the involvement of women much like those who would later be recognized in Norse written sources as the vǫlur. Indeed, the number nine would further associate the vǫlur with Maiden-mythology; The vǫlva of Eiriks saga was the last in a company of nine sisters, and the vǫlva of Örvar Odds saga had nine apprentices of either sex in her following. Gullveigr died three times and was reborn three times; a three-by-three count resulting in the number nine. A ritual enactment of the myth could, at some point in history, easily have involved a vǫlva both as master of initiation, as suggested in chapter 9.6, and as the representative of the goddess herself, ladling out the precious mead and offering her cup and her embrace to the consecrated.

SUMMARY AND CONCLUSIONS

Throughout this study, I have argued the existence of a "Maiden mythology" hidden behind the texts of the Poetic Edda. "Maiden mythology" is revealed through a common structure of themes, a pattern that may be traced in widely different poems from the Hávamál to the Heroic Poems. The center of this mythology is the "Maiden", a supernatural young woman who receives a god or hero in her hall and offers him a cup or a horn of "precious mead", a "drink of memory". The offering is accompanied by a marriage between the Maiden and the hero. Before being granted the drink and the embrace of the Maiden, however, the hero has to undergo some fierce trials beginning with vision quests, visions, and a descent into the realm of the dead.

In chapter 3.1, I explained the term "initiation", basing myself on Eliade's "Encyclopedia of Religion". Whether the initiation be part of a "puberty rite" or an initiation into a secret society or a mystical vocation (such as shamanism), the initiation usually includes isolation from society, secret revelation, and a ritual death followed by resurrection or rebirth. As Schjødt has pointed out, it is important that the one undergoing these trials actually receives a new position in society or cult after that, in order to call it an "initiation".

In Maiden mythology, the hero descends into the underworld, receives secret revelations, and returns to the living. Several of the poems, such as the Hávamál and the Hyndluljóð, indicate that the hero experienced a very severe "ritual death" involving the sacrifice of himself. Many of the poems, particularly the Hávamál and the poems of Sígurðr also indicate that the hero returned from the trials a sage, a poet, a healer, even a king. It appears that the Maiden-mythology reflects the typical basics of initiation rituals into a sacred office.

I have frequently touched upon the kind of initiation ritual that is revealed, without arriving at any certain conclusions. The indications in the myths are varied at best. My main aim, as stated in the Introduction, is not to decide what the hero is initiand into, but to prove that the pattern, the structure of themes, exists, and thus, a "Maiden mythology" reflecting initiation. Our study has, however, made it possible to get a vague idea about the nature of the initiations, and I have pointed out significant similarities not only with shamanism or royal inauguration through sacred marriage, but also to ancient Mystery religions.

We may still see these myths as products of a religious tradition unique to pre-Christian Scandinavia, yet one that may have drawn from many different traditions which are related to and thus similar to other world traditions of the kind just mentioned.

Firstly, the initiation is centered around the Maiden figure, whom we have identified as the Great Goddess. The initiation culminates in marriage. Since the Maiden is a goddess or other supernatural entity, we are talking about a sacred marriage, a Hieros Gamos as defined in chapter 3.1. Sacred Marriage is closely connected to kingship inauguration in many ancient cultures, and was known in Scandinavia during the Bronze Age, probably an idea imported from the great civilizations of the south such as the Sumerian, where sacred marriage was the central ritual of the religion.

In Scandinavia, sacred marriage appears to have had a new "boom" from around the fifth century A.D, when the Germanic tribes started to constitute little kingdoms. From comparative sources such as the Sumerian and the Irish, the sacred marriage of the king and the goddess had to do with the consecration of a king by the Great Goddess of the land: only through her authorization may a king enter his sacred office.

From the studies of Steinsland, it seems clear that sacred marriage was closely connected to kingship and it would seem as if the king had to undergo trials of initiation before claiming the throne. However, I have frequently referred to the nature of the teachings in "Maiden mythology" and had to conclude that the myths of the Maiden seem to cover a lot more than kingship initiation. The art of healing, poetry, galdr, seiðr, magic, sorcery and journeys into the Underworld were hardly the unique domain of the king in Norse nor in Germanic society.

In chapter 8, I showed that so-called "masters of initiation" were present at the trials, and that they could be identified with actual religious professionals operating in Scandinavia and Germania in pre-Christian times. These masters could not have been ignorant about the trials and teachings of the neophyte; on the contrary, we would assume that they were experts. They would become experts only by going through the same kind of trials beforehand.

In some cases, these experts would appear to be working in the service of kings, such as Atli, Sinfiǫtli and Skírnir. The relationship between kingship and the Maiden is visible in the Heroic Poems, where the heroes are royal princes. The focus in the Heroic Poetry is not so much on kingship, however, as on the continuity of the relationship between the hero and the valkyria through lives and deaths. The theme could very well be about the journey of the soul through different lives, as Kragerud suggested, and, as I suggested, about the valkyria perhaps being the actual divine, immortal soul of the hero.

This does not out rule the importance of kingship and sacred marriage, but it could show that the union with the Maiden is a far broader and more universal theme than that of kingship. Looking back to "masters of initiation" such as the Atli figure, we will recall that Atli not only brings a Maiden back to the king, but also a Maiden for himself. Atli is certainly not a king, but an earl's son, "earl" being the echo of an ancient religious office. Thus, the marriage to a Maiden from the Other World is not restricted to kings.

Atli's expertise has to do with journeying in the Other World, journeys that begin with vision quests and visions of a thoroughly ecstatic character. We should not ignore the ecstatic nature of the heroes´ experiences. The vision quests and visions followed by journeys to a different realm, a realm of giants and of the forces of death, are vividly described and I, at least, do not get the impression that these are descriptions of organized, routinized ritual. I am convinced that, if these myths reflect actual practice, that practice must have been of a highly ecstatic character. The ecstasy is not induced only among royal candidates. It would rather appear to have been part of the religious practice of Old Norse cult, performed by professionals – the initiand.

I have pointed out the likeness to shamanism, yet it is impossible to decide whether we are dealing with shamanism in its strictest, classical sense or something that only resembles it in greater or lesser degree. Shamanism was certainly known and even used by the Norse population, who lived very close to the shamanistic Sámi, whom they apparently approached for help in magical matters. In chapter 8.5, I pointed out the likeness of Óðinn's role as divine archetype and the role of Siberian "ancestral shamans".

Óðinn is certainly the most shaman-like character in the Norse sources, if we should believe Snorri's descriptions of the god in the Ynglinga saga. I have touched upon the subject of shamanism in the Norse sources quite often, because I believe it is too prominent to be ignored, particularly in the context of Maiden-mythology. As far as I have been able to investigate, the classical shamans' relations to great female divinities is a subject rather more prominent than Eliade ever suspected, but this is a subject which reach beyond the scope of this thesis.

In any case, shamanism in some way appears to have had some influence on Norse mythology, whether it be because there were shamans in Norse society, practitioners who resembled classical shamans to some degree, or perhaps the influences were only remnants of a distant past. In the Encyclopedia of Religions, Eliade gives the impression that many scholars believe shamanistic rituals and tribal initiations were the structural and mythical origins of different kind of ritual behavior such as the type detected in Antique mystery cults. In this second edition of my original thesis, I have put greater emphasis on this possible resemblance.

While shamanism certainly could involve marriage to supernatural beings, such a union is also known from Mystery religions. Such religions also involved a "journey" (how ritualized or how personally experienced we do not know) through the Underworld, leading to a mystic union with the primary deity, very often the Great Goddess. This kind of initiation also involved esoteric teachings, and one of its central ideas had to do with overcoming death: how to earn a blessed existence after death. The emphasis on the life-death opposition in the Maiden mythology (as seen in the ogress-Maiden polarity) could in fact resemble mystery religions.

We know for a fact that Germanic religions were influenced by Celtic and (often through them) other Indo-European religions such as the Greek and the Mediterranean ones, so that a link to Antique mystery religion would not be an impossibility. Michael Enright has pointed out that the emerging Germanic warrior tribes were greatly influenced by Celtic culture and religion at the end of the Celtic Iron Age (which started from about 500 B.C.). Enright shows that the ideology of the lady with a mead cup and the German liquor ritual was borrowed from the Celtic upper classes when Germanic tribes evolved their own class hierarchy.

The Celts again were certainly influenced by Mediterranean culture through mercenaries and merchants. This period is the same that saw a wide variety of mystery cults in the Mediterranean. In fact, the way the Maiden mythology is conveyed certainly indicates a degree of secrecy and "mystery": it has to be deciphered through intricate symbols and is never explained or presented in complete. All in all, Maiden mythology is not restricted to covering consecration of kingship. It appears that the Maiden will teach anyone who seeks her through the realm of death and who has the power to withstand that realm.

As to the idea that Maiden mythology reflects cultic practice, we have the archaeological evidence pointed out by Enright, as referred to in chapter 9.5. The Maiden with the Mead had her living counterpart in the world of Germanic tribal society. She was a woman holding a spoon sieve or other equipment for the ladling and serving of mead, and she was buried with cauldrons which designs were often of great antiquity and elaboration, and of obvious cultic purpose. She was also buried with jewelry showing her high rank, equipment for spinning and weaving which was forever associated with divination and fate-magic in the Germanic world.

Finally, she would often have a staff which was exclusively for women of her rank, identified as a "cult staff" by the archaeologists, as well as objects that she had carried in a pouch in her belt. She has been found in burial sites from before the birth of Christ up to the last pagan strongholds in Scandinavia. Her cult was old and of great continuity and popularity. Her grave always holds a special position in the burial site, showing her as a revered and important person: in one site she is at the center with all the other graves laid in a half-moon formation around her. The finds strongly suggest a religious function, and Enright identifies the women as the "prophetesses" who held such authority in early Germanic societies. He also sees the connection between them and a goddess cult. According to Enright, the queens offering mead in later medieval literature were their descendants.

Michael Enright has argued that the (non-religious) literary evidence shows that the living Mead-Lady's main function was to establish brotherhood and social positions through a ritual in the king's hall. This would appear to be true and reminds me of the idea of Freyia "arranging seats in the hall". The arrangement of seats was important in Norse and Germanic society, showing the exact social position of each individual.

Freyia's arrangement of seats takes place, however, in an afterlife-realm. Extending our idea of the living Mead-Lady to the supernatural Maiden figure, we see that the Maiden, first and foremost, initiands and consecrates. Perhaps, reflecting how the living Mead- Lady established the social positions of men within a warband by the chieftain's table, the Maiden established the spiritual (and thus social, religious) position of the neophyte. Regarding the possibility of an actual ritual setting behind the Maiden mythology, the women's´ staffs could perhaps indicate the involvement of women much like those who would later be recognized in Norse written sources as the vǫlur.

Indeed, the number nine would further associate the vǫlur with Maiden-mythology; The vǫlva of Eiriks saga was the last in a company of nine sisters, and the vǫlva of Örvar Odds saga had nine apprentices of either sex in her following. Gullveigr died three times and was reborn three times; a three-by-three count resulting in the number nine. A ritual enactment of the myth could, at some point in history, easily have involved a vǫlva both as master of initiation, as suggested in chapter 9.6, and as the representative of the goddess herself, ladling out the precious mead and offering her cup and her embrace to the consecrated.

INITIATION NARRATIVES IN THE SAGAS

In the beginning of 2022, I began working on the last part of a new work titled Fjǫlkyngi – Stories of Seiðr and Initiation, which may be published in 2023. This last part of a compilation of stories with my commentaries on the diverse arts of fjǫlkyngi – "great knowledge", centers around the many underlying initiation narratives of diverse sagas – mostly sagas about the "old times" (fornaldarsögur), where spiritual mentors appear who are evidently described as people (or dwarfs and giants) with fjǫlkyngi.

I have titled this part "Witches and Warriors – Initiation Narratives and Mentors in the Sagas." Within the context of the larger project on seiðr and other forms of fjǫlkyngi, I wanted to show that women and men who have magical knowledge played a crucial role in the education and initiations of young men – and also of young women.

The stories possess a remarkable amount of details and are too many to retell in full, but they are also relevant to this work on the Maiden with the Mead, so allow me to offer up a little summary:

Kjalnesinga saga is set to the 9th century and the era of Haraldr Hárfagri Dofrafostra. It follows a structure of initiation that seems to go through three subsequent cycles.

FIRST CYCLE

☞ *The hero, Búi, is sent into "fostering" – in fact a way of saying "apprenticeship" – with a wise, old woman called Esja, who knew well "the old ways".*
☞ *While in her custody, he starts roaming around without any weapons apart from a sling, and is accused of unmanliness because he is "armed like a woman" and refuses to arm himself in the traditional manners of his male peers.*
☞ *He proves himself capable of protecting himself one against many with this sling. He is called einrænn – "one who runs alone" – a loner.*
☞ *Towards the end of this cycle, he enters a temple dedicated to Thor, where he commits a crime that has him outlawed.*

SECOND CYCLE

☞ *Outlawed, Búi must travel into the unknown.*
☞ *He walks into the king´s hall and asks for a chance to redeem himself.*
☞ *The king sends him to find a tafl – a gameboard – at the mountain giant Dofris abode.*
☞ *Nobody knows where this is, and the king says that Búi must find his own way.*
☞ *Búi offers a gold ring to a man who turns up and shows him the way to Dofri´s mountain and tells him how to enter it.*

THIRD CYCLE

☞ *Búi reaches the entry to the gnipahellir – the protruding cliff-cave of Dofri - on the eve of Yule.*
☞ *He strikes his hammer three times while invoking Dofri, and ends with breaking the shaft of the hammer.*
☞ *A woman opens the portal into the mountain, the giant´s daughter Fríðr [Peace, Truce, Beauty], and she lights the path through the labyrinthine caves of the mountain giants.*
☞ *She offers him the ágætan drykk "famous drink".*
☞ *Búi stays the winter with the giants and sleeps in the arms of the giant´s daughter, who later helps him obtain the game-board and get back to the world of men.*

Let us go through the structure of initiation in Búi´s story:

☞ *Separation/Apprenticeship: Búi leaves home to be "fostered" by a woman who knows the "ancient ways".*
☞ *Ordeals/Humiliations: Búi walks a solitary path where does not partake in the ordinary roles of the young men of his class, and where he must be near unarmed, using only a sling for protection, which is said to be a woman´s weapon.*
☞ *Test & Quest: Búi enters a pagan temple. He also commits sacrilege in said temple, killing a praying priest, which is why he must be exiled. But if we are to look for the underlying struc-ture with roots in a pagan worldview, the important thing may be that he enters a pagan temple where something happens that leads him on to his path.*
☞ *Separation/Humiliation: Búi loses all status and becomes an exile. Being pulled away from your ordinary life and surround-ings is a typical feature in an initiation narrative.*
☞ *Ordeal/Humiliation: Búi faces death (when he seeks the king).*
☞ *Test & Quest: Búi shows his cleverness and his eloquence, and instead of being killed, he is offered a quest to prove his worth (and to exonerate him from his sacrilege). The quest is to retrieve a magical game-board from the hands of the mountain giant.*

☞ Separation: Búi must wander alone in the cold and uninhabited wilderness and lose his way.

☞ Apprenticeship: Búi must seek the aid of another cunning man, Rauðr, who tells him how to get to the other world. Búi pays Rauðr a gold ring for his trouble.

☞ Ordeal: Búi must spend the night in a magical place where contraries meet, a peaking cave.

☞ Ritual: Búi must beat his hilt with his hammer while invoking Dofri to open his hall three times, and then beat his hammer with strong emotion so that the hammer breaks apart (Ritual Act):

☞ Descent: Búi is approved of by the lady who guards the gate, and she leads him into the cave and guides him through its labyrinthine interior, opening doors and lighting the paths. He learns that many have come to the mountain before him, without having shown themselves worthy, and it has been their death.

☞ Consecration/Test/Escape: Búi is served the Famous Drink, before he and Fríðr enjoy a long erotic adventure together within the mountain during winter. At spring, the maiden assists Búi in his quest for the magical game-board, and it is stated that he could not have done it without her help, just like Óðinn stated that he would not have gotten out of the world of the giants without the help of the giantess who loved and embraced him in the Hávamál.

☞ Return: Búi returns with the game-board, is exonerated from his crimes (freed from imminent death) and re-welcomed into the human world with a new status.

The cave and the mountain, especially the inside of the mountain, the cold, the winter and the wilderness are all typical Norse metaphors for death and the underworld, as is the theme of making love to a giantess in the underworld. The game-board itself is symbolic of fate, and the story faintly echoes the initiation story of the god Óðinn´s adventure with a giant´s daughter inside the mountain of Suttungr.

ᘄ

In Egils saga einhenda ok Ásmundar berserkjabana, we find several different initiation narratives, all coming together for a grand climax. This is also one of the few sagas that detail the initiation of a woman sorceress, Arinnefja [Eagle Beak].

Arinnefja experiences servitude and humiliation as the youngest in a group of 18 "sisters".

☞ *She makes sacrifice (of goats) and invokes a god (Thor).*
☞ *The god helps her. She has intercourse with the god. The god helps her retrieve her legacy.*
☞ *She can now change shape.*
☞ *She meets a sorceress of great power, who possesses a power that Arinnefja wants.*
☞ *The sorceress tests and outwits Arinnefja. In order to redeem herself, Arinnefja is sent to the underworld to collect several magical powers.*

Arinnefja goes into three different underworld realms:

1. First, she meets a mysterious king Snow, offers goats (like she did to Thor) and gold, until he sells her the drinking horn (divine wisdom, poetry).

She learns to survive poison.

2. Second, she meets the three norns and fights for their game board (control of fate). She conquers the rulers of fate, takes control of her own destiny.

3. Third, she meets a god (Óðinn) and has intercourse with the god, who tells her how to reach the innermost realm of the Depth Below, where she jumps the fire fence which surrounds the hall of immortality in the world of the dead, and retrieves a cloak that can withstand fire. This is, likely, a cloak of immortality, or else a cloak of shape-changing.

☞ *She "loses her skin" after this, which is probably a way of saying that she no longer has a definite shape of form. Shape-changing is often referred to by another word for skin, hámr.*

☞ *A shape-shifter either has a "strong skin/hide" (hamrammr) or not one single skin. This is probably what is also hinted at in the case of the name of her daughter, Skinnefja – "Skin Beak".*
☞ *Arinnefja returns with the gifts. She now becomes a healer, a master surgeon, and a spiritual mentor to two young warriors who wander into her cave one evening, seeking the famous Game-Board.*

In the same saga, Arinnefja becomes spiritual mentor to two young men and two young men, as well as to her own daughter by Thor, Skinnefja [Skin Beak]. The first to go is Ásmundr:

FIRST CYCLE OF ÁSMUNDR'S INITIATION:

☞ *Ásmundr is special and very talented: While a teenager, Ásmundr is lost in the wilderness for three nights – a symbol of the underworld.*
☞ *Ásmundr meets a mysterious man in the forest, engages him in combat and sport competitions before the man takes him onto a fate-changing path.*
☞ *They swear themselves to each other in a ritual equivalent "marriage", as in a family commitment between friends.*
☞ *Ásmundr becomes a king-maker and gains power in a foreign land.*

In this story, we see that there is a repeated theme of going into the underworld, facing dangers, conquering death before returning with new treasures and a new social status, such as the right to contend for the throne at parliament.

SECOND CYCLE OF ÁSMUND´S INITIATION

☞ *Ásmundr sits in a burial mound for three nights*
☞ *Ásmundr must combat his foster-brother's draugr and escape the grave.*
☞ *He retrieves the treasures that had been laid in the grave.*
☞ *Ásmundr now has the right to contend for the throne at parliament.*

<u>Third Cycle of Ásmund´s Initiation</u>

☞ *Ásmundr is to be sacrificed to Óðinn on a burial mound.*
☞ *Ásmundr breaks free, turns the tables and escapes death.*
☞ *Ásmundr again becomes a king-maker, winning a valuable friendship and gets a new nickname. He also gets a ship and a crew to make his way in the world.*

Second to go is Egill

<u>First Cycle of Egill´s Initiation</u>

☞ *Egill is special and outstanding*
☞ *Egill seeks a distant and mysterious island in the wilderness*
☞ *Egill loses his way due to dark mist and cold wind – symbolic of the underworld.*

On the third day, Egill finally reaches the distant island and finds himself in the giant world.

☞ *Egill is taken as slave and must work as a goat-herder and live in a cave with his jǫtunn master. This is a typical stage of an initiation narrative where a high-standing person (a prince) must live the life of a humble slave herds boy before he can prove himself.*
☞ *Egill must use wit and cunning to escape slavery and has the help of the gold-eyes of a cat, and there is a theme of being able to see in the darkness.*
☞ *Egill must survive in a dark cave without anything to eat or drink.*
☞ *Egill assumes the hide of a he-goat – a typical sacrifice to Thor and to the giants.*
☞ *Egill receives a gold ring from the cave-giant, as if the giant had been his mentor all the while.*
☞ *Egill escapes the cave and becomes a leader of men.*

SECOND CYCLE OF EGILL´S INITIATION

☞ *Egill goes to a clearing – a sort of grove – what was in itself a sort of natural temple back then.*
☞ *In a hole (or on a mound) in this grove, he sees a giant and a sorceress, fighting over a gold-ring.*
☞ *Egill helps the sorceress but loses a hand to the giant.*
☞ *Egill walks into the forest*
☞ *Egill seeks to relieve his pain in a healing water-stream*
☞ *A dwarf pops out from a rock*
☞ *Egill offers his gold ring to the dwarf*
☞ *The dwarf invites Egill into the rock (=the underworld), where his wound is healed*
☞ *Egill receives a sword that has been made to replace his lost hand in battle*
☞ *Egill returns to the world healed and with a new weapon to overcome his handicap.*

The third cycle of Egill´s Initiation is intertwined with the other main characters of the saga as they become apprenticed to the sorceress Arinnefja. There are two sisters, one warrior woman, and one wise woman, who have been abducted into the mountain of the giants. Egill and Ásmundr must meet up and help these two women, whose stories are also indicative of initiation trials. The women also contribute to their own rescue by showing their magical skills before a court of giants.

The four youngsters receive the help of their mentor, Arinnefja, whom they must seek in a cliff-cave on a distant shore. Arinnefja´s skills as a surgeon are such that she is able to heal Egill´s hand completely by putting the hand that she had taken care of and preserved with life-giving herbs – she was the sorceress that he helped while in the grove that day when he lost his hand.

In Bósa saga ok Herrauðs, two young friends set out to exonerate themselves on an impossible journey with no certain outcome, one that takes them north and east – the direction of death and giants. They are first apprenticed to a "foster-mother" called Búsla, who is clearly a sorceress of great power, a shape-shifter and a spell-song master. She directs them to where they have to go to find their trials. The young men end up on a distant shore where they have to roam the wilderness, and end up having a proper journey of initiation:

First Cycle of Bósi and Herrauð´s Initiation

☞ *Both the prince and the karl´s son are outstanding persons, even as young boys. The one is a prince, and the other the son of a warrior woman and the "foster-son" of a wise woman, Busla, who offers to teach him galdrar and töfr [witchcraft]*
☞ *Bósi and Herrauðr are doomed to die but are helped by their mentor, Busla, and her magical powers. They may be exonerated if they go on a quest for the Vulture´s Egg with Golden Inscriptions, a journey that has no certain outcome.*
☞ *Bósi and Herrauðr are "fostered", as in mentored, by the sorceress Busla, who tells them where to go and what to do.*

Second Cycle of Bósi and Herrauð´s Initiation

Bósi and Herrauðr enter the wilderness and have little to eat (liminal phase)

☞ *The foster-brothers find a mysterious farm with three helpful people; an "inhabitant", a "húsfreyia" and a "farmer´s daughter". The "inhabitant" is later referred to by name; Háketill, which means "High Cauldron" – ketill meaning cauldron and often referring to a temple cauldron or a sacrificial cauldron.*
☞ *Bósi pays a gold ring and asks the farmer´s daughter for sex. It is his first time. They both enjoy the sex, and she rewards him for the good banging with good counsel on their quest for the Vulture´s Egg, explaining exactly the dangers and what they must do and where to go, as such she acts as the second mentor on their initiation journey.*

☞ They butcher a slave and a cow. The prince assumes the disguise of a slave, and they use the hide of the cow in order to trick the temple bull.
☞ They enter the temple and face obstacles – the vulture of death and the powerful giantess (of death)
☞ They find the sacred treasures of the temple
☞ They enter the inner sanctuary
☞ They find a priestess seated on a chair like an oracle, and free her. She is the priestess apprentice of the temple.
☞ The prince gets a promise to marry the princess, and they both return to society with proof of their ordeals, and are exonerated.

THIRD CYCLE OF BÓSI AND HERRAUÐ´S INITIATION

The third cycle in the saga of Bósi and Herrauðr begins where the second ends; the king-to-be has acquired a queen for his kingdom, but Bósi stands wife-less. He is an ordinary karl and has so far only had fun with women of his own rank and standing. But some improvement should be offered to one who had stood the new king so near and helped him in all matters. In fact, it is Búi who was responsible for finding the way and for knowing what to do, as if he himself is on his path to become a king´s mentor, a counsellor and confidante with great magical powers. He has, after all, been raised by a powerful sorceress. But now, he too needs a wife.

The third cycle begins much like the two previous ones, with a journey through the wilderness and a three day long visit to a certain farm, much like that of the High Cauldron Man. Here, he manages to please the farmer´s daughter so much that she declares that sex with Bósi was better than drinking the finest mead, before she tells him to thrust his "brush" real hard once more. When Búi has passed his test of grand lovemaker, he finally dares to ask for her counsel.

And now, the wise woman of the forest and the High Cauldron Man, who evidently has no other designs on Búi than good sex and fun company, finally grants him a more ambitious marriage match, happily helping him to find and retrieve for a bride the daughter of the Bjarmian king. Her name is Edda, whose name means Great Grandmother, and which is also the term used for the sacred lore of the pagan religion. She is, of course, a good friend of the farmer´s daughter.

The wise daughter of High Cauldron now leads Bósi to a grove of walnut trees, in which he meets his Edda, and takes her home as his bride. This time, Bósi pays the wise woman three golden walnuts for her guidance.

⸙

In Þorsteins saga Víkingssonar, we are first introduced to "Viking", Thorsteinn´s father. He goes through a trial that involves a woman with a drinking horn – in fact, she is called Hamhleypa Dís – "The Shape-Shifting Goddess":

☞ *Viking goes on a solitary quest into the wilderness (the unknown, the underworld)*
☞ *Viking arrives at a grove/clearing (natural temple)*
☞ *Viking is met by a woman in the grove with a drinking horn (poetry, wisdom, inspiration, divine resurrection). She is "The Shape-Shifting Goddess"*
☞ *Viking drinks the precious drink and sleeps in the mead-woman´s embrace.*
☞ *Viking returns to society, marked by his experience.*

IN VIKING´S SECOND CYCLE OF INITIATION, HE HAS THE HELP OF A WISE FRIEND, HALFDAN:

VIKING´S 2ND CYCLE OF INITIATION

☞ *Friend/Foster-brother Halfdan walks into the wilderness and finds a grove (natural temple)*
☞ *There is a magical rock in the grove*
☞ *RITUAL: Halfdan taps the rock with his wand*
☞ *A dwarf representing the drink (he is called Lítr – a common term for the drink, such as the mead of poetry in Hávamál) comes out, and is the "foster-parent" (=mentor) of Halfdan.*
☞ *The dwarf appears with the drinking horn, stolen from the shape-shifting goddess. He knows how to pour the drink correctly, and now, Viking is healed and fulfils his fate in life.*

Thorsteinn´s First Cycle of Initiation

☞ *Thorsteinn is exiled and must live in hiding on a deserted island in a lake (separation-liminal theme)*
☞ *Has an omen dream about animal fylgjur, warning of imminent death*
☞ *Must survive magically invoked storm (invoked against him)*
☞ *Is drowning (dying - Initiation Death Experience)*
☞ *Is taken to a cliff-cave (hellir) by a woman of fjǫlkyngi (Skellinefja)*
☞ *Must promise to fulfil her wishes in order to get healed*

Thorsteinn´s Second Cycle of Initiation

☞ *Thorsteinn is wounded and falls down cliffs*
☞ *Is dying beneath the ground*
☞ *Is saved by Skellinefja a second time*
☞ *Is taken to her cliff-cave*
☞ *Must swear to marry her and have sexual intercourse with her*
☞ *She heals him*
☞ *She returns his sword to him (his power)*
☞ *He returns to society*

Later, Skellinefja appears as his beautiful bride, Ingibjörg, having resumed her human form. They have a daughter, Véfreyia: the Freyia of the Shrine, who has been conceived, born and raised in the cliff-cave of the giantess and shares the wisdom of her mother, Skellinefja/Ingibjörg.

There are many, many more such stories, many of which I go through in great detail in the oncoming book project. They are, in fact, too many to render here. In the saga of Bósi and Herrauðr, we see that events are happening in a pagan temple – in most of the stories, they happen within a hellir – a cliff-cave, where the helpful sorceress tends to live. Her identity is always something between a giantess and a woman who has taken the hide of a giantess for some reason. Often, the cave is situated in a place called Gandvík, which means the Bay of Magic or the Bay of Wands (as in the wand carried by a vǫlva).

The sagas show different layers of attitudes towards paganism, but they all build upon exactly the same structures, where young men must venture into the unknown – wilderness, mist, storms, darkness, until they find a woman and other supernatural beings who may test and challenge them, but who often turn out to be benevolent. They often include mention of a drink or a drinking horn, but not always. However, it seems clear to me that the theme of initiation is so widespread in old myths and legends that we may conclude that such a theme was once vital and central to the pre-Christian religion of Scandinavia.

BIBLIOGRAPHY

Primary Literature in Original Language:

Bugge, Sophus, ed. (1867 / 1965): SÆMUNDAR EDDA HINS FRÓDA Norrøn Fornkvædi -Islandsk Samling av Folkelige Oldtidsdigte om Nordens Guder og Heroer Universitetsforlaget, Oslo

Jónsson, Finnur, ed. (1907): EDDA Snorra Sturlusonar. Reykjavik

Jónsson, Finnur, ed.(1912): Den Norsk-Islandske Skjaldedigtning (800-1200) udgiven af Kommisjonen for det Arnamagnæisk legat B: rettet tekst, 1. bind Gyldendalske Boghandel –Nordisk Forlag Kjøbenhavn og Kristiania

Primary Literature in Translation:

Byock, Jesse L. (1998): The Saga of king Hrolf Kraki. Penguin Classics, England

Byock, Jesse L. (1999): The Saga of the Volsungs –the Norse epic of Sígurðr the Dragon Slayer. Penguin Classics, England

Eggen, Erik (1978): Snorre Sturlason: Den yngre Edda Det Norske Samlaget, Oslo

Faulkes, Anthony (1987): EDDA Snorri Sturluson. University of Birmingham. Everyman, London

Fisher, Peter (transl.)/Ellis Daidson (ed) (1979): Saxo Grammaticus. The History of the Danes, Volume I English Text. D.S. Brewer, Rowman and Littlefield, Cambridge

Hatto, A.T. (1969): The Nibelungenlied. Penguin Books, London, New York, Victoria

Holm-Olsen, Ludvig (1985): Eddadikt. Cappelen, Trondheim

Larrington, Carolyne (1996): The Poetic Edda. Oxford University Press, Oxford, New York

Lie, Hallvard (1970): Egils saga Skallagrimsonar [Norsk]. Aschehoug, Oslo

Mattingly, H. (1970): Tacitus: The Agricola and the Germania

Mortensson-Egnund, Ivar (1993): Edda-Kvede Det Norske Samlaget, Oslo

Pálsson, Hermann/Edwards, Paul (1985): Seven Viking Romances. Penguin Books

Rindal, Magnus (1974): Soga om Volsungane. Det Norske Samlaget, Oslo

Translator not named (1944): Snorres Kongesagaer Gyldendal Norsk Forlag, Oslo

Secondary Literature

Acker, Paul/ Larrington,Carolyne (eds) (2002): The Poetic Edda: essays on Old Norse mythology. Routledge medieval casebooks, New York

Ahlbäck, Tore (ed.) (1990): Old Norse and Finnish Religions and Cultic Place-Names. Almqvist & Wiksell International, Stockholm

Bartha, Antal (1992):Myth and Reality in the Ancient Culture of the Northern Peoples (in Hoppál, Pentikäinen,1992)

Bessason, Haraldur/Glendinning, Robert J. (eds)(1983): Edda: a collection of essays. University of Manitoba Icelandic studies; 4. Winnipeg: University of Manitoba Press

Blundell, Sue/ Williamson, Margaret (eds) (1998): The Sacred and the Feminine in Ancient Greece Routledge: London and New York

Bogoras (1904-1909): The Chuckchee. The Jesup North Pacific Expedition, edited by Franz Boaz. Memoirs of the American Museum of Natural History

Bäckman, Louise (1975): Sájva – Föreställningar om hjälp och skyddsväsen i heliga fjäll bland samerna Almqvist & Wiksell, Stockholm

Clover, Carol J./Lindow, John (eds)(1985): Old Norse-Icelandic literature: a critical guide. Islandica; 45, Cornell University Press

Clunies-Ross, Margaret (1987): Skáldskaparmál –Snorri Sturlusson's Ars Poetica and Medieval Theories of Language. Odense University Press

Clunies-Ross, Margaret (1994): Prolongued Echoes -Old Norse Myths in Medieval Northern Society, Volume I: The Myths Odense University Press

Davidson, Hilda Ellis (1964): Gods and Myths of Norhtern Europe. Penguin, London, New York, Toronto

Davidson, Hilda Ellis (1998): Roles of the Northern Goddess. Routledge, London and New York

Demant Jacobsen, Merete (1999): SHAMANISM –Traditional and Contemporary Approaches to the Mastery of Spirits and Healing Berghnan Books, New York, Oxford

Diószegi, Vilmos (1968): Tracing Shamans in Siberia, The story of an ethnographical research expedition. Translated by Anita Rajkay, Oosterhout cap. Anthropological publications

Dronke, Ursula (1997): The Poetic Edda, volume II: Mythological Poems. Clarendon Press, Oxford

Eliade, Mircea (ed.et al.) (1987): The Encyclopedia of Religion. New York: Macmillan

Enright, Michael J. (1996): Lady with a Mead Cup -Ritual, Prophecy and Lordship in the European Warband from La Tène to the Viking Age. Four Courts Press, Dublin

Fari, Camilla Helene (2003): HIEROS-GAMOS En sammenlikning mellom symbolets uttrykk i den nordiske bronsealderens helleristningstradisjon og myteverdenen i det østlige middelhavsområdet Hovedoppgave i nordisk arkeologi, Universitetet i Oslo

Flood, Jan Peder (1999): Volver, Seidmenn og Sjamaner: en komparativ analyse av norrøn seid Hovedoppgave i religionshistorie, Universitetet i Oslo

Grim, John A. (1983): The Shaman. Patterns of Siberian and Ojibway Healing. University of Oklahoma Press

Grimstad, Kaaren (1983): The Revenge of Volundr (in Bessason / Glendinning, eds., 1983)

Hammer, Anita (1999): Inanna in Hieros Gamos, A Processual representation. Skriftserie fra Institutt for Kunst og Medievitenskap 3. Trondheim

Haugen, Einar (1983): The Edda as Ritual: Odin and His Masks (in: Bessason / Glendinning, eds., 1983)

Hedeager, Lotte (1999): Skygger av en annen virkelighet – Oldnordiske myter Oversatt av Kåre A. Lie Pax Forlag, A/S, Oslo

Heide, Eldar (1997): Fjölsvinnsmål. Ei oversett nøkkelkjelde til nordisk mytologi Magisteravhandling i norrøn filologi. Universitetet i Oslo

Hjelde, Sígurðr/Ruud, Inger Marie (red) (1998): Enhet i mangfold? 100 år med religionshistorie i Norge Tano Aschehoug

Hollander, Lee M. (1986): The Poetic Edda. University of Texas Press, Austin

Holm-Olsen, Ludvig (1995): *Norges Litteraturhistorie bind I: Fra runene til det Norske Selskab –Middelalderens Litteratur i Norge* J.W. Cappelens Forlag A.S, Oslo

Hoppál Mihaly/ Pentikäinen, Juha (eds.)(1992): *NORTHERN RELIGIONS AND SHAMANISM ETHNOLOGICA URALICA 3.* Budapest Akadémiai Kiadó, Helsinki. Finnish Literature Society

Hultkrantz, Åke (1953): *Conceptions of the Soul among North American Indians. A study in religious ethnology.* Ethnographical Museum of Sweden, Stockholm

Hultkrantz, Åke/Bäckman, Louise (ed.) (1978): *Studies in Lapp Shamanism. Acta Universitatis Stockholmiensis. Stockholm studies in comparative religion.* Almqvist & Wiksell International, Stockholm

Hultkrantz, Åke (1992): *Shamanic Healing and Ritual Drama. Health and Medicine in Native North American. Religious Traditions.* Crossroad, New York, 1992

Hultkrantz, Åke (1992) (b): *Aspects of Sámi (Lapp) Shamanism* (in Hoppál, Päentikainen, 1992)

Hødnebø, Finn/ Fjeld Halvorsen, Eyvind (et al) (1992): *Eyvindarbók: Festskrift til Eyvind Fjeld Halvorsen 4.mai* Universitetet i Oslo

Jakobsdóttir, Svava (2002): *Gunnlod and the Precious Mead (Hávamál). Translatedby Katrina Attwood* (in Acker and Larrington, eds., 2002)

Kragerud, Alv (1989): *Helgediktningen og Reinkarnasjon. Scripta Islandica –Isländska sällskapets årsbok 40/1989.* Almqvist & Wiksell International, Stockholm, Sweden

Kramer, Samuel Noah (1969): *The Sacred Marriage Rite Aspects of Faith, Myth and Ritual in Ancient Sumer.* Indiana University Press, Bloomington, London

Larrington, Carolyne (ed.) (1992): *The Feminist Companion to Mythology.* Pandora Press, HarperCollins, London

Motz, Lotte von (1983): The Wise One on the Mountain: form, function and significance of the Subterranean Smith: a study in folklore Göppingen, Kummerle Verlag

Motz, Lotte von (1993): The Beauty and the Hag, Female figures of Germanic Faith and Myth. Filologica Germanica 15. Fassbaender, Wien

Motz, Lotte von (1997): The Faces of the Goddess. New York: Oxford University Press

Mundal, Else (1974): Fylgjemotiva i norrøn litteratur. Universitetsforlaget, Oslo

Mundal, Else (1990): The Position of the Individual Gods and Goddesses in Various Typse of Sources –with Special Reference to the Female Divinities (in Ahlbäck, 1990)

Mundal, Else (1992): Heiðrun –den mjødmjølkandegeita på Valhalls tak (in Hødnebø, Fjeld Halvorsen, 1992)

Mundal, Else (1994): Mytar og diktning (in Schjødt, 1994)

Narby, Jeremy/Huxley, Francis (eds) (2001): Shamans through Time –500 Years on the Path to Knowledge. Penguin Putnam, New York

Näsström, Britt-Mari (1998): Frøya –Den store gudinnen i Norden
Oversatt av Kåre A. Lie Pax Forlag, A/S, Oslo

Näsström, Britt-Mari (2001): BLOT –Tro og offer i det førkristne Norden Oversatt av Kåre A. Lie Pax Forlag A/S, Oslo

Pollan, Brita (2002): Noaidier –historier om samiske sjamaner De Norske Bokklubbene, Oslo

Schjødt, Jens Peter(ed.) (1994):Myte og ritual i det førkristne Norden – et symposium. Odense Universitetsforlag, Odense

Simek, Rudolf (1996): Dictionary of Northern Mythology. Translated by Angela Hall. D.S. Brewer, Cambridge

Skretting, Atle (1980): Innvielsene i antikkens Isis-mysterier
Hovedoppgave i Religionshistorie, Universitetet i Oslo

Solli, Brit (2002): SEID Myter, sjamanisme og kjønn I
vikingenes tid Pax Forlag A/S, Oslo

Steinsland, Gro (ed.) (1986): Words and Objects, Towards
a Dialogue Between Archaeology and History of Religion.
Norwegian University Press, Oslo

Steinsland, Gro (1991): Det Hellige Bryllup og Norrøn
Kongeideologi En Analyse av Hierogami-Myten i Skírnismál,
Ynglingatal, Háleygjatal og Hyndluljód Solum Forlag, Larvik

Steinsland, Gro (1992): Døden som eroitsk lystreise (i Hødnebø,
Fjeld Halvorsen, 1992)

Steinsland, Gro (1997): Eros og død i norrøne myter
Universitetsforlaget, Oslo

Steinsland, Gro (1998): Hedendom mot kristendom i norrøne
myter (i Hjelde/Ruud (ed.) (1998)

Steinsland, Gro/Meulengracht Sørensen, Preben (1999): Voluspå
Pax forlag A/S, Oslo

Steinsland, Gro (2000): Den Hellige Kongen –om religion og
herskermakt fra vikingtid til middelalder Pax Forlag A/S, Oslo

Ström, Folke (1954): Diser, nornor, valkyrjor Fruktbarhetskult
och sakralt kungadöme i Norden Almqvist & Wiksell, Stockholm

Ström, Folke (1985): Nordisk Hedendom –Tro och Sed I
förkristen tid Akademiförlaget, Göteborg

Strömbäck, Dag (2000): SEJD och andra studier I nordisk
själsuppfatning Kungl. Gustav Adolfs Akademien för svensk
folkkultur, Gidlunds förlag, Uppsala

Turville-Petre (1975): Myth and religion of the North: the religion
of ancient Scandinavia Greenwood Press, Westport

ABOUT THE AUTHOR

Maria Kvilhaug was born in Oslo, Norway, in 1975. She studied History of Religions and Old Norse Philology at the university of Oslo. She has written several non-fiction and fiction books concerning Old Norse Pre-Christian culture and religion.

http://www.bladehoner.wordpress.com
http://www.youtubecom/user/ladyofthelabyrinth

NON-FICTION:
The Maiden with the Mead
(2004/2009/2023)
The Seed of Yggdrasill (2013/2018/2020)
The Poetic Edda, Six Cosmology Poem
(2017/2021)
The Trickster and the Thunder god, Thor
and Loki in Old Norse Myths (2018)
The Goddess Iðunn (2022)

FICTION:
Blade Honer Series:
The Hammer of Greatness
My Enemy´s Head
The He Rune´s Claim
A Twisted Mirror

The Three Little Sisters

The Three Little Sisters is an indie publisher that puts authors first. We specalize in the strange and unusual. From titles about pagan and heathen spirituality to traditional fiction we bring books to life.

https://the3littlesisters.com

www.ingramcontent.com/pod-product-compliance
Lightning Source LLC
Chambersburg PA
CBHW070907120626
46546CB00001B/166